UDR
DECLASSIFIED

Micheál Smith is an advocacy case worker with the Pat Finucane Centre. He had previously worked as a diplomat with Ireland's Department of Foreign Affairs and Trade, and was privileged to work as Irish government observer and a liaison for the families at the Bloody Sunday Inquiry in Derry and London. He lives in Belfast with his wife and three stepchildren.

MICHEÁL SMITH

MERRION
PRESS

First published in 2022 by
Merrion Press
10 George's Street
Newbridge
Co. Kildare
Ireland
www.merrionpress.ie

9781785374272 (Paper)
9781785374289 (Ebook)

A CIP catalogue record for this book is
available from the British Library.

Typeset in Sabon LT Std 11/15 pt

Cover design by Fiachra McCarthy

Front cover image: UDR vehicle checkpoint, Belfast, Northern
Ireland, 1971. Image courtesy of Victor Patterson, Belfast, UK.

Merrion Press is a member of Publishing Ireland.

CONTENTS

ACKNOWLEDGEMENTS

This book could not possibly have been completed without the assistance and guidance of my colleagues at the Pat Finucane Centre (PFC) and Justice for the Forgotten (JFF). Adrienne Reilly, Alan Brecknell, Anne Cadwallader, Margaret Urwin, Paul O'Connor and Sara Duddy each dove deep into the archives, as did intern Ulrike Hillerkuß from NUI Galway. I have been very fortunate indeed to have worked with such fantastic colleagues and friends.

The book includes many written contributions throughout by my PFC/JFF colleagues. Margaret Urwin gave great assistance with the sections on the Miami Showband killings, and on the attacks on Belturbet and Pettigo, while Anne Cadwallader, lent her talents for the section on weapon UF57A30490.

I also relied upon previously published works, including Paul O'Connor and Alan Brecknell's article 'British Counter-Insurgency Practice in Northern Ireland in the 1970s – A Legitimate Response or State Terror?' and the Pat Finucane Centre pamphlet *The Hidden History of the UDR: The Secret Files Revealed*. Both documents disclosed the stunning extent of collusion between the UDR and loyalist paramilitaries, the penetration of that regiment by loyalist paramilitaries, and the extent to which all of this was known about, tolerated and encouraged by Whitehall and the MoD.

viii ACKNOWLEDGEMENTS

I have been aided in compiling this research by the work of many others, and there is hardly space to acknowledge them all here. Nevertheless, deserving of special mention are journalist and researcher Tom Griffin, Ciarán MacAirt (of Papertrail. pro) and Alec Ward (of the University of Virginia), who were particularly generous with their time and research, and Orla Smith, who kindly provided her time and the mysterious arts of transcription and speed-typing.

I am especially grateful to my wife, Sharon McDaid, and our children, Tara, Michael and Ryan, for their constant love and support. Thank you also to the Smith and McDaid families, especially Deirdre, Orla, Seamus and Geraldine.

Thanks to Conor Graham, Patrick O'Donoghue, Maeve Convery, Wendy Logue and all at IAP/Merrion Press for guiding me through the process of turning a pile of words into a book, and to the editors who left me humbled by the thoroughness of the deep clean done to my text.

Many thanks are owed to Colin Wallace who generously provided a foreword for this book. As a former member of the Ulster Special Constabulary, a Captain in the Ulster Defence Regiment, and a senior Psychological Operations Officer at Army Headquarters in Northern Ireland from 1970 to 1975, Mr Wallace's thoughts on the book's subject matter gave a complementary perspective which it was important to present.

Finally, I am grateful to the many families fighting for justice whom I have met as an advocacy case worker with the Pat Finucane Centre. Your spirit, courage and endurance through every challenge has been constantly inspirational. I have been privileged to share in your victories and honoured to gather strength from you whenever we have faced defeat. This book is dedicated to you.

Micheál Smith

FOREWORD

Colin Wallace,
former senior Psychological Operations
Officer, Army Headquarters

Before you judge my life, my past or my character, walk in my shoes, walk the path I have travelled, live my sorrow, my doubts, my fear, my pain and my laughter. Remember, everyone has a story of their own. When you've lived my life, then you can judge me …

Anonymous

This is an important but, for many, a potentially painful book. It highlights that, to 'walk in another person's shoes', we need to shift our own perspective on occasions to see and feel the world as another person sees and feels it. In particular, it is about making a genuine effort to grasp the other person's point of view emotionally. Once we understand that our own hitherto apparent 'truth' is only one perspective, it allows us to view the same situation differently. Such a shift in perception is the foundation of empathy and is of immeasurable help in resolving conflicts, as South Africa's truth and reconciliation process has shown. Our perception is our reality and, if our perception is flawed, our reality also becomes flawed.

My parents were both born in Scotland, but I was born and grew up in Northern Ireland where my grandparents lived. My father had been shot and severely wounded serving with the British army in France in the First World War. He survived, but died while serving with the Royal Air Force in the Second World War. Another family member was killed in the First World War during the battle for Vimy Ridge. I suppose my family background isolated me, to some extent, from the more extreme sectarian undercurrents that brought havoc to so many lives in Ireland over the years.

As one would expect, I am not a natural critic of the security forces who served honourably in Northern Ireland. I am, however, unashamedly a critic of those individuals who abused their positions within the security agencies and undermined the good work done by those who genuinely tried to bring about peace to that community. Ireland as a whole was, and remains, one of the most hospitable and friendly places on earth, but it has also been a place of unimaginable cruelty.

In his report of the Dublin and Monaghan bombings, Judge Henry Barron summed up my attitude to my role in Northern Ireland as follows:

> Though he has reasons enough to be bitter – the abrupt and unjust ending of a promising career in Northern Ireland, five years spent in prison on a conviction which has since been quashed – he displays no outward signs of resentment towards individuals or institutions. He remains intensely loyal to his country and to the Army: insofar as he has a quarrel, it is with individuals rather

> than the institutions concerned ... When speaking of
> matters directly within his own experience, the Inquiry
> believes him to be a highly knowledgeable witness.

When the British army deployed in Northern Ireland on peacekeeping duties in 1969, I was already working as an information officer on the staff of the British army's HQ on the outskirts of Belfast. By 1971, I had become a member of the army's Psychological Operations (PsyOps) unit. My work required me to 'walk in the shoes' of the paramilitaries involved in the conflict to achieve a better perspective on their activities and motivations, and to use that perspective to disrupt their operations.

In October 1971, Brigadier Denis Ormerod became the first Roman Catholic to be appointed Commander of the UDR. Following discussions between Major General Robert Ford and my then superior officer, Colonel Maurice Tugwell, it was decided that, in addition to my overall PsyOps role with the army as a whole, I should also take on special responsibility for PsyOps activities within the UDR and report directly to Brigadier Ormerod. As a result, I became an officer in the UDR in October 1972 and continued to serve with the regiment until 1975.

The nature of my role in the regiment was highly sensitive and the Ministry of Defence still claims that it cannot find my army record for that period. In a letter dated as recent as 20 September 2021 the MoD stated:

> We have contacted various sources and have been
> unable to locate your service records. We can only
> locate your medal card for the General Service Medal
> with the Northern Ireland clasp.

I had a high regard for Brigadier Ormerod. His role was certainly a 'poisoned chalice', and he was well aware of the challenges facing the regiment – many of which were outside his control.

Micheál Smith has produced a remarkably well researched and documented account of the UDR's troubled history, but he also makes it clear from the outset that his book is not:

> an attempt to demonise one community, or the many ordinary people who wore a UDR uniform. Thousands of people living in the north of Ireland will have relatives who did so. To them they are 'Granda' or 'Nana', 'Uncle' or 'Auntie'. They were as much a victim of colonial policies here as anyone else.

From my own personal experiences, I wholeheartedly agree with that comment. Most of the UDR members I met with during the 1970s were thoroughly professional and were dedicated to protecting the community as a whole. Many of them, including three officers who were well known to me, paid the ultimate price in the process.

There is little that I can add to Micheál Smith's impressive research, but I would like to put his narrative in the context of the wider background to the events that he has recorded. To avoid any suggestion that I am disaffected because of my own experiences in Northern Ireland, and to avoid falling foul of the Official Secrets Acts, I have attempted to make my points through disclosed official documents and the recorded comments of others whose knowledge of those events is beyond challenge.

From the outset, it is important to debunk the myth that abuses by members of the security forces were solely the work of 'rogue elements'. Such behaviour, if true, would have been detected not tolerated.

Interviewed by BBC's *Panorama* programme on 28 May 1985, Baroness Nuala O'Loan, who was Northern Ireland's first police ombudsman, appeared to be taken in by that myth when she asserted that the security forces 'failed to control their undercover operatives' and that state agents were involved in murder: 'They were running informants and their argument was that they were saving lives, but hundreds and hundreds of people died because these people were not brought to justice.' Her comment is, however, very important in the light of the current government's inexplicable decision to abandon legacy cases.

In 1973, Warrant Officer Ken Connor was one of a team of highly experienced SAS soldiers who were sent to Northern Ireland to assess the effectiveness of the army's undercover Military Reaction Force which was then based at Palace Barracks near Holywood. In his memoirs, he comments on the culture of intelligence that existed at that time:

> MI5 and MI6 had only one thing in common: a shared contempt for the RUC Special Branch, which they regarded as staffed by incompetents.
>
> MI5 and MI6 had diametrically opposed agendas for the conflict. While MI6 pursued a political solution through secret contacts with the Dublin government and the Provisional leadership, MI5 sabotaged their efforts. The judicious spin put by MI5 upon a Provisional IRA document discovered during a raid on their Belfast HQ convinced Harold Wilson's government that the IRA were about to launch terror attacks on whole Protestant communities.
>
> In fact it was a contingency plan, only to be put into effect in the event of another wave of Protestant attacks such as the ones that had ushered in the new

era of the Troubles in 1969. As MI5 intended, however, their misleading information both discredited the
political overtures engineered by MI6 and stampeded
the government into a rapid expansion of undercover
army operations.

Government officials and ministers have repeatedly and
falsely denied that any such activities to undermine Harold
Wilson's government ever existed.

In his report into collusion, published on 17 April 2003,
Sir John Stevens, former Commissioner of the Metropolitan
Police, stated:

> My enquiries have highlighted collusion, the wilful
> failure to keep records, the absence of accountability,
> the withholding of intelligence and evidence, and the
> extreme of agents being involved in murder. These
> serious acts and omissions have meant that people
> have been killed or seriously injured.

Eight years later, during a debate in parliament, the now
Lord Stevens said:

> There was the RUC, MI5 and the army doing different
> things. When you talk about intelligence, of the 210
> people we arrested, only three were not agents. Some
> of them were agents for all four of those particular
> organisations, fighting against each other, doing things
> and making a large sum of money, which was all against
> the public interest and creating mayhem in Northern
> Ireland. Any system that is created in relation to this
> country and Northern Ireland has to have a proper
> controlling mechanism.

Given the very high level of infiltration of paramilitary groups referred to by Lord Stevens, is it really credible that the extensive collusion he identified went totally unnoticed by the security authorities?

The report by The Right Honourable, Lord MacLean in 2010 into the shooting of Mid-Ulster loyalist paramilitary leader, Billy Wright, illustrates in graphic terms the techniques used by the Special Branch (and other intelligence agencies) to cover up knowledge of collusion and other abuses.

A former head of the RUC Special Branch, Assistant Chief Constable Sam Kinkaid, explained to the inquiry what he meant by the phrase 'plausible deniability':

> It was, he said, a practice or culture that existed in an organisation where the members did not keep records, so there was no audit trail. Nothing could be traced back, so that if they were challenged they denied it, and that denial, being based on no documentation, would become 'plausible deniability'. The system in SB was such, he said, 'that it didn't give proper audit trails and proper dissemination, and at times it would appear that it allowed people at a later date to have amnesia, in the sense that they couldn't remember because there was no data on the system'. This admission, from a senior PSNI officer appointed by the Chief Constable to explore the apparent lack of documentation supplied to the Inquiry, is an eloquent indication of the shortcomings inherent in the system.

What became of the old-fashioned policy of telling 'the truth, the whole truth, and nothing but the truth'? This strategy of plausible deniability has bedevilled investigations into a wide range of incidents ranging from the bombing of

McGurk's Bar to the sexual abuse of boys at the Kincora Hostel.

The role of the civilian intelligence services in Northern Ireland, particularly MI5, was pervasive. During the Terry Inquiry in 1982 into allegations of a cover-up of sexual abuses at the Kincora boys home, the RUC wanted to interview a senior MI5 officer, Ian Cameron, who was based at army HQ in Lisburn. It was claimed (correctly) that an army intelligence officer, Brian Captain Gemmell, had been ordered by Cameron to stop investigating the abuse allegations. A message sent from MI5 at the Northern Ireland Office to the Director General of MI5 in London said that the RUC had been told of the Director General's policy that: 'no serving or former member of the Security Service (MI5) should be interviewed by the police'. It is no surprise that the RUC were never permitted to interview Cameron. Moreover, Sir George Terry's report on Kincora failed to inform parliament of the MI5 Director General's directive.

Indeed, the fact that parliament has now passed legislation permitting MI5 agents to commit crimes illustrates how standards have been lowered still further to the extent we now have two levels of law – one for 'Crown servants', and one for the rest of the community.

In 1973, the army gave me a written brief about loyalist paramilitary leader William McGrath and his employment at the Kincora. That document was clearly marked for dissemination to the press. Despite that clear instruction to me to disclose the information, Ian Cameron later reported to MI5 HQ in London that by giving the information to a journalist I was breaching security!

It is clear from the foregoing that, even during the 1970s, MI5 regarded themselves as being above the law and that they 'justified' their actions as being 'for the greater good'.

Moreover, the acts of collusion by members of the security forces referred to in Micheál Smith's book were based on the highly questionable principle that: 'my enemy's enemy is my friend'.

The result of that flawed philosophy was highlighted very graphically in an article by Kevin Myers in *Hibernia* magazine in which he referred to the close links between the UVF and army intelligence officers from army HQ at Lisburn:

> By 1973 (Jim) Hanna had become the senior military commander for the UVF in Northern Ireland. He had become a close friend of Captains Anthony Ling and Anthony Box and Lieutenant Alan Homer, all of 39th Brigade at Lisburn, and a Timothy Golden, who is not listed as a member of the Intelligence Corps but was possibly a SAS man attached to Intelligence. They were frequent visitors to Hanna's home near Lisburn, and group photographs of Hanna, Homer and Golden were taken away by the police after Hanna was murdered last year. The remarkable thing is that Hanna remained on good terms with Intelligence when he was masterminding the bombing offensive.

The *Hibernia* article contained a photograph taken in Hanna's home with two of the army intelligence officers. The photo showed Hanna posing with a regulation British army rifle belonging to one of the officers.

In the mid-1970s, the commander of the UVF in Mid Ulster was a former soldier, William 'Billy' Hanna – no relation to Jim Hanna. His wife told the press that army officers from Lisburn frequently visited her husband at his home in Lurgan and also took him away on fishing trips at a nearby lake. In May 1974, Billy Hanna led the UVF's bombing attacks on Dublin and Monaghan, but it is almost certain that Jim Hanna was involved in the planning of these attacks.

Similarly, the wife of Charles Harding Smith, UDA leader in West Belfast in the early 1970s, told the press that army officers in civilian clothes visited her husband at their home almost weekly to hold private meetings with him. It could, of course, be argued that such frequent and social visits to the leaders of paramilitary groups engaged in acts of violence were wholly justified. If so, they should have been recorded in military intelligence source reports and, not only circulated to senior army and intelligence officers, but also to the subsequent government inquiries such as those led by Lord Stevens, Sir Desmond de Silva and Judge Peter Cory. Although all three inquiries recommended the setting up of public inquiries on the basis of their findings, the British government ignored their advice. This indicates that despite the best efforts of those leading the inquiries, they were nothing more than 'window dressing' activities by the government to convince a concerned electorate that something meaningful was being done about these abuses of power.

MI5 also attempted to manipulate those inquiries. In 2002, while Canadian Judge Peter Cory was engaged in his investigation into allegations of collusion, MI5 officers visited his offices in London and removed all his team's computer hard drives 'in the interests of national security'. Judge Cory referred the matter to the Metropolitan Police, but, as expected, no action was taken by the police. Luckily, Judge Cory had made and retained back-up copies of the disks.

What is even more disturbing is that, although the finding of the inquiries by Stevens, de Silva and Cory were made known to parliament, no further action was taken on their recommendations that individuals, including intelligence officers, should be prosecuted and that the finding should be the subject of a public inquiry.

In a speech to parliament on 14 May 2003, the shadow secretary of state for Northern Ireland, Kevin McNamara, referred to the Stevens' inquiries saying:

> The public have been kept in the dark for too long. I believe that the Government have colluded in the unlawful activities of their agents, and that the guilty must be called to account, however high up they are. Where there is sufficient evidence, they must be prosecuted and punished – no more *nolle prosequis*. It is clear that existing mechanisms for the oversight and scrutiny of the intelligence services have failed. A Committee of Members of this and the other House, appointed by the Prime Minister, meets in secret and has its reports vetted in advance of publication, and so cannot provide the accountability that we are entitled to demand.
>
> When the Government themselves stand in the dock, what is the appropriate remedy? The charges made by Sir John Stevens are the most serious to be faced by any Government in Britain. They go right to the heart of our democracy. Our commitment to human rights, the rule of law and justice in Northern Ireland will count for nothing if we cannot address these matters openly and honestly.

I feel increasingly very sad as I write this foreword because, in doing so, I have been reminded that many of the things I was brought up to believe in during the early part of my life turned out to be totally false. My grandmother, who embroidered handkerchiefs to send to the troops during the

First World War repeatedly claimed, 'British justice was the envy of the world.' Sadly, Micheál Smith's book shows that my grandmother's genuinely held belief was far removed from reality. What is even more disturbing is that our elected representatives at Westminster appear to be allowing the erosions of parliament's sovereignty to go unchallenged.

The violence that engulfed the whole of Ireland during the so-called 'Troubles' stemmed from a deeply held sense of injustice. The way in which successive British governments have failed to handle the injustices raised in this book shows that nothing has fundamentally changed, other than that many young people throughout Ireland now have a very different outlook on the conflict from the one that most people had fifty years ago!

LIST OF ABBREVIATIONS

CID	Criminal Investigation Department, RUC
DS10	Defence Secretariat 10 of the MoD
DUP	Democratic Unionist Party
ECHR	European Commission of Human Rights
FCO	Foreign and Commonwealth Office
GOC	General Officer Commanding
HET	Historical Enquiries Team
HMG	Her Majesty's Government
HQNI	British Army Headquarters Northern Ireland
INLA	Irish National Liberation Army
IRA	Irish Republican Army
JFF	Justice for the Forgotten
MoD	Ministry of Defence
NAI	National Archives of Ireland
NIO	Northern Ireland Office
PFC	Pat Finucane Centre
PPW	Personal Protection Weapon
PRONI	Public Records Office Northern Ireland
PSNI	Police Service of Northern Ireland
PUS	Permanent Under-Secretary

RSR	Review Summary Report of Historical Enquiries Team
RUC	Royal Ulster Constabulary
SDLP	Social Democratic and Labour Party
SLR	Self-loading rifle
SMG	Sub-machine gun
TAVR	Territorial Army Volunteer Reserve
UCD	University College Dublin
UDA	Ulster Defence Association
UDR	Ulster Defence Regiment
UFF	Ulster Freedom Fighters
USC	Ulster Special Constabulary
USCA	Ulster Special Constabulary Association
UVF	Ulster Volunteer Force
UWC	Ulster Workers' Council
VCP	Vehicle checkpoint

PREFACE

EXTRACT FROM *A LONG LONG WAR*
BY KEN WHARTON

It was early evening 4th January 1976. The CO put his head through my office door and said, 'What are you up to RSM?' 'I'm going to Glennane [*sic*] Sir!' I replied. 'I'm going there too, ride with me,' said the CO.

... We drove off into the misty cold Armagh night, the CO, myself and the female Greenfinch driver and my driver who came as additional escort.

... Halfway through the journey we started to pick up radio traffic of a shooting incident close to Glennane at Whitecross just outside the base and on our route. Three dead was mentioned and the RUC were at the scene. We drove into Whitecross over the crossroads and down into a lane and down into the muddy yard of the house where we had been directed on the radio.

'... No need to go in,' whispered a policeman. 'Just look through the window; it's a bloody awful sight.' I looked and saw the shot-up bodies of two dark-haired young men, teenagers. Blood spattered the wall above one of them. A wounded third man was being attended to upstairs. He sounded to be in the most terrible agony.

An older woman arrived back at the cottage and was spoken to by a policeman. She tried to rush to the house, but was stopped from entering. She then let out an immediate howling sound of the most dreadful grief, it continued on for some minutes and then she collapsed, she came to, and the grief started again.

... I stood by a police Land Rover and spoke with the Greenfinch driver. My words to her were, 'Jesus Christ! Just imagine rearing those boys to see them come to this.' She made no immediate reply and then said quietly, 'Good enough for the likes of those.' Before I could reply to her, my driver, himself a Catholic, squeezed my arm to keep quiet.

On arrival back at Gough barracks I made a written report of her words. I felt she should be sacked ... I heard no more of it for a while, then about a week later the Training Major (Light Infantry) came into my office and sat down.

... After a silence he said, 'RSM, don't become involved in Irish politics, leave it alone or you will be the loser.' He left my office, and as I sat in thought, I just thought, 'What a hopeless situation!'[1]

INTRODUCTION

'Narrowing the Permissible Lies'

The recollection on the preceding pages comes from a regular British soldier, a member of the Royal Regiment of Wales, on a two-year attachment to the Ulster Defence Regiment (UDR).[1] The soldier is recalling the aftermath of the murder of the Reavey brothers – John Martin (24), Brian (22) and Anthony (17) – on 4 January 1976. The attack was carried out by the infamous Glenanne Gang, comprised of members of the loyalist extremist Ulster Volunteer Force (UVF) and members of the local state security forces – the RUC (Royal Ulster Constabulary) and UDR. The gang was responsible for about 120 murders on both sides of the border.[2]

The many contradictions within this soldier's brief recollection encapsulate all that is divisive about the UDR and the difficulties in trying to capture and present its history and legacy. The soldier was apparently sympathetic to the plight of the victims and their mother, reflecting the army's role as 'Military Aid to the Civil Power'[3] and the UDR's designated role as 'a locally recruited, part-time, military defence force'.[4]

Yet members of his regiment – the UDR – were culpable, along with members of the UVF, for the Reaveys' murder. One of the killers was named by a member of the Glenanne Gang as Robert McConnell, a serving UDR soldier.[5] Also, weaponry used to kill the young men had been stolen from Glenanne UDR base.

Meanwhile, the reported reaction of the 'Greenfinch' (as female UDR personnel were known) at the scene reflects her own sectarianism – the three brothers were innocent civilians, and the family had no involvement in the simmering conflict. The regular soldier instinctively reacted negatively to her callous words. He saw himself as separate from the Irish around him. Indeed, he was. He was on an 'attachment' to the UDR from his regular British army unit. While nominally a British army regiment, the UDR was in many ways an entirely separate entity.

From its formation in 1970, the UDR was on continuous operational service for a period of twenty-two years, a distinction held by no other regiment in the long history of the British army. On 1 July 1992, the UDR merged with the Royal Irish Rangers to form the Royal Irish Regiment, and was effectively no more. By the time of its dissolution, the regiment numbered 6,300 soldiers and was the largest infantry regiment in the British army. On 6 October 2006, the British monarch awarded the Conspicuous Gallantry Cross to past members of the UDR for their unique 'contribution to peace and stability'.[6]

To many people in the Protestant, unionist or loyalist tradition, service in the UDR was a noble act – and in many cases a family tradition, with family members sometimes recruited to the same units of the regiment. And yet in the experience of the Catholic community (and the UDR didn't differentiate between nationalist and republican), an encounter with the UDR was frequently hostile, often brutal, and sometimes fatal. For many it was simply a loyalist militia.

In this book, we aim to set out the background to the regiment and the traditions from which it was born; we attempt to reflect the experience of those who served in the UDR and acknowledge their losses; we also aim to show the range of illegal, collusive and murderous acts of some of its number, and, as ever, attempt to understand this in the context of British colonial military practice.

One of the assertions of this book is that London knew the UDR was bound to attract active loyalist recruits but pressed ahead to form the regiment anyway, with one of its unspoken functions being to, at least partially, contain loyalist violence. As a result, infiltration was widespread, but – far from containing loyalist violence – it led to the UDR becoming a training and arming facility for loyalism.

For elements of the British establishment, the UDR was used as a surrogate 'counter-gang'. Although unacknowledged in public, officers and the Ministry of Defence (MoD) knew UDR weapons were systematically stolen and used to murder Catholics. Although the term 'collusion' has been derided by those sympathetic to the British narrative of the conflict in Ireland, the British were in fact well aware of what was going on and frequently referred to it internally as 'collusion' from the early 1970s.

Evidence of collusion continues to emerge. A long-awaited report by the Police Ombudsman in January 2022 into the RUC's investigations of attacks by the UDA between 1989 and 1993, including 19 murders, identified what the ombudsman called a range of 'collusive behaviours [that] raised significant concerns about police conduct'.[7] The Ombudsman reported that a significant number of serving and former UDR members had links with senior UDA figures and that this 'allowed paramilitaries access to weapons, training, intelligence, and uniforms which added to their effectiveness in carrying out sectarian attacks'.[8]

It is important to note the context in which the book was written. In July 2021, Brandon Lewis, the British secretary of state for Northern Ireland, set out universally rejected proposals for dealing with the legacy of the conflict in Northern Ireland. The proposals were about shutting down current and future investigations and procedures, with a view to protecting the state from discovery of its role in a very dirty war. For many families the proposals were about shutting down access to the truth.

This book is based on files and evidence that were uncovered by hard slog and sometimes pure good fortune. It is interesting that, aside from Chris Ryder's sympathetic history of the UDR ('extraordinary men and women doing an extraordinary job'),[9] first published in 1991, and former UDR major (and regimental secretary) John Potter's quasi-official history of the regiment, *A Testimony to Courage* (which was vetted by the Ministry of Defence prior to publication in 2001),[10] not much has been published about the UDR or indeed by its former members. Perhaps a true telling of the regiment's history would prove too contentious.

The book is not an attempt to list all of the wrongdoings of what was probably the most controversial element of the British army in its long and bloody record. It was not possible to detail all of the victims of loyalist killers who wore a UDR uniform. Where victims are named, it is because of a connection to a file or a theme we sought to develop. A family might turn to this book, hoping to see the name of a loved one. This book is not about the deaths of individuals so much as it is about the machine that killed them.

Nor is the book an attempt to demonise one community,

or the many ordinary people who wore a UDR uniform. Thousands of people living in Northern Ireland will have relatives who did so. To them they are 'Granda' or 'Nana', 'Uncle' or 'Auntie'. They were in many ways, victims of British colonial policies themselves. As the *Andersonstown News* headline of 17 July 2021 put it, when news of the British government's legacy proposals broke, to the British all were just 'Paddies'.

This book is not a history of the UDR. It is rather an attempt to tell what Whitehall, Number 10 and the MoD had to say about the regiment in papers found among declassified files.

It is about narrowing the permissible lies.[11]

CHAPTER ONE

'A Dangerous Species of Ally'

The Good Friday Agreement in 1998 was a de facto peace treaty that ended a thirty-year armed conflict between Irish republicanism and the British state. Increasingly, that conflict is being situated by modern historians in the broader geopolitical framework of 'an unfinished colonialism'.[1] It is legitimate, then, to examine the role of the British military in Ireland through the prism of colonialism.

In the Franco–British negotiations over the division of West Africa in the 1890s, a key concern of both imperial powers was ownership of the best military recruiting lands.[2] The European powers traditionally used locally raised militias to rule over their subjugated colonies. A good example is the colonial police in the British Gold Coast (now Ghana), which was partly modelled on the Royal Irish Constabulary (RIC). The British recruited what they called 'Hausas', Muslim men from the northern interior of Ghana, and deployed them in further conquest of territory, and also in strike-breaking, in supervising convict labourers and in guarding banks.[3]

This, written of the Hausa, may sound familiar to Irish ears: 'All too often a uniform seemed a license to loot and extort, and as a result ... [they] were despised and hated by those they affected to police. Preeminently they were hated as unaccountable representatives of an alien colonial power imposing a range of new laws and measures of social control which lacked any semblance of popular consent.'[4]

Similarly in Ireland, from the end of the eighteenth century onward, the British found it preferable to leave the colonial policing of the population to locally raised Yeomanry – voluntary, part-time and locally organised groups of men, serving under commissioned British officers, paid, armed and equipped by the British government. The Irish Yeomanry, a force with a reputation for 'ill-discipline and brutality',[5] provided armed strength to the Protestant Ascendancy, which was determined to maintain power through domination over the Catholic majority.

Allan F. Blackstock's 'A Dangerous Species of Ally': Orangeism and the Irish Yeomanry reveals how the Yeomanry was often inseparable from the Orange Order.[6] For example, Blackstock reports:

> between 1809 and 1831 the Lurgan Infantry made recruits take an unofficial, de facto Orange oath. Their liberal Protestant captain, William 'Papist' Handcock, disapproved, but admitted that owing to 'high political and religious feelings ... it is found difficult to constitute a yeomanry force free from objection'. This corps was involved in various disturbances, eventually forcing Handcock to dismiss the permanent sergeant, a local Orangemen, for admitting unattested men and allowing arms to leak into the community. Thus the yeomen themselves became a 'dangerous species of ally'.[7]

The dangers inherent in the Yeomanry are revealed in records of the governments of the day. In 1798 the Lord Lieutenant of Ireland lamented to the prime minister: 'How impolitic and unwise [it was] ... to refuse the offers of Protestants to enter with the Yeomanry ... yet how dangerous [was] even any encouragement to the Orange spirit.'[8] In 1815, the chief secretary for Ireland (and later prime minister) Sir Robert Peel wrote of the Yeomanry, 'Admitting that the Yeomanry are generally speaking unfit for those very duties in the performance of which their main utility would consist, namely in relieving the army from the maintenance of internal order and the collection of revenue, I am not quite prepared to come to your conclusion that it would be the wisest measure to disband the whole force.'[9] Peel was saying that while the Yeomanry was unfit for its duties in maintaining order, he couldn't agree to getting rid of them. By the 1830s the force was described by Sir Frederick Stoven, inspector general of police, as 'more than useless ... they are dangerous'.[10]

The Yeomanry was eventually stood down and replaced by a professional police force, the Irish Constabulary, in 1822. Yet all of the problems associated with it – 'admitting unattested men', difficulties in establishing a force 'free from objection', and 'allowing arms to leak into the community' – would be revived under its twentieth-century successors, the B Specials and then the UDR. Like these forces would, the Yeomanry had proven (as Blackstock describes them) a 'dangerous species of ally ... using them was risky, yet disbanding was politically difficult.'[11]

During the Irish War of Independence, the passage of the Government of Ireland Act in 1920 would provide for a separate unionist statelet secured through partition. But before partition, violent conflict flared across the island. Vigilante groups, comprised of soldiers demobbed after the First World War and remnants of the Ulster Volunteer Force,[12] emerged in unionist areas. These unionist vigilante groups drove Catholics from factories and towns across the north, 'condoned by the hard-pressed British army and RIC who turned a blind eye on the basis that they were on the same side'.[13]

In the autumn of 1920, a force of special constables was raised for use only in the north. Alongside a full-time force, to be known as A Specials, under the command of the RIC, a force of voluntary part-timers – called B Specials – was also proposed. These men, in the company of an RIC officer, would do duty one night in ten in their local area. A third category – C Specials – would comprise a 6,000-strong reserve force for use in emergencies.

After the state of Northern Ireland had been established, the A Specials and RIC were assimilated into a new police force there, the Royal Ulster Constabulary (RUC). The B Specials were retained as a reserve paramilitary force, part-time and unpaid, operating at night and weekends; their command structure was kept separate from that of the civil police force.

Recruitment to the B Specials was corrupted from the outset by the former vigilante gangs referred to above, which were behind much of the anti-Catholic violence that flared across the north before and after partition. In a report to London, a British army officer criticised the selection committees, accusing them of 'a want of moral courage ... in excluding undesirables'. The outcome, according to the officer, was that the B Specials were comprised of 'a large leaven of a bad type'.[14]

Ryder provides a contemporaneous report by a Belfast RIC officer who warned, 'There can never be any possibility of establishing confidence and security so long as the B force, the ordinary Protestant countryman and, in many cases, the corner boy, is supplied with arms and clothing by his government and authorised to "get on top", as it were, of his neighbour.'[15]

In March 1921, *The Manchester Guardian* editorialised about the B Specials:

> The Special Constabulary, drawn almost exclusively from the ranks of the Orange Lodges[16] and the Unionist 'Volunteers', was nominally raised to protect life and property and to maintain order, not to become a force of terrorists exercising powers of death over their Catholic neighbours ... It will be a bad beginning for the Ulster parliament if its establishment coincides with the dragooning of the Catholic minority in the six counties by an armed Protestant force administering a sort of lynch law.[17]

Despite the 1921 July truce between the British government and the fledgling Irish state, serious violence continued in the north-east of Ireland. In one notorious incident, six members of the McMahon family were murdered at their home in Belfast in March 1922.[18] The murders were committed under cover of curfew, and eyewitnesses asserted that members of the B Specials had been among the assassins. The crime was described by none other than Winston Churchill as 'worse than cannibalism'.[19] In a foreshadowing of a pattern of violence to come from state forces in the 1970s,[20] the McMahon family were prosperous Catholics – they owned several pubs in Belfast – with no connections to the IRA. Owen McMahon was a supporter and personal friend of Joe Devlin, the Irish Parliamentary Party member of parliament, an Irish nationalist who rejected republican violence.[21]

A contemporaneous account of the fear prevailing in Belfast in 1922 was recorded by a visiting Catholic priest, Fr P.J. Gannon:

> Two days after my visit this sector of the front was to waken up to renewed activity in which five Catholics were killed and seven wounded. In a house some four doors from the one we were looking at two women were shot dead in cold blood. 'The Irish Independent' for April 13, 1922, stated that on the previous day a Lancia car manned by 'Specials' patrolled the city with the inscription in chalk on its sides – 'Papish blood is sweet'. It would seem so, and very particularly the blood of women and children.[22]

Gannon's account of his visit continued: 'The powerlessness of the military during two years of this sort of situation, recurring almost weekly, is one of the mysteries of Belfast. It is pathetic indeed when fear-frantic women have to appeal to powerless soldiers against the Special Constabulary of Northern Ireland.'[23]

Over the following decades of unionist rule, the B Specials were feared and despised in equal measure by Catholics and the nationalist community. Supported by the unionist community in Northern Ireland (who saw it as a bulwark against republicanism), the B Specials became established as a unionist auxiliary force, with a deserved reputation for sectarian brutality.

Flash forward to 1969 when, following widespread civil unrest, thousands of refugees from the nationalist-republican community in Northern Ireland fled across the Irish border to camps set up by an ill-prepared Irish army.[24] They were fleeing attacks from loyalists, aided and abetted by the RUC.[25]

By that time, the B Specials were the only remaining class
of the original three Ulster Special Constabulary classes. In
1969 they numbered around 8,000 men and were deployed for
military-type duties, such as road checks and mounting armed
guards on certain installations. An official review described
them as 'a partisan and paramilitary force recruited exclusively
from Protestants'.[26] Critically, they were deployed in the areas
in which they lived, 'policing' their own Catholic neighbours.

In 1968, the civil rights movement was growing in
strength, inspired by the civil rights movement in the United
States. The demands of the movement in Northern Ireland
included the introduction of universal franchise, an end to
the practice of gerrymandering to manipulate elections, fair
and equal access to housing, the reform of draconian security
powers and the outlawing of religious discrimination. The
initial response of the Unionist government was to concede
nothing and to unleash the RUC and the B Specials to sup-
press the movement.

The willingness of the B Specials to carry out this task
is evidenced in the words of a former RUC officer who had
previously served as a member of the B Specials:

> The USC [B Specials] regarded every Catholic as an
> enemy. It was as far as I know one hundred percent
> Protestant. I am not impartial and I have never believed
> in impartiality but it had got to the stage where our
> backs were up against the wall and something had to
> be done. After all our country and our government was
> being attacked. The Ulster government belonged to the
> Ulster people and the people who cared about Ulster.
> The Civil Rights movement was nothing more than
> the IRA. The Unionist government knew that but the
> British wouldn't listen.[27]

Perhaps the most notorious event was the loyalist mob attack, abetted by security force personnel, on the People's Democracy civil rights march at Burntollet Bridge, just outside Derry, on 4 January 1969. Eyewitness testimony was gathered by two student activists, Michael Bowes Egan and Vincent McCormack. They concluded that 'the attack was organised locally by representatives of the Orange order and the Special Constabulary (B Specials) ... It may well be that local branches of the clandestine organisation known as the Ulster Volunteer Force were involved. But the overlap of personnel between these organisations render such distinctions of purely academic significance.'[28]

Paddy Devlin, an MP at the Belfast parliament (Stormont) for the nationalist Social Democratic and Labour Party (SDLP) – which was closely aligned to and associated with the civil rights movement – later established that a significant number of the attackers were members, or former members, of the B Specials,[29] though no prosecution or disciplinary action was taken against them.

In the aftermath of Burntollet, the unionist establishment circled the wagons in defence of the B Specials. On 5 January, Prime Minister of Northern Ireland Terence O'Neill issued a statement in which he said, 'Ulster has now had enough, we are all sick of marchers and counter-marchers. Unless these warring minorities rapidly return to their senses we will have to consider a further reinforcement of the regular police by *greater use* [emphasis added] of the Special Constabulary for normal police duties.'[30]

The escalating crisis arising from the confrontation between the Northern Ireland state and civil rights protesters was to become the subject of two royal commissions, subsequently published as the Cameron Report (1969) and the Scarman Report (1972). The Cameron Commission, which reported in October 1969, concerned the RUC; it accused the force of illegal violence and failures of discipline, but stopped short of calling out serious institutionalised misconduct. The Scarman Commission investigated the violence of August 1969 – which many pinpoint as the start of 'the Troubles' – including the murder of John Gallagher in Armagh. Gallagher was shot dead by a platoon of B Specials in circumstances severely criticised by the Scarman Commission, yet none was charged with any offence. Gallagher's killing prompts many questions, including: Is this where we see the beginning of the policy of non-prosecution in cases of killings by state forces? And how many of these B Specials – including the killer of John Gallagher – subsequently joined the UDR?

The violent security force reaction to the civil rights movement over 1968 and 1969 led the British government to define the RUC and B Specials as a major part of the problem. Both forces were contributing to the breakdown of British authority in Northern Ireland.[31] So it was that the British government placed primary responsibility for public order and internal security there in the hands of the British army. On Thursday, 14 August 1969, the army, under Military Aid to the Civil Power provisions, was ordered onto the streets.

The arrival of British troops was initially seen by many in the nationalist-republican community as a welcome sign that London would intervene and protect them from the worst excesses of the regional Unionist government in Belfast and their armed forces. On 15 August 1969, the Stormont government decided themselves to request 'the assistance of troops' in Belfast;[32] at the same time, it was absorbed in finding 'a useful role' for the B Specials.[33]

In London, however, there was little trust in the B Specials. A Home Office memo from 18 August describes them as 'not a Special Constabulary in the English sense'. Instead, 'they are a sectarian group of citizens trained in the use of firearms … vulnerable to the suggestion that they are a private army, but lacking the knowledge of policemanship essential to their employment on police duties.'[34]

Prime Minister Harold Wilson himself is said to have regarded the B Specials as the Unionists' 'private army'. William Beattie Smith reported the view of Irish diplomat Eamon Gallagher: 'Wilson considered that the possession of such a force by the white minority administration had wrecked his Rhodesia policy, and he was determined not to repeat the mistake in dealing with the settlers of Northern Ireland.'[35]

The key concern for London was doing away with this 'private army'. Another Home Office memo dated 18 August 1969 reflects a discussion among senior officials in which they resolved to 'put strong and urgent pressure' on James Chichester-Clark – the recently installed successor to O'Neill as leader of the Unionist Party and prime minister of Northern Ireland – to remove the B Specials from street duty, as 'the majority of "B specials" were a poor type, attracted by firearms training'.[36] It is noteworthy that all these discussions were happening just days after John Gallagher's killing.

Tellingly, London was alert very early on to the divided loyalties among the B Specials' rank-and-file. An internal Whitehall memo of a call between Chichester-Clark and the British home secretary, James Callaghan, on 18 August 1969 reflects concerns that the suggestion of disarming the B Specials could 'give rise to something approaching mutiny … and there was also the danger that arms might be passed to the UVF, or members of the B Specials might join that force. The UVF – Ulster Volunteer Force – was the first armed loyalist paramilitary group to emerge, formed by Gusty Spence in 1966, whose violence predated the notional start of the conflict in 1969. The UVF – a notional revival of the UVF of 1914, which formed to prevent Irish Home Rule, and in large part marched off to die in the British army during the First World War – was outlawed after it was responsible for three murders in June 1966. But the question *was whether these* [mutiny, or passing arms to the UVF] *were greater evils than the evil of allowing the B Specials to continue in their current form* [emphasis added].'[37]

According to Beattie Smith, Wilson and Callaghan had not intended to replace the B Specials after their disbandment.[38] But if the RUC was to shoulder purely civilian policing, then some force would be needed, they felt, to protect infrastructure in the event of a republican insurgency, such as the (relatively minor) IRA campaign of 1956–62. In the absence of this, withdrawing the army would be difficult.

As Beattie Smith has written, an additional factor was that 'London did not welcome the prospect of there falling outside its control a network of over 8,000 committed Protestants, trained, armed, disaffected, and with a sudden surplus of time and energy.' It was reasoned that, under army command, the former B Specials' 'commitment to public service could be channelled into harmless activities'.[39]

The Hunt Committee

On 21 August 1969, amid increasing anxiety at Stormont and public pressure over the actions of the security forces, an advisory committee was established to report on the effectiveness and organisation of these forces under the chairmanship of John Hunt, a well-regarded army officer esteemed for having led the 1953 Mount Everest expedition. His committee colleagues were Robert Mark, deputy commissioner of the Metropolitan Police, and James

Robertson, the chief constable in Glasgow. Robertson's appointment was perhaps a sop to unionists, among whom he was apparently well regarded.[40]

Hunt's committee convened for the first time on 29 August and, over the course of its meetings, interviewed dozens of witnesses and took written testimony. A file in the National Archives contains the committee's notes and reports, and it is often revelatory. To cite just one example of evidence to Hunt, an English chief inspector of police attached to the army's Northern Ireland Command disparaged the B Specials as 'a militia'. He reported on the reaction of B Special commandants to the possibility of disbanding or disarming the force, where one warned him – 'I need time to consult my men or there could be a bloodbath.' The chief inspector warned that if the Specials were disbanded, the membership would instead turn to the loyalist paramilitaries, 'if indeed some members do not already belong to them'.[41]

In the committee's travels to barracks around Northern Ireland, B Specials regularly gave similar warnings. Among the committee members' notes, it is recorded that many admitted without hesitation that they would join paramilitary groups if the force were disbanded.[42] One such report states, 'The feeling that Ulster needed to be defended against the IRA was so strong that if an armed USC [B Specials force] ceased to exist many men would join proscribed volunteer forces.' Furthermore, the B Specials saw themselves as 'an essential shield for Ulster'; in its absence, 'there were hints that alternative forces might assume the load'.[43] In another report, the somewhat mixed message is recorded that 'It was better that Ulster's determination to defend itself should find expression in the USC than in volunteer forces [sic], which would not be disciplined, organised or amenable to control.'[44]

By contrast, Hunt and his team found RUC members to

be looking forward to a relief from security duties so that they might instead focus on ordinary police work – 'We are robber-catchers at heart,' one said.[45] Visits to stations in Armagh, Keady, Newry, Crossmaglen and elsewhere revealed RUC men and officers expressing this desire to return to ordinary police work. The file recorded comments such as: 'D.I. Armstrong would prefer to be divorced from security duties'; '"Would love to be a policeman." Joined force to be one. Hasn't been one for 11 years in Londonderry'; and 'All said, "We don't want to carry arms"'.[46] RUC personnel also frequently complained that B Specials they had worked with had been deployed with no training whatsoever, and that their poor conduct had soured public opinion against the RUC. The RUC's Antrim Consultative Board told Hunt's committee 'some men were taken straight from labour exchanges into the mobilised U.S.C. and put on police duties without training'. 'This tended to bring the R.U.C. into disrepute,' they said.[47]

The Hunt Report

Chichester-Clark's cabinet received an advance copy of the Hunt Committee's report on 6 October. It recommended the disarmament of the regular RUC and their relief from 'all duties of a military nature as soon as possible', bringing them into line with standard policing practice in Britain, perhaps so as to 'acquire a "British Bobby" image'.[48]

But the issue of most interest is what was to become of the B Specials. Hunt's committee proposed the wholesale disbandment of the B Specials, whose auxiliary policing functions were to be taken up by a new RUC volunteer reserve force under the ordinary RUC chain of command. But if the RUC was to be a civil policing force, then some other force would be needed to take on a defence role in the event of insurgency. In the absence of this, withdrawing the army would be difficult.

The Hunt Report was released to the public on 10 October 1969. The reaction among the Unionist leadership was hostile. The Belfast *News Letter* warned, 'The recommendation is a victory for the Roman Catholics and the Civil Rights Movement, who demanded the Stormont Government abolish all the Protestant Specials. Opposition will come from the men themselves ... It is unlikely that they will respond to the invitation to join a Roman Catholic–Protestant volunteer force.'[49]

Firebrand street preacher and loyalist agitator Ian Paisley called Hunt's recommendations 'an absolute sell-out to the republicans and the so-called civil rights movement which is only a smokescreen for the republican movement', and called on the prime minister to resign.[50] The loyalist Shankill Defence Association called the report 'a capitulation to the Civil Rights agitators' and warned 'that a day is fast approaching when responsible leaders and associations like ourselves will no longer be able to restrain the backlash of outraged Loyalist opinion'.[51]

Soon after this, loyalists rioted across the north, one shooting dead Constable Arbuckle in Belfast – the first member of the RUC to be killed during what became known as 'the Troubles'. The reaction from the Dublin government was cold, with the Irish ambassador in London informing Labour MPs that 'the creation of any British armed force for use in Ireland could only be regarded by us as "utterly repugnant" (even apart from the "disguised B Specials" aspect).'[52]

To the nationalist minority in the north, however, the report's recommendations must have looked promising. The disbandment of the B Specials would see a hated and feared hostile paramilitary force removed from their lives. A plan for significant reform was on the table, but it would be another matter entirely to see it implemented.

CHAPTER TWO

Formation of the New Force

The White Paper setting out the arrangements and organisation for the formation of the UDR was published on 12 November 1969. Minister of State for Defence Administration Roy Hattersley told parliament that:

> The nature of the new military force will be governed by its operational task. That task will be to meet what the Hunt Committee called 'armed guerilla-type attacks'. This calls for a force to guard key points and installations, to carry out patrols and to establish check points and road blocks.
>
> This force will be an integral part of the Army. It will be controlled by the Secretary of State for Defence, and will be under the command of the General Officer Commanding, Northern Ireland. Its immediate commanding officer will be a brigadier of the regular Army ...
>
> Of necessity, the new force will draw substantially on the Ulster Special Constabulary [B Specials] for its

initial recruitment, but there will be a campaign to enrol recruits from all sections of the Northern Ireland community. Apart from the formal qualifications of age, residence and nationality the sole criterion for acceptance will be suitability for service in a military force. There will be a strict security vetting.

The force will be called the Ulster Defence Regiment ...

Officers of the new force will be subject to military law at all times ...

The success of this force is vitally important to the people of Northern Ireland. It must be representative of the community as a whole. Recruits must come forward from all sections. We are confident that they will.[1]

Regimental headquarters was established in Thiepval Barracks, Lisburn, and Brigadier Logan Scott-Bowden was named the new regiment's commander.

The UDR was organised into seven battalions – one for each of the six counties and one entirely for Belfast – as follows:

- 1 UDR (County Antrim) Battalion; Battalion HQ – Ballymena
- 2 UDR (County Armagh) Battalion; Battalion HQ – Armagh
- 3 UDR (County Down) Battalion; Battalion HQ – Ballykinler
- 4 UDR (County Fermanagh) Battalion; Battalion HQ – Enniskillen
- 5 UDR (County Londonderry) Battalion; Battalion HQ – Derry

- 6 UDR (County Tyrone) Battalion; Battalion HQ – Omagh
- 7 UDR (City of Belfast) Battalion; Battalion HQ – Holywood

Each battalion was to be commanded by a local member of the force. In fact, all seven were initially handed to former B Special county commandants.[2]

According to Potter, an officer at UDR headquarters said that there was some 'concern' at former B Specials retaining positions of command: 'We regarded the Training Majors as sort of commissars. We had them half-watching their COs to ensure that they were behaving as military commanders and not as USC County Commandants might have done.'[3] A decision was taken to appoint regular army commanding officers to each battalion, but this was not universally popular. Potter, again, quotes a former county commandant, who wrote, after his sole year in command of 5 UDR had to be given up, that:

> [He,] whose home and family had long been established in Co. Londonderry, handed over command to Lieutenant Colonel Lys, an officer with no previous experience of Northern Ireland and, in accordance with MOD policy, a Roman Catholic. His religion did not affect in any way those who had already joined the battalion, but to the people of the county, from whom it was hoped to draw still more recruits, the appointment was attributed as a gesture to encourage the inherently disloyal section of the community to enlist, with the result that the Loyalists decided they would keep out.[4]

A couple of weeks after the first regular army CO took over command of 3 UDR, a bomb was exploded close to his headquarters ('An empty hut just behind BnHQ was badly damaged in an explosion, thought to have been the work of Protestant extremists').[5] Potter suggests this was the work of 'loyalist extremists as a protest against his [the regular army CO's] appointment'.[6]

If it was intended that the B Specials' replacement force was to have the support of all citizens of the northern state, the name of the regiment was the first politically loaded issue. Northern Ireland is composed of six of the nine counties of the province of Ulster, yet the terms 'Ulster' and 'the province' stand for Northern Ireland almost exclusively among its Unionist population. Hunt had recommended a neutral title for the regiment – the Northern Ireland Defence Regiment. The decision to name the force the 'Ulster Defence Regiment' was, as recently uncovered state files show, of clear concern at the top levels of the British government as early as October 1969. In a minuted discussion between ministers, reasons advanced for not using the politically loaded 'Ulster' in the title included, 'a. It fails to differentiate sufficiently between the new force and the USC which it replaces … b. It could prove a bar to Catholics joining the force.'[7] It is arguably quite telling that this document comes from a declassified MoD file entitled 'Ulster Defence Regiment – Reorganisation of B Specials'.

These concerns were reflected in the debate on the establishment of the UDR in the House of Lords. Hunt argued, 'Ulster, as we know, is … a historic fact which has strong Party political and partisan connotations, whereas Northern Ireland is simply a geographical fact of life. I am sorry that that name [Northern Ireland] has not been attached to the force [instead of Ulster].' Hunt lamented, 'I regret that this force has been given a name which is anathema to many Catholics who might be disposed to do their civic duty and join the force.'[8]

Meanwhile the army was exercised over the inherent dangers of raising this new force. At a meeting of the Army Board – 'The 82nd Meeting [on] The Formation of the New Northern Ireland Local Defence Force' – note was made of the 'real possibility that the hasty forming of this politically inspired force will end as a military failure' and that 'The crucial factor is the recruiting problem'.[9]

The first two men to enlist in the UDR were sworn in on 18 February 1970. One was a nineteen-year-old Catholic and the other a forty-seven-year-old Protestant, yet their signing-in ceremony was a cause of some anxiety for the military. The week before the ceremony, the head of the adjutant general's secretariat wrote to the civil adviser to the general officer commanding (GOC) setting out the protocol that was to be carefully followed. It was assumed 'that "representative" recruits [would] include both Roman Catholic and Protestant, USC and ex-Service applicants, and that no speeches on matters of substance' were to be made. In fact, in his speech the UDR commander was to 'confine himself to the sort of "pleasantries" that one uses on such occasions, if I can put it this way'.[10] In short, Commander, whatever you say, say nothing!

If that brief guidance betrays a certain anxiety, it is clear from the files that recruitment to the UDR was a major worry for the British army from the very outset. In fact, according to minutes of an Army Board meeting in October 1969, the adjutant general's secretariat envisaged certain difficulties in raising the regiment, so much so that 'There must be doubts whether it can be raised at all.'[11]

Some of the concerns were quite cryptic – 'What USC members [B Specials] may accept now, may not be acceptable when the force becomes part of the British Army. It may not match their philosophy of service. It may not suit the North Irish [sic] temperament.' Was the AG's staff anticipating conflicts of loyalty among this significant new addition to Her Majesty's Armed Forces?

In that context, is a degree of sarcasm detectable in a reference, in the same document, to the B Specials' 'inherent discipline'? How would 'imposed military discipline be received'? Might it again provoke a conflict of interests to those loyal to the northern state, who had also taken an oath to serve the army? And did the army anticipate a clash between army discipline and the criminal intentions or activities of potential UDR troops when particular 'Difficulty is foreseen for those who are permitted to keep weapons at their homes'?

Within the same file lies a question that leaves a lot to ponder: 'Can there be harmony between Protestants and the RC [Roman Catholic] members when the force leadership is completely ex-USC from inception?' It appears the army was aware of the corruption embedded in the process – in other words, the duplicity of the Stormont regime which planned to subvert the Hunt reforms from the outset with regard to the UDR, all of which is exhibited in the archived files. This was especially relevant regarding recruitment.

The UDR was, as already mentioned, organised into seven battalions, 'one for each of the six counties and one for Belfast',[12] with each battalion to be commanded by a local member of the force. Immediately, 'ex-commandants of the USC ... were given commands of all seven.'[13] Political wrangling between Stormont and Westminster saw that the B Specials were to be 'replaced', as opposed to 'disbanded'. Callaghan felt that this 'seemed a small concession to make ... as they felt so strongly about it'.[14] Accordingly, Stormont began work on simply 'replacing' the B Specials.

On 12 November 1969, Roy Hattersley stated in parliament that, 'of necessity', the new force would 'draw substantially on the Ulster Special Constabulary for its initial recruitment'. Of these, a majority were 'men who have given good and honourable service to Northern Ireland'.[15]

A month later it transpired that Hattersley had committed to write to the members of the B Specials outlining clearly the methods and the terms of recruitment: 'That promise was given because there had been some evidence that the B Specials were not joining as individuals but were joining as groups, and that this was as a result of a meeting of an unofficial committee within the Regiment.'[16]

As it happens, Stormont's minister of home affairs, Robert Porter, had already consulted the B Specials, apparently attending at least one large meeting in Newtownards in mid-October 1969. Porter warned that there had already been mass resignations from the B Specials and aired demands that its members be enrolled in the new force 'en bloc'. Stormont agreed to announce as soon as possible their intention to accept B Specials into the new force by default and to require applicants to take an oath of allegiance.[17]

On 15 October, Stormont issued a press release addressing how they would recruit for the new force. It said, 'Members of the USC who wish to [join] will be accepted for service with the new defence force'; the only qualification expressed was that this was 'subject to satisfying requirements as to age and physical fitness which have yet to be determined'.[18]

On 19 November 1969 Bernadette Devlin MP challenged then Secretary of State for Defence Denis Healey over this seemingly proactive recruitment-by-stealth of B Specials to the as yet unformed UDR:

> If I heard the Secretary of State correctly, on two occasions during his speech so far he has stated that recruitment will not begin until the Bill becomes law. I therefore want to draw his attention to an article in

the *Guardian* of 19th November 1969, written by John Cunningham, which begins in this way: 'Application forms for Northern Ireland's new security force were sent to all B Specials last week, the Minister of Home Affairs, Mr. Porter admitted at Stormont yesterday.'[19]

Healey disowned this application form as 'not an official army document'. It was, he said, merely 'circulated to enable USC leaders to form an impression of the numbers of their men who would wish to join' – although that was not the understanding received by the B Specials. Regimental historian John Potter said of these 'application forms that weren't', that they 'sowed in the minds of the Nationalist MPs, and therefore the Catholic community, the first seeds of distrust about the new Regiment'.[20]

UDR Advisory Council

In December 1969 an advisory council was convened to begin the task of recruitment and getting the regiment operational. It had been announced, almost as an afterthought, during the debates on the UDR Bill. This council was to come solely under the remit of the Ministry of Defence and so, aside from the inevitable rollover of B Special personnel, recruiting was notionally set to proceed straightforwardly and free of sectarianism.

Nevertheless, the advisory council was clearly seen as a terrible imposition by the army in particular, and also by the advocate general's office; in November 1969, the latter wrote that the 'AG would prefer not to have any committee at all on various grounds. There might be difficulty in containing its activities and there would be a real risk of escalation into fields for which it was not designed.'[21]

In other words, perhaps, an oversight body that included civilians might well begin to point out things the UDR ought not to be doing. The advocate general's office wrote that 'It might seem to carry an implication that the Army is not capable of complete impartiality, which goes entirely against the fundamental principle of transference of this USC function to the Army.'[22] Indeed it might, and yet it was still deemed necessary by London.

Nonetheless, if 'in the last resort' it was 'considered necessary to make some concession', the advocate general was willing to accept a vaguely 'limited' body, which would only 'produce bright ideas or give advice on how to improve recruiting in difficult areas' ('difficult' here clearly meaning Catholic or nationalist).[23]

The advisory council's composition was carefully managed to meet the appearance of balance and fair play. In one memo from the Home Office to the adjutant general's secretariat, there is an air of *well, if we must have a Catholic about the place*:[24] 'It is important that formally, at any rate, we should get away from the joint Protestant/Catholic concept. The men on the Committee should surely be men able to help in specific aspects of recruiting ... Having decided on this it would be wise to arrange that some of them were Roman Catholic ... In present conditions there must', they suggest, 'be some commonsense about who is taken in.'[25]

That 'commonsense' included distinguishing between *Castle Catholics* and *Cardinal Catholics*. In the home secretary's view, 'not too many of the Roman Catholic members of the Advisory Council should be "Castle Catholics" ... some of them at least should be persons whom responsible and orthodox Roman Catholic leaders such as Cardinal Conway would not regard as Government stooges.'[26]

It appears that, in late November 1969, General Freeland, the army's top officer (GOC) in Northern Ireland, proposed a draft committee membership. The proposed chairman was Sir John Anderson, the soon-to-be Colonel Commandant (purely an honorary or ceremonial title) of the UDR, said to be 'highly respected by all sections of the community and known to be completely impartial'. Anderson, from Downpatrick in County Down, would be the UDR's colonel commandant from 1969 to 1977, during which time he would also hold the annually appointed office of High Sheriff of County Down in 1974.[27]

The draft membership of the council included a former Lord Mayor of Belfast, an architect, a surgeon, a scientist and a judge, all with past or contemporary links to the military: 'The sort of members we had in mind were people who are not concerned with politics in any way and are known to be liberal minded and respected by all sections of the community.' That is, people upon whom the phrase 'politics doesn't interest you when you have no interest in changing a world that suits you so well'[28] sat comfortably.

A degree of horse-trading was to follow, with the home secretary in London suggesting that one of the Catholic nominees 'had already been used too much – he is the man whom everybody thinks of'. The man had 'outlived his usefulness as a Roman Catholic ... for this type of assignment'.[29] Oliver Wright, London's liaison with the Stormont government, agreed with these sentiments, and is reported to have said, 'we shall have difficulty finding distinguished Roman Catholics willing to serve on the Advisory Council, and that we may have to settle for whoever we can get'.[30]

Attached to the office of Stormont PM Chichester-Clark, Wright's official title was 'United Kingdom Representative in

Northern Ireland' (the first such appointee). He was formerly a deputy under-secretary at the Foreign and Commonwealth Office, and until recently had been the British ambassador to Denmark. This influential figure's main duties included warning 'that government [Stormont] if they proposed action which the British government would not approve and to inform the British government of the situation in Northern Ireland generally'.[31]

Soon after his arrival in Belfast, Wright explained to Cardinal Conway, the Catholic Primate of All-Ireland, over dinner at the palace in Armagh that he was 'unprejudiced by knowledge as far as Northern Ireland was concerned'. Yet within a fortnight of this meeting, he was bold enough to report to London that:

> Ulster is an essentially colonial situation. The present Protestant settler majority fears the unimpeded progress to an eventual Catholic majority caused by a higher Catholic birth rate ... Most people who have given any thought to the matter assume a Catholic majority in about two decades ... The majority also fear not only the loss of political power within his own community, but his absorption into the larger society of Southern Ireland, alien in smell, backward in development and inferior in politics. What was the Reformation about if not to liberate men from the tyranny of priests?[32]

Despite these sentiments, Wright evidently forged a working relationship with the cardinal. A memo from December 1969 shows Conway's influence on the British agonies over membership of the advisory council. It is reported that the cardinal, 'gently and diffidently', objected to a Major Beaumont on the basis that he 'was a staunch Unionist and would not, therefore, be considered by Northern Ireland Catholics as being representative of their section of the community'.[33]

Not long after Wright made his lament about the difficulty of finding Roman Catholics willing to serve on the Advisory Council, happily, a useful Catholic made himself known: a Mr Guckian, writing to the secretary of state for defence, Denis Healey, expressing gratitude to the army upon the departure from Derry of the 1st Queen's Battalion.[34]

Sensing an opportunity for some propaganda, Healey asked the army to 'find out a little more about' his correspondent.[35] The army reported Guckian to be:

> a very distinguished and respected Roman Catholic ... He is a staunch O'Neill supporter [O'Neill was the previous Stormont prime minister] ... He is held in great esteem by both the Army and the RUC and has in particular been a close friend of 1 QUEENS during recent months ... In short he is clearly an admirable fellow and probably worth logging as a reserve, should one be necessary, for the UDR Advisory Council.[36]

By 23 December 1969, this man had been 'given a clean bill of health by Cardinal Conway' and likewise was said to be 'entirely acceptable' to both Stormont and London's man, Oliver Wright.[37] That same day, less than two weeks after he wrote to the Ministry of Defence, this man was confirmed as the last member of the UDR Advisory Council. He had not been on any prior list of possible candidates; in fact, he had not been on the radar at all.

Nonetheless, it is apparent from recently uncovered files that Mr Guckian did not restrict himself to solely producing 'bright ideas' or giving 'advice on how to improve recruiting'.[38] The PFC has a letter on file from Guckian, dated 6 September 1971, actualising the army's fears of the advisory council and the 'real risk of escalation into fields for which it was not designed'.[39] By this time the UDR had been operative for just under a year and a half, and Guckian here sets forth his thoughts on future directions for the regiment:

> It is now proposed that a major increase in numbers will take place over the coming weeks, as a result of demands from a wide section of the community. The demands would appear to emanate from a variety of sources such as:
>
> a. Men who wish to fight the IRA.
> b. Men who wish to fight for the Constitution of N.I. and defend the border.
> c. Men who wish to protect their homes and families.
> d. Business people in urban areas who desire protection.
> e. Men who are frustrated at the state of the community and want to do something about it.[40]

Guckian wrote that the 'majority of groupings aforementioned' are clamouring for a 'third force', while 'we are being asked to supply arms to people who may exercise a considerable local power and autonomy in small communities throughout the province' (incidentally, it is interesting to note Guckian's identification with the UDR through the use of 'we' here). He also warned, 'When it is realised that under paragraph 2a, b and c, *we will be largely arming one section of the community* [emphasis added], then the operation is frought [*sic*] with serious political implications.' The three-page memo closes with 'a final word ... Above all, we cannot and must not adopt measures which in the public image will make us a force which can be associated with the force which we were created to replace.'[41]

A matter of days before this note was written, the Unionist prime minister at Stormont, Brian Faulkner, had urged British Prime Minister Edward Heath to permit the recruitment of UDR units in workplaces such as the Harland & Wolff shipyard in Belfast as a 'means of avoiding further pressures for the formation of irregular Protestant armed groups'.[42] In response, Guckian writes, 'It has been suggested that individual firms should provide units of the UDR for their own protection. I know we all agree that this is "not on" so I will not deal further with it.'[43]

What was 'on' was the expansion of the UDR when already, as Guckian acknowledges, 'It is widely accepted that there are far too many weapons in private hands.' The planned expansion of the UDR would mean 'that the majority of weapons will be held at home with the resulting allegations that we are arming one side of the community. On the security issue, it is clear that the more arms held in homes the greater the danger of them falling into the wrong hands.'[44]

Meanwhile, Stormont had manipulated Westminster and successfully removed the proviso that all applications to join the new force would be considered 'without discrimination'. These words were deemed by Stormont to be 'objectionable and unnecessary'.[45]

Is there evidence of discrimination in the UDR's recruitment practices? In his insightful 2015 article 'The Ulster Defence Regiment and the Question of Catholic Recruitment, 1970–1972', Gearóid Ó Faoleán illustrates how 'there is still no consensus as to how many Catholics enlisted during the first year': 'Potter ... stated that 25% of applicants were Catholic. Ryder estimated 22%, while a

Fortnight article from 1976 stated that "the proportion of Catholics in the regiment never got higher than 16%" ... By July 1970, of the 180 officers appointed within the UDR, just nine were Catholics.'[46]

With encouragement from moderate Catholic politicians and clergy (who had an influence on the composition of the UDR Advisory Council), Catholic recruitment to the UDR stood at 17 per cent by November 1970.[47] British Prime Minister Jim Callaghan apparently believed that this figure alone 'was sufficient to show that the UDR was not just the B-Specials under another name'.[48]

Major military operations in Northern Ireland saw the deployment of significant numbers of UDR members. Concessions made to Stormont during the formation of the UDR may have had a chilling effect on Catholic recruitment, but a correlation may certainly be seen between the use of the regiment in certain roles and a significant drop in Catholic membership. The brutal imposition of the Falls curfew on 3 July 1970, in which, over three days, the British army flooded Catholic neighbourhoods with CS gas, ransacked hundreds of homes and killed four people, was seen by the nationalist population as having been supported, or abetted, by the UDR. By providing personnel for roadblocks, and patrolling elsewhere, they allowed the army to deploy large numbers of regular troops in Belfast that weekend.

On 9 August 1971, internment without trial was implemented. As with the Falls curfew the previous year, UDR deployments elsewhere allowed huge numbers of regular British troops to launch pre-dawn raids across Belfast. Over 3,000 UDR members were deployed to assist while young men, exclusively from the nationalist community, were rounded up and held without charge or trial. In the ensuing three days, more than a dozen civilians were shot dead by the army, including ten people in the Ballymurphy Massacre.

Outrage at the internment raids led the IRA to lift their self-imposed ban on targeting UDR personnel. On the very day of the IRA's announcement, the first UDR member to be killed, Winston Donnell, was shot by republicans at a vehicle checkpoint in west Tyrone.

Then IRA chief-of-staff Seán MacStiofáin, later wrote:

> From internment on, UDR and RUC personnel, like British soldiers, were treated as legitimate combatant targets at all times, whether on duty or not, armed or not, in uniform or not. This may sound a harsh ruling, but the facts of life were that IRA members were liable to be arrested or shot by any of these forces at any time. In addition, the RUC and UDR were the eyes and ears of the enemy intelligence machine, particularly in the detailed knowledge of rural districts which would be so difficult for the occupation forces to obtain on their own.[49]

Ó Faoleán described internment as 'the principal watershed in terms of Catholic attitudes to the UDR, appendage to the regular British Army as it was'.[50] In the wake of internment, a senior SDLP figure, Austin Currie (whose own brother was a member of the force), publicly withdrew his support for the regiment, stating, 'As far as I am concerned internment was the last straw. The brutality which accompanied it certainly helped to break the camel's back.'[51]

In his history of the UDR, Potter writes that internment was a disaster for the regiment – one which its commander, Brigadier Scott-Bowden, had foreseen would happen: 'It accelerated the loss of Catholic soldiers.'[52] In Ryder's words, 'one-sided application of internment ... smacking as it did of a return to the bad old days of Unionist repression, left the Catholics in the UDR in a disillusioned and vulnerable position.'[53]

The Irish government kept a concerned eye on developments; one official in the Department of External Affairs noted, 'The UDR was supposed to be a non-sectarian unit of the British Army, representative of all sections of the community. It seems to me that ... it is becoming a refuge for ex-B Specials, and such members of the minority who may still be in the UDR in these [border] counties will soon be "encouraged" to resign.'[54]

During Operation Motorman (the 31 July 1972 assault on the 'no-go' areas in Derry and Belfast), over 5,000 UDR men were deployed. A subsequent meeting of the UDR Advisory Council on 12 August 1972 noted a rise in recruitment in 'response to operation Motorman'. However, the meeting also detailed declining recruitment from within the Catholic community, with only 389 remaining in the regiment out of a total strength of 8,917. The minutes record: 'The reasons for the high Catholic wastage were being analysed; this was probably due to Catholic members who had long been inactive finally tendering their resignations.'[55]

While that may have been considered a possibility in certain circles, it is more likely, as Ryder allowed, that the hostility encountered by many Catholics within the regiment in the lead-up to internment, the anger they felt at the frequent brutality meted out at checkpoints, 'and the emphasis on patrolling and oppressing Catholic areas on the basis that they were the monopoly suppliers of disorder' were the reasons for the decline in Catholic representation. Ryder also reports the words of one Catholic man who resigned from the UDR and said, 'It was made clear we weren't wanted.' Ryder says of Catholic UDR personnel that 'their loyalty was also being called into constant question by Unionists despite the fact that all Catholic soldiers had taken an Oath of Allegiance to the Queen'.[56]

Nevertheless, both Potter and Ryder lay the blame for Catholic under-representation in the UDR mostly on republican attacks. UDR personnel were considered 'legitimate targets' by republicans from the introduction of internment onwards. Both writers agree that there was deliberate targeting of Catholic UDR members to deter Catholics from joining the force.

The first Catholic UDR man to be killed by republicans was Sean Russell, a thirty-two-year-old father of five, shot dead by the IRA in his home on 8 December 1971, four months after the introduction of internment. According to Potter, Russell 'lived in a predominantly Catholic estate at New Barnsley and was a committee member of a Republican club ... He saw the Regiment as playing a part in the running of the community, and with Catholics taking a hand in it for the first time.'[57]

Between February and October 1972, a further three Catholic UDR men were killed by republicans. The Provisional IRA shot dead Thomas Callaghan in Derry city in February. John Ruddy was killed in Newry eight months later. The third Catholic UDR victim of republican violence that year, Marcus McCausland, was shot by the Official IRA.

In the fourteen months following internment, seven Catholic UDR soldiers were killed. According to Potter, 'it is hard not to believe that those Catholics were murdered deliberately to persuade their co-religionists to resign from the Regiment.'[58] Both Ryder and Potter ascribe a cause-and-effect dynamic to these figures. Ó Faoleán has interrogated this, however, and argues that 'the facts do not fit such interpretations.'[59] He asserts that the deaths of many Catholic

UDR members fit with patterns other than a sectarian motive – Catholic and Protestant UDR men alike were killed because they were, to use a horrible phrase, 'soft targets'. A look at the figures perhaps supports Ó Faoleán's argument: in the same period, from internment in August 1971 to the end of 1972, thirty-two members of the UDR were killed in total,[60] Catholics comprising 22% of that figure (and not the 28% Potter suggests).[61]

Perhaps internment was the final straw for many Catholic members of the force. It is arguable that the sheer number of ex-B Specials within the ranks was also significant. This aspect is minimised by Potter, who asserts that all UDR battalions – 'including those with a predominately USC [B Specials] background' – had some Catholic members, who 'were willingly accepted and respected for their courage'.[62]

He cites the experience of one officer who recalled:

> There I was, an ex-USC officer, commanding a patrol of eight men, of whom I was the only Protestant. We got along fine, both then and in the years ahead. Some time later a Catholic member of the company, who later became Regimental Quartermaster Sergeant, said to me one evening over a few drinks in the canteen after we had come back from a Border operation, 'Sir, I've just heard you were a Special. It's a remarkable thing that everyone I like best in this company seems to have been in the USC.'[63]

Remarkable indeed. Is it too cynical to suggest that this is a tall tale? Ó Faoleán is sharply critical of Potter's treatment of the sectarianism that existed within Potter's own regiment (Potter rose to the rank of Major in the UDR). Of the UDR's cadre of former B Specials, Ó Faoleán argues that 'it is highly doubtful that all but a few rejected sectarianism following the transition into the UDR'. Potter's dismissal of sectarianism as a factor, he says, 'undermines his assessment of Catholic alienation from the force'.[64]

A letter among recently discovered files dated 15 November 1984 – from an official (named Coulson) in the Law & Order Division of the Northern Ireland Office (NIO) – offered the following views to the secretary of state for Northern Ireland:

> I wonder whether it is not an over simplification to attribute the run down in the proportion of Catholics in the UDR merely to murder and intimidation. These are clearly factors; however there were other factors which could be reflected, because they do account in part for the attitude of the minority community towards the UDR ...
>
> I suspect that this process was hastened by the staunchly Loyalist and anti-Nationalist inclinations of many members of the force – some of whom had been directly recruited from the B Specials. There is no doubt that, although the Ulster Special Constabulary might have been disbanded, most people in the minority community perceived its spirit living in the UDR. I suspect that this perception was shared by many people in the Loyalist community, which may well account for their sensitivity at any prospect of its role being diminished.[65]

There can be no doubt that the fear of IRA retribution was intended to deter potential recruits from the minority community. At the same time, in the aftermath of internment, Catholics turned away from the UDR in droves in protest at a security policy aimed exclusively at the nationalist-republican population.

If internment was 'a disaster for the UDR', this was mitigated by the surge in Protestant enlistment to the force following its introduction. Potter attributes this surge to the perception within the Protestant community that the government was 'at last taking resolute action against the IRA', adding that applications rose from an average of forty a week to seventy-two in the week following internment – 'then 169, then 376', with 1,290 new applications having been made by the end of September.[66] If there had been doubts or suspicion among the unionist majority population as to the loyalties of the UDR – a fear that it would not be their force, like the B Specials had been – the internment campaign got rid of any lingering doubts. In September 1971, the press was reporting that the UDR was experiencing an increase in recruitment at the very time that the Catholic exodus was underway.[67]

Despite alarming signs that the UDR was rapidly becoming a regiment drawn from only one side of the community, the advisory council nonetheless 'agreed that the Regiment had succeeded in preserving its non-sectarian spirit to a much greater degree than the statistics of Catholic membership suggested'. However, the council also laid emphasis upon 'the need ... to prevent certain companies in Protestant areas from becoming irreversibly Protestant'.[68] Ultimately, the surge in recruitment after internment would highlight another uncomfortable reality for the UDR – infiltration by loyalist paramilitaries.

CHAPTER THREE

Citizens of Good Character?

We have seen how the army was preoccupied with whether or not 'imposed military discipline' would be tolerated by the UDR. Might this provoke certain conflicts of interest? The legislation creating the UDR provided 'full opportunity for all citizens of Northern Ireland to serve the community as a whole. To this end, enrolment [was to be] open to all male citizens of good character of the United Kingdom and Colonies, normally resident in Northern Ireland, whatever their denomination.'[1] Presumably, citizens of less than good character were to be weeded out at the application stage.

At Westminster, in the debates around the Ulster Defence Regiment Bill, the Labour MP Manny Shinwell skewered the absurdities in trying to apply such fair-minded principles to the sectarian statelet ruled from Stormont by Unionists: 'Who will be responsible for the interpretation in the Six Counties? What will be the interpretation of those members of the Orange order, the Unionist Party or the extremists associated with them? What is the interpretation of "desirable character"?'

Shinwell continued:

> I will deal with the proposed Army. Somebody goes
> along, fills in an application form and is security vetted.
> I suppose that he would be asked a few questions –
> for example, what is his religion? He might reply that
> he is a Roman Catholic. That is all right. He might
> then be asked, 'What is your opinion about partition?'
> I would be interested to know what the reaction would
> be. He might be asked, 'What is your opinion about
> the Stormont Government?' I can imagine what the
> answer would be. Or have you ever been associated
> with the Civil Rights Movement? Have you ever been
> arrested for anything in the nature of turbulence in
> recent months in the Six Counties – in other words,
> 'Are you a desirable character?' I doubt very much
> whether there would be many recruits accepted from
> the minority section in the Six Counties. Indeed. I do
> not suppose that those on the other side of the fence
> want them.[2]

The regular army was to be wholly responsible for recruiting
and vetting, with the Army Security Vetting Unit based at
army HQ at Lisburn. According to Potter, it consisted of
'some thirty-five vetting officers, mainly retired officers from
outside Northern Ireland with no experience of local nuances,
including a Vice Admiral and several Major Generals'. With
no experience of local nuances, what could go wrong?

Every applicant had to nominate two referees, and the
procedure was that the vetting officer was to interview both
of them. Applications were also to be referred to the RUC
Criminal Investigation Department and Special Branch.[3]
With the RUC casting the final judgment on applicants'

character, as British Labour MP Kevin McNamara put it, 'it would not be beyond the bounds of possibility for us to be a little suspicious of the information being laid.'[4]

A further weakness was highlighted in 1973 by a senior official in the army's Directorate of Security; he described the UDR's 'security vetting process' as 'in fact only a screening procedure [which] has no relationship to normal security vetting carried out on people who require to have access to classified information ... The screening procedure was initiated to dispel fears that the UDR would perpetuate the USC ("B" Specials) in a different guise.' Furthermore, while the requirement for recruits to provide a reference 'has probably been successful as part of the PR exercise ... it can have had little effect in improving the value of the screening'.[5]

A memo dated 20 August 1973 from the Director of Security (Army) to BGS (Int) (Brigadier-General Staff with responsibility for Intelligence) alludes to the 'security vetting process' in the UDR and notes that it was introduced to dispel fears that the UDR would evolve into the B Specials 'in a different guise'. Although the injection of the interview has probably been successful as part of the PR exercise, it can have had little effect in improving the value of screening.

As weak as it was, there was to be a steady erosion of the vetting process over time. In May 1974 a lieutenant colonel informed the under-secretary of state in the Ministry of Defence – referred to as the 'US of S (Army)' – that 'the RUC may have attempted on some occasions deliberately to conceal criminal records', a fact the under-secretary of state found 'very disturbing'.[6]

By then, violent loyalist passions had found expression with the formation of a number of paramilitary groups, the UVF and subsequently the Ulster Defence Association

(UDA), and various smaller groups that would ebb and flow in influence through the 1970s right up to today.

In another secret memo a couple of months later, the head of DS10 (Defence Secretariat 10, an important division within the British Ministry of Defence that provided information and policy advice to ministers and British military staff during the conflict in the early 1970s) admits there had been 'some relaxation of security screening for UDR' recruits and that 'If news of this ... [were] to leak out ... it could be distinctly awkward.'[7]

Even with the weaknesses embedded in the system – RUC concealment of criminal records, and the 'relaxation of security screening' – it was still too troublesome for the UDR to carry out properly. Potter says it was decided that, for the purposes of establishing the UDR:

> it would take far too long to adhere to that system. Instead, it was officially agreed that applicants would be divided into three categories: Those who were apparently acceptable and could be cleared without further ado; those who were obviously not and should be rejected; and those about whom there was some doubt. Only the third category was subject to a more detailed vetting.

It should be noted that the actual usefulness of the vetting process was hardly improved over the duration of the UDR's existence. A 2012 review by Desmond de Silva QC[8] of the UDA's murder of lawyer Pat Finucane in 1989 (using stolen UDR weaponry) referred to vetting problems in the UDR as still a live issue in the late 1980s. He reported that 1,350 adverse vetting reports had arisen in relation to individuals seeking to join the UDR during the period 1988–9. Despite these adverse reports, 351 of these individuals were enlisted in the UDR.[9]

Potter waves away concerns at what he describes as the 'rough and ready system' of vetting, because 'at that time [the spring of 1970] the only Loyalist paramilitaries were the few in the Ulster Volunteer Force (UVF); the Ulster Defence Association (UDA) had not yet been formed.'[10] That may have been so, but was soon set to change. The UDA was to grow rapidly, becoming the largest loyalist paramilitary organisation – and it would remain so throughout the conflict. The UDA used the cover name 'UFF' when claiming sectarian killings, which enabled the UDA to avoid proscription until 1992. By December 1972 the UDA was 'the largest non-state paramilitary organisation in the Western world', with a membership of 26,000 men[11] – concerns about the UDA had already been aired at meetings of the UDR Advisory Council.

At one such meeting in June 1972, the UDR's then commanding officer, Brigadier Ormerod, reported that 'certain recruits were motivated primarily by the wish to obtain access to arms'. Ormerod assured the council that 'those who operated the vetting procedure were very alive to the need to identify political extremists ... although it was inevitable that from time to time extremist sympathies would not be revealed by a candidate's record or references'.[12]

As 'alive to the need' as the vetting staff may have been, by July 1972 Brigadier Ormerod, as the UDR's commanding officer, was concerned enough to write the following memorandum to his staff:

1. It is clear that the UDA attracts considerable sympathy for its political aims amongst some UDR soldiers. It is suspected that a minority of UDR soldiers are actually active members of the UDA. This is not in

itself a military or civil offence but it raises problems of loyalty which I am going to discuss in the following paras.

2. The mission of the Security Forces is to support the Government's policy and no action can be tolerated if it might jeopardise this. The UDA are a large and volatile factor in the development of the political situation in the Province. This is the most important consideration, at the present time, in deciding how COs are to react to membership or support of the UDA by men in their battalions.

3. The second most important consideration for UDR COs is the maintenance of morale in their battalions. This has a close bearing on the future of the Regiment. As a principle therefore soldiers are not to be forced into declaring a political allegiance now nor are they to be punished simply for being members of the UDA. Nevertheless joint membership clearly stretches loyalties and is for that reason undesirable.

4. Bearing in mind those considerations the following guidelines are issued to COs:

   a. If an officer either declares that he is, or is shown to be, an active supporter of the UDA he is to be asked to retire or to resign (subject to the procedures in ... UDR Regulations).

   b. Soldiers who are suspected of sufficient sympathy for UDA aims to affect the performance of their military duties or call their future loyalties into question are to be warned.

   c. If an officer or soldier's conduct, arising out of his membership of the UDA, constitutes a military offence, disciplinary action will be taken against him either under the Army Act or the UDR Act

1969, whichever is applicable. Such action must be
authorised by Commander UDR.
5. A military offence envisaged in 4.c. above would be,
for example … carrying AD [possibly 'Active Duty']
weapons or wearing AD uniform at a UDA assembly,
connivance with the UDA in the provision of military
information or in the theft of AD weapons, or
encouraging other soldiers to commit such acts.[13]

Ormerod went so far as to provide a briefing document for
officers to assist them in warning UDR soldiers about these
vexed issues – a briefing document that was to guide 'oral
briefing' only and was not to be disseminated outside battalion
headquarters. 'Particular importance' was attached to this
last instruction.[14] Clearly the threat of divided loyalties was
taken seriously by the UDR's commander and was deemed so
dangerous that it needed to be dealt with secretly.

By October 1972, such was the 'disturbing rise in the
number of cases involving UDR men in the courts' that
Fortnight (the influential political and cultural magazine
published in Belfast) noted, 'the number of charges brought
against UDR personnel strongly suggests that the supposed
careful screening of potential UDR conscripts has failed
to weed out the sort of people which so discredited the
"B" Specials. There is a danger that in our highly sensitive
situation, the UDR is shortly to become equally discredited.'[15]

Nevertheless, in November 1972 Ormerod was telling
the audience at a Belfast Rotary Club event that while joint
membership of the UDR and the UDA was not welcomed,
the prevailing policy was that membership of the UDA was
not necessarily a bar to membership of the UDR. But he said
that they would not expect an officer in the UDR to remain
with the regiment if he was also a member of the UDA.[16] The

UDR was, it seems, co-operating with UDA members in a kind of 'don't ask, don't tell' policy.

Why was this significant? In his discussion of the nature of pro-state terrorism in *The Red Hand: Protestant Paramilitaries in Northern Ireland*, Steve Bruce says that 'any pro-state terrorist organisation [such as the UDA or UVF] has the problem that it competes with the government's security forces for personnel ... the state and the pro-state terror group recruit from the same population'.[17]

What this means, in practice, is the legitimisation of the offensive or defensive impulses of one part of a divided community: 'A working-class Protestant who wishes to ... defend Ulster can do [so] in a variety of high status, well-rewarded channels. He can join the RUC or the UDR. If he wants to combine such a commitment with a full-time job, he could join the RUC Reserve or become a part-time UDR soldier.' Bruce agrees that 'many committed loyalists, who on the Catholic side might be members of the IRA, join the RUC Reserve or the UDR'.[18]

Bruce gives the example of one senior UDA man who, he reports, had tried to join the RUC in the 1950s but had been rejected because he was too short. According to the UDA man himself, 'When things started to get bad, I tried to join the Specials but they were being stood down. I put my name down for the UDR but for some reason – they never tell you the reason – I was rejected. So I had to look elsewhere. I got involved with my local vigilantes and just went on from there.'[19] Bruce asserts that 'compared with loyalist paramilitary organisations, the police and the army are selective'; he writes that so 'many of the people who in only slightly altered circumstances might have become competent terrorist operators have been siphoned off, and the UDA and UVF are left to recruit from the least competent sections of their population ... The Crown forces have the advantages of being legal, respectable, and paying well.'[20] The UDR had the advantage then, it follows, of having the first pick of potential 'competent terrorist operators'.

On 17 July, Lt Col J.L. Pownall at the MoD wrote to the civil adviser to the GOC in Northern Ireland, John Howe, expressing his concerns at the extent of UDA infiltration of the UDR becoming public knowledge. This was brought about because the under-secretary of state for the army had been told of the problem while on a visit to Northern Ireland and because the magazine *Private Eye* had recently made it public.[21]

Pownall included the *Private Eye* piece in his letter of concern, not least because it exposed the fact of UDR officers confronting British soldiers while masked and acting for the UDA – 'One set of British officers, in other words, have been negotiating with another set, with the latter openly threatening to shoot down the former.' The *Private Eye* article also noted the 'sudden rise in "missing equipment" from UDR headquarters' and concluded, 'The most absurd aspect of the forthcoming war is that the British army may well find itself fighting troops trained by fellow officers and armed with British army weapons and radios.'[22]

The appalling vista of a forthcoming war between British soldiers was hardly likely. In the same letter of concern, Pownall communicated his assumption that 'it is generally agreed that the UDA is to be regarded as an "extremist" organisation', membership of which was 'incompatible with membership of the Regiment'; he sought advice on how to proceed, or at least how to be seen to have been 'taking steps' in case of parliamentary scrutiny.[23]

The reply from Howe, at army headquarters in Northern Ireland, starkly illuminates the relationship between the UDR and violent loyalism:

It is inevitable that part of the Protestant element of a part-time regiment in Ulster will sympathise with the aims of the UDA, and it is suspected that there are cases where this sympathy is carried to the extent of active membership ...

One important (but unspoken) function of the UDR is to channel into a constructive and disciplined direction Protestant energies that might otherwise become disruptive ...

I am sure this moderate line towards UDA supporters is the right one in light of the role of the UDA as a safety valve. In my opinion it would be politically unwise to dismiss a member of the UDA from the UDR unless he had committed a military offence.[24]

While the UDR was taking this 'moderate line' towards UDA supporters, the UDA was busy killing people. Over the course of July and August 1972, loyalist paramilitaries were killing Catholic civilians at a rate of one person every second night.[25] The UDA murdered at least twenty people in July alone – the same month the letter was written.[26]

Yet in June 1972, when HQNI was taking stock of the UDR's disposition (it had by then come within 15 per cent of its 10,000-man target strength), concerns were raised by HQNI that 'there would be disappointment amongst the Protestant members of the population at any announcement that the recruiting ceiling was to remain at 10,000. This could lead to men joining a paramilitary organisation such as the UDA as an alternative to the UDR.'[27] That British army HQ should seek to actively recruit extreme loyalists who might otherwise join a paramilitary organisation is in itself an extraordinary admission.

The reply from Howe continues: 'I recognise the reasons

why Ministers might wish to be able to say unequivocally … that membership of the UDA is not compatible with membership of the UDR and that we have no evidence that any UDR member is actively associated with the UDA. But I fear it would be wrong to offer categorical assurances on either point.' Instead, it is proposed that ministers simply say that the UDR is a 'non-sectarian' force, the members of which represent 'a wide range of political viewpoints'.[28]

This disingenuous construction ignores the fact that while by no means all serving UDR men were linked to paramilitary activity, the vast majority would have been unionists. The British government would have been well aware of this and so to say the regiment represented a 'wide range of political viewpoints' was a breathtakingly cynical equivocation, technically true but functionally a lie.

On 11 September 1972, a meeting was held in London of the GEN 79 security committee, a secretive committee comprising cabinet ministers (including British Prime Minister Heath) and senior figures from the military and security services. At the meeting, the prime minister said that 'the question of members of the UDR who were also associating with the UDA required further consideration'.[29] Significantly, the letter confirms that the prime minister was aware of loyalist infiltration of the regiment.

The extent to which the government was concerned to ensure the UDR was not seen as sectarian, while at the same time privately acknowledging that this was indeed the case, is illustrated in a letter, dated 21 June 1972, from an official (MacDonald) in the Ministry of Defence to Howe, the civilian adviser to the GOC in Northern Ireland. Howe had asked (on 2 June) about the possibility of extending the UDR's range of duties.[30]

In MacDonald's careful reply, it is clear that the UDR's

sectarianism was a concern to the military and to politicians, so much so that they tried to limit the UDR's activities, keeping them away from interface areas and the west bank of the river Foyle in Derry. Their presence could lead to what is described as the risk of escalated violence: 'An exchange of fire in such circumstances would be bound to put at risk immediately the reputation of the UDR for impartiality.'[31] The very necessity of the letter proves the UDR had no such reputation. In fact, the letter discloses that the UDR could not even be entrusted with 'helping to enforce the car parking ban', which was imposed in response to the IRA's tactic of leaving car-bombs in commercial areas.[32]

On 24 November, as the British prime minister was preparing to meet Taoiseach Jack Lynch to discuss, among other issues, the UDA, the prime minister's officials provided a background brief to explain security force policy towards the UDA. This confidential army document was classified and designated as too sensitive to be passed in writing below battalion level. It stated, 'i. Operations against UDA should be directed against their criminal extremist elements whilst making every endeavour to maintain good relations with law abiding citizens in the organisation. ii. Contact should be maintained at company commander level with the UDA. iii. Unarmed, locally resident vigilante type patrols should be tolerated provided they do not break the law.'[33]

The prime minister was informed that the RUC had similar instructions. The official view was therefore that loyalist violence was confined to criminal extremists. This official denial of the extent of loyalist violence is exemplified in the minutes of a meeting in London in 1974, where an official from the attorney general's office asked, 'why only Roman Catholics had been interned before 1973'. A Treasury solicitor representative replied that it was the view of the security forces that there was 'no serious Protestant threat in that period that led to death or serious injuries'.[34] The British government was denying the fact of 143 assassinations carried out by loyalists during 1971–2.

The UDA was not actually declared an illegal organisation until August 1992. The UVF were an illegal organisation throughout the conflict, since shortly after their third fatal attack in 1966, apart from a brief period in the early 1970s (seventeen months from May 1974 to October 1975). As brief as this period was, it should not be glossed over. The UVF was legalised two days before their involvement in the fatal Dublin and Monaghan bombings, the attack on the Miami Showband, and other murders.

Up until the early 1990s, the UDA was responsible for numerous sectarian murders from 1973 onwards, using the barely veiled conceit of claiming its victims using the soubriquet 'Ulster Freedom Fighters' (UFF). The British government, which publicly denied the UDA's murderous campaign for two decades, was aware from an early stage, however, of the nature of the organisation. An internal British briefing paper said of the UDA and UFF in September 1976:

> The UDA is the largest and best-organised of the Loyalist paramilitary organisations. It tries to maintain a respectable front and, to this end, either denies responsibility for sectarian murders and terrorist bombings or claims them in the name of the ULSTER FREEDOM FIGHTERS (UFF), *a proscribed and essentially fictitious organisation* [emphasis added] which is widely known to be a nom de guerre for the UDA.[35]

Writing to the British government in July 1972, General Sir Harry Tuzo, the senior British military officer in Northern

Ireland, warned that the UDA's 'militant action will lead to widespread inter-sectarian conflict and eventually civil war'.[36] Nevertheless, the view was that this organisation, handled correctly, would be a valuable ally in the war against the only real enemy, the IRA. This was 'the Tuzo plan', which was prepared in anticipation of the breakdown of the IRA ceasefire and presented to the Northern Ireland secretary William Whitelaw on 9 July 1972. Even before the end of the IRA ceasefire, Tuzo was planning an all-out offensive against the IRA in which both the UDR and the UDA would have a role to play.

Tuzo accepted that the British army should 'acquiesce in unarmed UDA patrolling and barricading of Protestant areas'.[37] Indeed, the UDA was often allowed to patrol 'Protestant areas' in uniform, sometimes wearing masks. The authorities even went so far as to turn a blind eye to the UDA patrolling with arms, and sometimes even allowed it to patrol with British troops.

Tuzo's proposals were prepared with the approval of the British army's chief of general staff, Field Marshal Michael Carver, and can therefore be taken to reflect the view of Britain's military establishment on how best to conduct operations against the IRA. In Tuzo's view, 'Vigilantes, whether UDA (Ulster Defence Association) or not, should be discreetly encouraged in Protestant areas to reduce the load on the Security Forces.'[38] After all, as William Beattie Smith put it, the British government 'depend[ed] on the Protestant community for its foot soldiers ... the point was made at a meeting of the MoD's Northern Ireland Policy Group on June 1, 1972, that "the killing of IRA members by Protestants might be no bad thing from our point of view".'[39]

The essence of the Tuzo plan would permeate British strategy throughout the conflict. Its influence could be felt almost two decades later, when the British command would discuss a strategy and planning dossier called 'Defeating Terrorism', which made no reference at all to loyalist violent extremism.[40] Also in 1990, Secretary of State for Northern Ireland Peter Brooke would write to Secretary of State for Defence Tom King requesting that two additional battalions be sent to combat 'Irish terrorism'. Again, loyalists are not mentioned once in the letter (subsequent documents show that both King and Prime Minister Margaret Thatcher disagreed with the request).[41]

Ian Wood recorded the reflections of a UDR officer on the army's relationship with the UDA in 1972:

> 1972 was the year of the UDA. Like Napoleon and Hitler, the Army had long worried about a war on two fronts, and this it got with the rise of the UDA ... In order to combat this threat, the Army chose quite deliberately to give the UDA tacit support ... Almost too late, in the winter of 1972, the Army realised that it had assisted in the birth of a monster. It sought to act but was only able to cage the beast: the secret of its destruction had been lost with its birth.[42]

An excellent illustration of the British military's relationship with the UDA, in 'the year of the UDA', comes from this short paragraph from a British army intelligence summary in the 39 Brigade Commander's diary for November 1972. In this instance, a UDA leader 'was visibly embarrassed' when British army 'searchers' he accompanied around a UDA club found 'Over half a ton of bomb-making equipment ... together with nearly 300 rounds of ammunition'. Visible embarrassment was the sum total of this man's discomfort, however, as he – the Officer Commanding, B Company, UDA – 'was released because of lack of evidence'.[43]

This cosy relationship is further exemplified in an army intelligence summary document from September 1973 that describes a meeting between security forces and the UDA in the Royal Bar, Newtownards, in County Down. The meeting was held 'to acquaint the new Battery Commander [British army officer] in Newtownards with the UDA hierarchy'. One of the UDA men named at the meeting is described as 'UDA PRO & SFLO', which presumably means he was the UDA's public relations and security force liaison officer.[44]

What was in it for the UDA? Ryder reported that in 1976, Andy Tyrie, then leader of the UDA, boasted of how his members were joining the UDR in order to receive weapons training.[45] The scale of weapons training reportedly given by UDR soldiers to the UDA, the UVF and other loyalist extremists, such as the Orange Volunteers, is unquantifiable. Mary Holland, writing in 1980, estimated that by then (ten years after the UDR's inception) the regiment had trained over 21,000 loyalists in the use of weapons.[46] Potter concluded that the reasons for loyalist extremists joining the UDR were self-evident: 'free training, plus access to weapons, ammunition and intelligence'.[47]

There was a high turn-over rate among UDR recruits. In 1973 a statistical analysis had been undertaken for the MoD to look into reasons for UDR 'wastage', as it was described. Of 900 separate cases of UDR personnel leaving the regiment, by far the most common reason given – one in four of those surveyed – was 'Failure to attend for duty'. Around one in seven gave 'no reasons'. Only one in twenty surveyed had left upon completion of their agreed term. This might support the idea that large numbers of people were joining the UDR in order to receive weapons training, and then resigning once they had been so trained.

Such 'wastage' was acknowledged in the UK parliament.

In July 1976, Robert Brown, parliamentary under-secretary at the MoD, said that 'in a volunteer force such as the Ulster Defence Regiment a constant turnover of personnel is both natural and healthy'.[48] In 1990 Secretary of State for Northern Ireland Peter Brooke, replying to former Secretary of State for Northern Ireland Merlyn Rees, agreed said that 'over the years the UDR has had a high turnover of people'.[49]

The issue of intelligence and the UDR proved controversial from the beginning. Numerous reports on file at the PFC by the PSNI's Historical Enquiries Team (HET)[50] point to UDR intelligence being used to target people for assassination. This was the case with Louis Leonard who was shot dead in his butcher's shop in Derrylin, Fermanagh, on 15 December 1972. The HET were in no doubt that local UDR members were involved in the murder.[51]

Likewise, with a series of UDA murders in and around Derry in late 1976 and early 1977, when the murders of four people – Kevin Mulhern, John Toland, Jim Loughrey, and Michael McHugh – were linked through ballistics or individuals with the trail leading back to the UDA commander in Derry at the time. According to the HET, this person had 'close links' to UDR members in the city.[52] One of those convicted in connection with these murders was a member of the UDR and the judge noted that he had used his position in the regiment to benefit the UDA.

The HET report into the murders of the Reavey brothers (see page xxiii) also notes information emanating from within the local UDR which falsely suggested that they were involved in the IRA and stored weapons and explosives in the the family home.[53] These smears were later rejected both by the HET and the RUC chief constable.

Access to UDR intelligence was a significant driver of

violence and not one restricted to the 1970s. In 1985 the Security Service assessed that 85 per cent of the UDA's intelligence originated from sources within the security forces.[54] The 2012 de Silva review examined a sample of security force leaks to loyalist paramilitaries between 1987 and 1989, for which the UDR was the branch of the security forces most culpable – especially for 'targeting information' (names, addresses, often photographs, pointing out nationalists, republicans or even simply Catholics, who the culpable security force members were happy to see killed).[55]

William Beattie Smith wrote of loyalist paramilitaries that 'They were not a mirror image of the IRA. Their objectives were more limited and reactive ... "localistic and politically primitive" ... But they had one significant asset which the IRA lacked: access to information, weaponry, and support from sympathetic individuals in the security forces, especially the Ulster Defence Regiment (UDR) and RUC.'[56] In November 1972, *The Observer* newspaper asked the very pertinent question: 'What happens to a militiaman, armed and trained by the British Army, who is also a member of a private army that isn't always on the same side?'

An editorial in *The Observer* – 'Some "Dad's Army" men stepping out of line' – described 'the schizophrenia apparent among the Ulster Protestants ... with talk about conflicting allegiances within the Ulster Defence Regiment'. It detailed 'two recent incidents ... both involving UDR men losing their arms to Protestant extremists', which helped to fuel views within the Catholic population that the UDR was 'synonymous with armed Protestants and everything that entails'. As a result of such incidents, 'many believe that Britain has simply raised another police force along the lines of the Black and Tans and Auxiliaries of the 1920s'. The article suggested that the UDR's 'failure to uphold a non-sectarian face' was forcing the regiment's commander, Brigadier Ormerod, to publicly 'explain the regiment's relationship with the UDA'.[57]

CHAPTER FOUR

'Arming One Section of the Community'

At least one UDR Advisory Council member was concerned that the army, through the UDR, was 'largely arming one section of the community'. What steps if any were to be taken to defend against these threats?

Files recovered from the National Archives reveal an astonishing degree of awareness among the British military and government of the scale of wholesale misappropriation (sometimes called 'theft' in the documents) from UDR armouries. Notes among the minutes of a UDR Advisory Council meeting in June 1972 show that the military was concerned at the rate at which weapons, being stored at home by UDR soldiers, were being 'stolen'.[1] Beginning 19 July 1972, a succession of reports summarising UDR weapons losses detailed instances of weapons 'stolen either from individual UDR soldiers or from their homes, or from UDR armouries or guard rooms'. In a number of cases reports say that 'collusion is suspected'.[2]

As early as 2 September 1971, when a .303 rifle was stolen from Newcastle, Co. Down, there is mention of the 'possibility of collusion'.[3] This document contains the first official reference to collusion in the conflict found to date. Significantly, that first mention was made in a note forwarded, in 1972, to the office of a British under-secretary of state – that is, to ministerial level. In a handwritten note on the memo, an official describes the losses as constituting 'an appalling list, which lends colour to recent allegations of connivance'.[4]

Discoveries such as these offer a stark rejoinder to anyone who says that the idea of state collusion with loyalism was invented by nationalists – internal British army documents dating back to at least 1972 see the word used routinely and repeatedly. What it all amounted to was a steady flow of modern military equipment from the British army straight into the hands of loyalist gangs.

Preparations for a ministerial response to a question in parliament on 3 August 1972 – Frank McManus MP seeking to know the numbers of weapons lost in the previous six months – show the minister of state for defence was advised that 'in a number of cases collusion is suspected'. Needless to say this did not find its way into the official reply.[5]

On 9 August 1972, an MoD official informed the chain of command that 'There is no clear explanation of why so many weapons were lost in July [1972]. As you are aware most of them were stolen by masked men and in several cases CID suspect UDA besides those where collusion is reported … As far as units are concerned the heaviest losses are in 2 UDR Armagh and 8 UDR Dungannon which possibly have the greatest problem of mixed population and active extremists.'[6] A meeting of the UDR Advisory Council on 12 August 1972 discussed the weapons losses and that there had been a number of media reports of UDA infiltration of the UDR.[7]

Such infiltration was already then suspected by Catholic and nationalist representatives. The circumstances of weapons losses were such that the SDLP's MP for Mid-Derry, Ivan Cooper, said, 'The UDR must believe they are living in a community of imbeciles', otherwise they would not have the 'effrontery' to provide the explanations they did for the losses. Cooper 'demanded to know how much longer the arming of loyalist extremists by the UDR would be tolerated'.[8] Cooper described the weapons losses as the UDR 'arming the UDA by stealth'.[9]

A note from the US of S (Army) showed that there were anxieties at ministerial level too. On 10 October 1972 he observed that UDR weapons and uniforms seemed to be stolen 'with some regularity', suspecting that more than 'sporadic thefts' were at the root of all this, and asking if there might have been 'any hint of a campaign building up'.[10] The official army line was that these were indeed merely 'sporadic thefts'. These thefts, while 'of course worrying', would be countered by the issue of new 'special instructions to UDR members' to assist them with the 'safeguarding of firearms'.[11] How successful that was may be judged by official figures which show that between October 1970 and March 1973, 222 UDR weapons were lost, 141 of which had *not* been recovered.[12]

The single biggest loss of arms by a UDR regiment occurred on the 23 October 1972 raid of the Lurgan UDR-TAVR (Territorial Army Volunteer Reserve) centre. A loose minute records how, in the early hours of the morning, a car pulled up to the front gates of the centre. Two men in berets approached the sentry there, 'confiscated' his weapon and held him at gun point. At this point, a group of up to ten men joined, and all took control of the guard room. There, they announced they were members of the UVF and ordered the remaining guards to lie on the floor. The raiders got away with eighty-three rifles, twenty-one machine guns, and ammunition, escaping in a British army Landrover taken from the base.

Suspecting collusion in the raid, Colonel Dalzell-Payne cautiously floated the 'remote possibility of a traitor in the guard' but also 'stressed that collusion in the LURGAN case is only a possibility'. However, a confidential army intelligence report decided that collusion in the raid was 'highly probable',[13] and a subsequent report by the HET confirmed that the weapons were used in a number of murders and attempted murders attributed to the UDA.[14]

In response to the raid, the GOC ordered 'a major review of the protection of all armouries ... to take account of the new factor of possible collusion'.[15] While the army periodically took pains to improve physical defences in response to arms thefts, they also admitted 'that the history of the recent raids would indicate that the human element is the main source of weakness'.[16] And so, despite the 'major review' of the protection of armouries, on 23 October 1973 – exactly a year to the day after the 1972 Lurgan raid – an almost identical raid was carried out on the UDR base at Portadown.[17]

Colonel Huxtable's report into this raid states that the raiders 'assured the UDR guard that they were members of the UVF and showed them a red hand medallion to prove it. In addition, some of the men were alleged to be wearing Royal Irish Rangers TA badges.'[18] This is glaring enough evidence of security force involvement in the raid, but there were also 'grounds to suggest that the raiders had assistance from members of HQ or B Coy 11 UDR'.

In this case, Colonel Huxtable writes that 'the circumstances were suspicious'.[19]

As well as raids on UDR armouries, a frequent occurrence was the routine 'loss' of weapons. They didn't need to be spectacularly stolen, they could simply disappear. Records show, variously, weapons listed as 'missing from armoury', 'taken from armoury', or 'Lost by unit'. There are reports from January 1973 of weapons simply going missing from 11 UDR's base at Lurgan ('pistols may have been missing for some six months') and 8 UDR's base at Cookstown ('Weapon found to be missing ... No indication that force had been used').[20] Some of the excuses found for missing weapons were flimsy, to say the least. It is almost as if there would be few, if any, repercussions for the loss of weapons. One note records that 'there was a considerable amount of weapon borrowing and as a result one rifle went missing'. An official has circled this and marked it 'awol' (possibly the colloquial term for 'absent without leave'), putting an exclamation point beside it.[21]

Weapons were also lost while in the care of individual UDR personnel. They might be roughly seized from UDR men by their pals ('on his way to duty when he was beaten up ... Collusion with UDA strongly suspected'). Often the UDR personnel didn't even fool their own superiors ('UDR soldier returning home from duty in his car was stopped by a number of armed men ... Strong feeling that weapon not stolen handed over'). One might reasonably think a degree more care might have been required of serving soldiers.

The files also show numerous instances where weapons were lost from UDR homes. In one example from 2 UDR in 1973, 'The soldier's home was broken into whilst it was unoccupied and his issued SLR, which had been stripped down and hidden, was stolen.'[22] It would hardly take a detective like Poirot or Columbo to wonder how the weapon had been stolen when it had apparently been so safely and secretly stored. The phrase 'collusion is strongly suspected' appears throughout reports of such incidents.

An alarming number of weapons were kept at home by UDR personnel. A note for the prime minister from the secretary of state in June 1972 reveals that, of the then total of 8,900 UDR personnel, some 3,500 kept their weapons at home.[23] A note from an MoD official in 1973 explains, seemingly quite reasonably, 'the weapons are usually kept in armouries' but *some* may be kept at home, 'where a soldiers' [*sic*] ability to do his duty is improved by allowing him to do so'. This, it explains, is when 'his unit armoury is more than thirty minutes travelling time from his home'.[24] The note reveals that in 1973 'the proportion of the UDR who have arms out for operational reasons [i.e. who keep their army-issued weapons at home] was about 27%'.[25] That was the average. In west Tyrone, that figure was 80%.[26]

Such was the embarrassment attracted by the UDR's weapons losses that no less a body than the USCA, or Ulster Special Constabulary Association (a kind of B Specials' ex-comrades group), sought to draw a distinction between the UDR's poor record and their own. In one note from February 1973, by A.P. Cumming-Bruce of DS7 at the MoD, we learn that the USCA had written to Robin Chichester-Clark MP (not to be confused with his brother, James, the former Northern Ireland prime minister) seeking details of UDR weapons losses from armouries and homes, as well as the number since recovered. Cumming-Bruce noted that the group had separately sought 'similar information about USC [B Specials] arms losses, presumably in order to draw unfavourable comparisons [between the UDR and the B Specials]'.

Providing answers to this group rankled Cumming-Bruce sufficiently for him to observe acidly, 'the USC[A] is a fundamentally mischievous organisation and it goes against the grain to feed them with ammunition'.[27] Of course, this is grimly ironic given that the subject was the UDR feeding actual ammunition to loyalists.

The appalling drain of weapons to loyalist extremists, often with collusion 'strongly suspected', led to pressure for explanations in the British parliament. In response to a parliamentary question from Bernadette Devlin MP as to the number of UDR weapons 'lost, mislaid or stolen' in 1972, government officials concocted a range of defensive positions in case of additional questions,[28] including that:

> Although the losses must be taken extremely seriously, it would be unjustifiable to infer that disciplinary standards in the UDR are deficient or that the Regiment's operational effectiveness and impartiality have been impaired ...
>
> We take any suspicion of collusion very seriously. There has not hitherto been any evidence of collusion sufficient to justify prosecution for it ...
>
> Even though a number of weapons have been stolen from UDR members' homes this year, our confidence in their trustworthiness to have weapons in these circumstances has been abundantly justified. Some 2225 weapons are on issue this way.

A letter, from one official at HQNI to their colleague at the NIO and dated 25 September 1972, shows officials wrestling with the question of how much information they might conceivably get away with suppressing in reply to Bernadette Devlin's repeated questioning:

> Nine self-loading rifles are missing from the UDR in Co Tyrone. Three others, which were formerly missing

have been recovered. In none of these cases has collusion been proven between the UDR and para-military
organisations, although in some cases there are suspicions of such collusion (perhaps in association with intimidation) and investigations are in hand. East Tyrone
is an area where we believe that certain UDR members
may be sympathetic towards the UDA.[29]

The letter's author proposes that 'the reply to Miss Devlin
should not quote specific figures'.[30] Instead, the response was
in fact diluted down to read, 'The thefts of 8 UDR weapons in
Co Tyrone are being investigated. In none of these cases has
any proof been found of collusion between members of the
UDR and para-military organisations. The appropriate action
would of course be taken if such collusion was proved.'[31] The
eventual reply to Devlin did not reflect the internal letters but
sought to mislead a member of parliament.

Despite such denials, in many cases of arms losses it is stated
in internal briefing documents that collusion is suspected. In
January 1973, the MoD informed the civil adviser to the
GOC that the US of S (Army) felt parliamentary questions on
arms raids were inevitable. Accordingly, officials were tasked
with providing a report on the army's investigations into the
raids, 'together with a defensive brief covering the collusion
aspect in particular'.[32]

Another note from February 1973 shows the US of S
(Army) requesting an update 'on the present position regarding UDR Arms' and asking, 'are any further plans to safeguard UDR arms in the offing?' A handwritten note beneath
this by, presumably, a senior civil servant says that he had
'agreed to take this on' and reveals his instructions from the
'APS' (assistant private secretary to the under-secretary of
state): 'APS tells me slow time, not above deadline. Response

is, for Defence debate (?15th), defensive use.'[33] The meaning of 'defensive use' here is open to interpretation, but it may be an indication of the pressure that was building to somehow explain the steady leaching away of UDR weaponry.

The impact of gun thefts from UDR bases (or donated to loyalists – depending on your interpretation of the facts) is possibly best illustrated by the history of one gun: a Sterling sub-machine gun, serial number UF57A30490. This weapon was 'stolen' from Glenanne UDR base and, despite its use in numerous attacks carried out by what has become known as the Glenanne Gang, there is no evidence that its theft was ever investigated by the RUC.[34] Much of the gun's known history comes from eight reports written by the HET, which in turn relied for its conclusions on information found within the RUC archive, so its conclusions are not conjecture, supposition or rumour. The weapon was destroyed on 27 April 1978 but before then it cut a bloody swathe through numerous families. Much of the following information comes from Anne Cadwallader's *Lethal Allies* and is used here with the kind permission of its author.

The first victim was Denis Mullen, a father of two living with his wife and two children, near the village of Moy. Denis, who was born in County Wicklow, was a significant figure in the civil rights campaign in County Tyrone and the chairman of his local branch of the SDLP. Olive was also an active SDLP member.

Denis Mullen was killed when his home was attacked on the night of 1 September 1975.[35] As he went to his front door to investigate a suspicious noise, Denis was hit by seventeen bullets. Police found no fewer than twenty-six bullet strike marks on the front of the Mullen's house, mainly around the front door. Garfield Gerald Beattie, a serving private in the TAVR based in Portadown, was convicted of Denis's murder, along with another man, eighteen-year-old William Parr. A former UDR man, William Corrigan, is also known to have been involved.[36] In this, the first record of the use of UF57A30490, a gun stolen from a UDR base in unexplained circumstances was used by a member of the TAVR (Beattie) and a former UDR man (Corrigan) to kill a leading member of the SDLP.

Less than two months later, on 23 October 1975, Peter and Jenny McKearney were shot dead in their home. Again, there is evidence of UDR involvement.[37] Half an hour after the shooting, the HET report into the McKearney deaths says, a British army foot patrol in Portadown (as yet unaware of the killings) stopped a car and recognised the four men inside as being UVF members – one of whom was also in the UDR.[38] The HET report into the murders goes on to say that having 'satisfied themselves' about the men's identities and movements, the patrol allowed two of the four men to continue on their way but detained the other two, one of whom was the UDR man.

Both men were taken to the local police station and interviewed. By then, news of the McKearney killings was out. The two men's hands were swabbed and were found to have traces of firearms residue. Thus, the RUC had two men in custody, whom they knew to be UVF members, shortly after a loyalist double murder – and with potentially incriminating forensic evidence on their hands.[39] Nonetheless, the presence of firearms residue without corroborating evidence, the HET report continues, was not considered sufficient to press criminal charges against the UDR man (as he was legally entitled to carry weapons).

The second man was also released, as he had an explanation ... of sorts. This was that he had shaken the hand of the UDR man and thus contaminated his own hands.

One might be forgiven for seeing this as something of a 'get-out-of-jail-free' card for all UDR men and their associates. The UDR men could always claim, if forensic evidence of being close to gunfire was found on their hands, that it was as a result of their legitimate UDR activities. Further, anyone arrested with them who was found to be contaminated with firearms residue also had a pat explanation: that they had shaken the hand of their associate.

Seven months after the murder of the McKearneys, soldiers searching the farm of a former B Special, Edward Sinclair, in County Armagh,[40] found firearms, firearm components, assorted ammunition, commercial explosives and bomb-making materials. One of the guns was a .38 Colt automatic pistol, serial number 36330, found in Sinclair's bedroom. It was examined, test-fired and found to be one of the guns used to murder Peter and Jenny. Police questioned Sinclair over two days in Portadown, during which time he told them he had bought the gun for £10 in a pub in Moy, three to four years before, for his own protection. He refused to say who had sold it to him. He then said he had loaned the weapon to a person he described as 'a boy', who kept it for five months. He would not name this 'boy' and could not tell police why he had wanted the gun.

Informed at this stage, by an interviewing officer, that this same gun might have been used in a shooting incident, Sinclair had replied, 'Well, I'm on a sticky wicket.' As for the other guns and ammunition, Sinclair said he was holding them for others, whom he would not name. The HET report into the McKearney murders comments, 'The natural course of the questioning should then have continued in regards to Peter and Jane's killings but, according to the statements, it appears it did not.' Sinclair was, however, charged with having illegal firearms; the following January he appeared in court, pleading guilty to various charges of possession of firearms and explosive substances – for which he received concurrent sentences, the longest of which was for six years. Sinclair left jail two years and four months later – on 24 May 1979 – three years to the day since he was first charged.

Almost exactly a year later, on 5 May 1980, he was arrested and questioned about another gun found on his farm, a .45 revolver, but there is nothing in the police papers to suggest he was questioned about the McKearney killings at that time either. Sinclair was arrested again in December 1981. This time he was questioned about Peter and Jenny's murder; he admitted he 'drove the car used in the murders' but 'could not admit' to carrying out the murder itself. For some unknown reason, what appears to have been a productive line of questioning was not followed, although the following day he said 'I am not denying I wasn't involved'. The questioning officer asked if he, Sinclair, was agreeing he was involved, to which Sinclair said 'I'm not saying anything, I can't afford to.' Four days later, he was charged with the McKearney killings. The charges were dropped six months later, however, as it was not considered that his admissions 'were sufficient to support a case'.[41]

In 1981, Garnet James Busby was convicted of the McKearney murders. He admitted involvement but claimed that a second man, whom he refused to name, had wielded UF57A30490. Busby pleaded guilty. He was sentenced to life imprisonment for the murders, to twelve years for possession of a Colt pistol, and to four further life sentences for his role in the Hillcrest Bar bombing – an incident, on St Patrick's Day 1976, in which four people, including two fourteen-year-old schoolboys, were killed.

The next attack in which UF57A30490 was deployed was mounted at Donnelly's, a small bar and filling station in the small village of Silverbridge in south Armagh. A gun and bomb attack on the evening of 19 December claimed the lives of Patsy Donnelly, Michael Donnelly and Trevor Brecknell.[42]

From eyewitness accounts, the gunman armed with UF57A30490 appeared to be a loyalist known to police from Portadown.[43] The detective sergeant in charge, Gerry McCann, circulated a photofit picture to Special Branch in Portadown but received no response. Knowing his suspect would be at the unemployment benefit office in Portadown at a specific time, McCann went there himself and brought along an eyewitness. The suspect duly put in an appearance – but to McCann's surprise had substantially changed his appearance. McCann found this highly suspicious. Had the suspect been tipped-off about the photofit circulating within Special Branch in Portadown?

The HET has established that the suspect was named within Special Branch databases as having been involved in the Donnelly's Bar attack. McCann was never told this, but his hunch had been correct all along. This individual was never arrested for questioning about the Donnelly's Bar attack.

No one was arrested in the months after the attack; three years later, however, more information emerged during an inquiry into a different murder. Two people arrested admitted involvement in the triple murder. They were RUC man Laurence McClure and Sarah Elizabeth Shields (known as Lily), housekeeper for another RUC man, James Mitchell, who owned a farm near the village of Glenanne. Both claimed to be unaware of the exact target and its purpose, but 'realised [it was] an illegal act'.[44]

McClure admitted that, on the night of the attack, he had been at James Mitchell's Glenanne farm – along with others, including UDR man Robert McConnell. McClure (who drove the killers to the target, and who lived close to

Mitchell's farm) and Shields had then waited, posing as a courting couple, at an Orange Hall, about 8 miles (13 km) from Donnelly's Bar. After half an hour, McConnell and two other attackers got into the car, and McClure dropped them off close to Mitchell's farm. Shields admitted her involvement and gave a similar story to McClure's, without naming the men they had picked up.

Both were charged with failing to give information, but three years later, all the charges were dropped. The prosecuting authorities said there was not enough corroborating evidence that those they had picked up (including UDR man Robert McConnell) had actually carried out the attack, or that McClure and Shields had known where it was to take place. For the same reason, more serious charges were not considered.

But other evidence against McClure and Shields comes from former RUC Armagh Special Patrol Group (SPG) officer John Weir; he named both of them, along with three UVF men who, he said, had gathered at Mitchell's farm after the attack.

McClure had contradicted himself during police interviews carried out in 1978. In one interview he said those involved in the 1975 Donnelly's Bar attack and the 1976 Rock Bar attack were not the same gang. In a second interview, however, he said both attacks were carried out by him and 'a crowd of ordinary fellows', adding, 'Silverbridge [Donnelly's] and Rock Bar was just arranged amongst ourselves.' The HET says, however, that detectives did not push home the contradictions to McClure, or ask what he meant by 'ourselves'. This oversight, deliberate or otherwise, precluded more serious charges being made against McClure.

Shields was also exposed as a liar. In her 15 December 1978 interview with the RUC, she admitted she had been the girlfriend of McClure's UDR co-conspirator, Robert McConnell, since 1971 – while maintaining that she did not know who he was when she and McClure collected him after the Donnelly's Bar killings. The HET, by implication again, criticises the RUC men who questioned her, adding, 'Her failure to name him [UDR man McConnell] as one of the three suspects was not challenged during the interview process.'

The rubble had hardly been cleared from Donnelly's Bar when, a mere sixteen days later, those who controlled UF57A30490 were murdering again. This time, they killed another three people – all brothers: Brian, John Martin and Anthony Reavey. They were at home watching television on 4 January 1976 when the gunmen burst into the family home and began firing.

The police moved into the Reavey home and began a forensic examination. No fewer than four guns had been used to attack the three brothers: UF57A30490; a second 9 mm Parabellum-calibre Sterling SMG (whose breechblock had been doctored[45]); a 9 mm Luger-type pistol; and a .455 Webley revolver.[46]

The HET report says the RUC made no arrests, and there is no evidence about whether Special Branch intelligence was passed to the detectives investigating the killings. John Weir claims in his 1999 affidavit that UDR man Robert McConnell was one of the gunmen. In its conclusion to its report into the murders, the HET report says an apparent motive was that the family was well respected and prominent, with influence in the local community. Murdering them, the report says, would 'frighten their friends, other Catholics and supporters of the nationalist agenda'.

On the same evening that the Reaveys were attacked, members of the same gang attacked the home of the O'Dowd family, who were enjoying a family party. Three gunmen burst into the house and opened fire, murdering three – Joe, Declan, and Barry O'Dowd. Barney O'Dowd, father of Declan and Barry, was shot five times and badly wounded. Like the Reaveys, the O'Dowds were fairly prosperous and prominent local Catholics – Barney O'Dowd had acted as an electoral observer for the SDLP.

The HET report into the Reaveys' murders says that post-incident intelligence indicates that the paramilitary organisation most likely to have been responsible was the Mid-Ulster UVF, and, 'as members of the RUC and UDR were involved with this group, it follows that similar collusion could have taken place in these murders' (a reference to other murders where the HET believes it has also established collusion).[47]

On the night of 15 May 1976, in the County Armagh village of Charlemont, a co-ordinated attack took place on two small local bars. According to a statement later made by one of the perpetrators, the gang lit the fuse on a bomb outside Clancy's Bar before moving on to open fire on a second bar, the Eagle, close by. Fred McLoughlin was mortally wounded when two gunmen – one using UF57A30490, the other a revolver – sprayed the window with gunfire. Fred McLoughlin died of his injuries on 31 May 1976.[48]

On 25 July 1976, Patsy McNeice was murdered outside his home. Two gunmen approached his house and, in what the HET described as a 'casual' manner, shot Patsy as he stepped outside his front door. They had no strategy to identify their supposed target, or even to ascertain whether he was at home when they arrived. 'This was irrefutably a callous, sectarian killing,' concludes the HET, '… they were content to shoot whoever came out … it was a cowardly attack on an honest, hard-working man, loved by his family and respected in the community.'[49]

Two days after Patsy's murder, on 27 July, police received intelligence naming TAVR private Garfield Gerald Beattie as having been involved in the murders of Peter and Jenny McKearney the previous October, as well as the attack on Clancy's and the Eagle just two months earlier. The RUC arrested Beattie on 11 August. At first he denied involvement in any murder – only admitting to minor offences. However, he then began to open up and led investigators to where UF57A30490 was hidden in Annaghmore bog. By now it had been used to kill in attacks where eleven people had died.

On Friday, 13 August, Beattie confessed to his involvement in Patsy's murder. In the following days, Beattie also confessed to his role in Denis Mullen's murder and the shooting of Fred McLoughlin at the Eagle in Charlemont. For an as yet unexplained reason, Beattie was never charged with the triple killing and bombing of Clancy's Bar in Charlemont village, virtually simultaneous with the Eagle Bar attack just 100 yards away, despite the fact that one of the perpetrators told police that Beattie had lit the fuse on the bomb outside Clancy's Bar.[50]

Beattie went on to implicate others in the attacks on the Eagle and Clancy's, including David Henry Dalziel Kane, a twenty-eight-year-old local orchard owner and former UDR man. Kane was then also arrested; four days later, he admitted to being a driver during the attack on the Eagle. He confirmed one of the gunmen was Beattie, but neither he nor Beattie would give the name of the second gunman. Given three life sentences and fourteen years, to run concurrently, Beattie served sixteen years. He was released from jail, on licence, on 29 March 1993.[51]

This left significant unanswered questions about the third man. Both TAVR man Beattie and former UDR man Kane said that he had been involved, but both refused to name him. The police still had no one accountable for the attack on Clancy's – where three men had lost their lives.

Two years after the attacks on the Eagle and Clancy's, and twenty-one months after Kane and Beattie were first questioned, police arrested a third man, Joseph Norman Lutton. He was duly charged with murdering Fred McLoughlin and the three victims at Clancy's Bar, along with possessing weapons and explosives with intent to endanger life. The RUC took no action against Beattie or former UDR man Kane, despite Lutton implicating them in the triple murder at Clancy's. There is no explanation for this failure, although they were both in prison and thus available for re-interview. Beattie, who had fired over thirty bullets into the bar full of customers – killing a father of four sons – was not even re-interviewed about Lutton's claim that he had lit the fuse of the bomb that devastated Clancy's Bar and killed three more people.

Lutton, throughout all his appearances in court and in all prosecution papers, is described only as a 'cheese processor', with no mention of his role as a constable in the RUC Reserve. When the HET checked police records, they discovered Lutton had joined the RUC Reserve in December 1974 and had resigned on 31 May 1978 – the very day he was arrested.

The McLoughlin family, and the families of the victims at Clancy's Bar, were never informed that all three men convicted of murdering their loved ones were either serving or former members of various branches of state forces. Jim McLoughlin has never been informed whether his father was killed by the RUC Reservist (Lutton) or the member of the Territorial Army (Beattie) or the former UDR man (Kane).

The bullet used to kill Fred McLoughlin was never recovered. It was removed from his chest during emergency surgery soon after he reached the South Tyrone Hospital in Dungannon, but there is nothing in police files about what happened to it after that. With no bullet and therefore no ballistic evidence – and since Beattie admitted to using the Sterling during the attack on the Eagle while Lutton confessed to using a revolver in the same attack – Fred McLoughlin's family are still unsure who killed their father.

In each of the six separate attacks where UF57A30490 was used, in which eleven people died, there is clear evidence of involvement by one branch of the security forces or another, whether that be UDR, TAVR or RUC.

The full story of all the links between the attacks is too intricate and numerous to fully detail. Suffice to say, there was a sharing of weapons and a multiplicity of perpetrators, not all of whom can be identified even today. At the time of writing, these links were being analysed by a team of detectives and former detectives under the leadership of the former Chief Constable of Bedfordshire, Jon Boutcher.[52] Among the issues to be resolved are the ballistic links between UF57A30490, the triple murder of the Reavey brothers and a gun-and-bomb attack on the Rock Bar, near the village of Keady, mid-Armagh, on 5 June 1976.

Ballistic evidence links UF57A30490 to the attack on the Rock through a 9 mm Luger pistol used in both. Whoever provided the Luger to the gunmen for use in both attacks has questions to answer about the provenance of UF57A30490.

The protagonists in the Rock Bar attack were all serving police officers, two of them on duty. Due to a subsequent series of unrelated incidents, several of the RUC men responsible were later interviewed. Surely, any kind of a detective who had in custody, fellow officers, who admitted their role in the gun-and-bomb attack at the Rock Bar, might think to go on and ask them the obvious question: 'Who gave you the gun?'

A clear opportunity presented itself to (a) find out who had carried out the attack on the ballistically linked shooting of the three Reavey brothers and (b) find out who had controlled the use of UF57A30490 in eight further murders. Only one of the RUC men questioned about the Rock Bar attack was asked any relevant questions about the origin of the weapons used. He was William McCaughey, and he refused to answer. The HET could find no evidence of relevant questioning.[53]

Less than two years after UF57A30490 was recovered from the bog at Annaghmore (12 August 1976), after multiple-murderer Garfield Beattie took police there, it was sent to the RUC's Weapons Control department for destruction (on 27 April 1978). The HET report into the triple murder at Donnelly's Bar comments only that this meant the weapon was 'not available' for the trials of William Parr (in 1979, for the murder of Denis Mullen), Joseph Lutton (in 1979, for the murders of Fred McLoughlin, Robert McCullough, Sean O'Hagan and Vincent Clancy) and Garnett Busby (in 1981, for the murders of Peter and Jane McKearney).

If it had chosen to, the HET could have added the names of the officers convicted in relation to the Rock Bar attack: Constable Ian Mitchell, Reserve Constable Laurence McClure, Constable William McCaughey and Auxiliary Constable David Wilson. The senior officers who investigated the attack on the Rock Bar have also escaped any accountability for their failure to follow the obvious ballistics trail leading to the attack on the Reaveys and other linked attacks. The UDR soldier responsible for the theft of UF57A30490 has never been questioned. No one has been held accountable for the fact that this weapon was later used in attacks that left eleven people dead. For that lamentable failure to investigate, no UDR officer has ever been held accountable, and neither has the RUC.

It is important to note that weapons thefts from the UDR were not merely a phenomenon of the 1970s. As but one example, a note on declassified files from an Irish diplomat details a UDA raid on a UDR base in February 1987. According to the sources, Davy Payne, the UDA's north Belfast commander, participated in the raid personally, and:

> On the night of 22 February, he [Payne] and three or four others arrived at the base. He was driving his own car and his colleagues had a van. The two UDR men met them at the entrance and took them inside in the boot of a UDR vehicle. When the driver of the van (waiting outside) suddenly panicked and drove off, the others had to load the weapons onto a UDR van parked inside the base. Payne drove off in his own car while his colleagues followed about half a mile behind in the UDR van. Payne was stopped by traffic police who had noticed that his car had an out-of-date number plate. They established his identity and his destination (a relative's house in Glengormley) and then let him proceed. A few minutes later they stopped the UDR van, found the weapons in the back and arrested the two UDA men driving it. Payne was subsequently arrested at the house in Glengormley. The UDR accomplices were also arrested. While Payne was later released (as there was no hard evidence to link him to the raid), the others are still in custody.[54]

It is important to note also that, while investigations into the 1989 murder of human rights solicitor Pat Finucane highlighted the role of RUC Special Branch and military intelligence (two of the UDA men involved were paid informers, and a third, instead of being arrested for the murder, was recruited as an agent) an often overlooked aspect is the role played by UDR Colour Sergeant Steven Fletcher. In his review of the case, Desmond de Silva QC identified Fletcher's as the first action by an employee of the state that contributed directly to the murder. In August 1987, Fletcher stole weapons from Palace Barracks, County Down, and sold them to Kenneth Barrett, a UDA member who in 2004 pleaded guilty to Pat Finucane's murder. The weapons stolen included a 9mm Browning pistol that was subsequently used in the murder. The Colour Sergeant was himself convicted in 1988 for his role in the theft.[55]

CHAPTER FIVE

Subversion in the UDR

Very early on, it seems, Secretary of State for Northern Ireland Whitelaw was being advised by senior civil servants who accepted, in private correspondence, that there was significant support for the UDA among the ranks of the UDR. It is little wonder that should be the case when official policy was for the state to secretly ally with loyalist paramilitaries.

In July 1972, Sir William Nield, permanent under-secretary of state at the NIO, wrote a letter to Burke Trend, cabinet secretary at the Cabinet Office, and copied it to Sir Robert Armstrong, secretary to the then British prime minister, Edward Heath. Nield expressed 'the Secretary of State's anxiety ... that he is not opposed by one violent and subversive force, but by two, the IRA and the UDA'. The truth was that while the British army could not openly side with the UDA – which was, after all, challenging London's authority – it nevertheless had 'considerable sympathy for the UDA, which 2½ years of bombings has aroused in the Army's auxiliary security forces, i.e. the Ulster Defence Force [*sic*] and the Royal Ulster Constabulary'.[1]

Shortly afterward, General Harry Tuzo – GOC of British

troops in Northern Ireland – presented a plan to Whitelaw to defeat the IRA in which:

> It will be even more necessary to acquiesce in unarmed UDA patrolling and barricading of Protestant areas. Although no interference with security forces could be tolerated, it would be as well to make the best of the situation and obtain some security benefit from UDA control of their own areas. Indeed it is arguable that Protestant areas could almost entirely be secured by a combination of UDA, Orange Volunteers and RUC. It may even be necessary to turn a blind eye to UDA arms when confined to their own areas.[2]

The effect of turning a blind eye was that, by the middle of 1973 it was clear that there was a significant, illegal and deadly relationship between loyalist paramilitaries and the UDR. The declassified documents from this period show that the military and political authorities were comfortable with a certain level of loyalist violence, and that they regarded the infiltration of the UDR by loyalist extremists as a 'safety valve' for loyalist tempers. In addition, there was an awareness of the wholesale departure of Catholics from the regiment, while the numbers of loyalists enlisting steadily rose. At the same time, the theft of weapons and ammunition from security force bases and personnel was ongoing. These were being used in a campaign of sectarian murder aimed at terrorising the nationalist population.

In August 1973, in an internal assessment, the British army admitted the extent of 'subversion' within the ranks of the UDR. An MoD draft report into 'Subversion in the UDR' was prepared by anonymous military intelligence personnel for the Joint Intelligence Committee (JIC), the top-level security committee advising the prime minister.[3] Needless to say, this detailed assessment was kept secret and under wraps, away from the public gaze. Nevertheless, in 2005 PFC/JFF discovered it among files at the National Archives in Kew; thereafter, its existence was publicised in an extensive analysis by award-winning journalist Steven McCaffery published in *The Irish News* in 2006.[4] His piece came to international attention when it was shortlisted in the 2007 Amnesty International media awards in London.

The 'Subversion in the UDR' report begins with a caveat, acknowledging the limitations imposed on those conducting the research. Attempting to present 'an exhaustive study of the state of subversion in the Ulster Defence Regiment' was not possible, they begin, given a 'lack of relevant intelligence'. Still, the authors saw merit in attempting to examine the available evidence and intelligence (personnel files; weapons loss reports; intelligence reports; questions submitted to UDR headquarters, army intelligence and security departments; and visits to UDR battalions). At the very least, they would be able to 'point up how limited our knowledge is in this field'.[5]

After presenting a mini history of the regiment, the authors asked, 'Why is there interest in subversion in the UDR?' The answer is revealing: 'Since the first days of the UDR the dangers of raising a local force from the two communities, at a time of intercommunal strife, has been clearly recognised.' These dangers were supposedly defused by the security vetting process for admissions to the UDR.

Nonetheless, by the time the report was being written, an impetus had been given to recruitment into loyalist extremist groups. The report's authors ascribed this to the suspension of the Stormont government and the imposition of Direct Rule from London in March 1972. By September 1972, they report, 'the UDA in particular was estimated to have a strength of 4,000–6,000 members in Belfast plus 15,000 supporters.' Thereafter, 'the problem of divided loyalties amongst UDR recruits became more marked. Joint membership of the UDA (which had objectives incompatible with those of HMG [Her Majesty's Government]) and the UDR became widespread, and at the same time the rate of UDR weapons losses greatly increased.'[6]

The report's authors consider subversion, in this instance, to include 'Strong support for, or membership of, organisations whose aims are incompatible with those of the UDR', and 'attempts by UDR members to use their UDR knowledge, skills, or equipment to further the aims of such organisations'. According to the report, seventy-three UDR personnel had been discharged between November 1972 and July 1973, and a further twenty had resigned. These are ascribed to 'subversive traces coming to light'.

This is broadly reflected in other declassified documents uncovered by the PFC. Minutes of the UDR Advisory Council meeting on 28 November 1972 marked 'the change in emphasis, which had now been agreed in the handling of members of the UDR who were found to be associated with the UDA'. Each battalion had been asked to compile lists of UDR members with UDA links. It was not felt that large numbers would be dismissed, but some 'weeding-out' would take place. 'Although it remained the case that a member of the UDR would not be discharged solely on account of his membership of the UDA, if his conduct cast in question his loyalty, or complete impartiality, he would be discharged as "services no longer required".'[7]

Subsequent meetings of the advisory council record the 'weeding-out' process and the numbers of UDR men described variously as 'being watched'[8] or 'under observation'.[9]

By April 1973, 'some 2–3 men were leaving the UDR, on suspicion of being extremists, per week'.[10] Minutes of the advisory council meeting on 6 July 1973 report that 'there had been little change in the numbers discharged [since the council's previous meeting on 25 May 1973] under the terms of the policy towards UDA members.'[11]

One would think from reading these extracts that the powers that be were doing their level best to weed out members of the UDA. However, the 'Subversion in the UDR' report confirms that 'the discovery of members of paramilitary or extremist organisations in the UDR is not, and has not been, a major intelligence target ... it is unlikely that our intelligence coverage of this area is in any way comprehensive.' The authors admit that 'it seems quite unlikely that the security vetting system, or subsequent intelligence material, can reveal all the members of subversive groups who have applied to join the UDR'.

Here the report makes a stunning admission: 'It seems likely that a significant proportion (perhaps 5% – in some areas as high as 15%) of UDR soldiers will also be members of the UDA, Vanguard service corps, Orange Volunteers or UVF.' Among this number, 'there will be a passing on of information and training methods in many cases and a few subversives may conspire to "leak" arms and ammunition to Protestant extremist groups'. To the report's authors, more alarming still is the potential for mutiny among the ranks: 'The presence within the UDR of members of extremist groups does, however, contain within it the danger that at some future stage, if HMG's actions were perceived to be unfavourable to "loyalist" interests, those men ... might even work within the UDR to make it unreliable.' The matter of loyalty to HMG within the UDR is one which we will examine later.

Examples of the subversive activity uncovered in the report include UDR members admitting to leadership roles within the UDA or UVF in Lisburn, Fermanagh, Ballymena, Randalstown and Belfast. On page four of the report, it cites the example of a member of 1 UDR who was described by his commanding officer as 'a model soldier'; the individual in question was deputy chair of a district council (Ballymena), the report states. He was also Officer Commanding of Ballymena UDA, had obtained arms for the UDA and was suspected of illegal arms deals – namely acquiring an SLR and an SMG in Scotland, and selling them to the UDA.

In 2006 this man was identified as Clifford Davison; he spoke to *The Irish News* to deny the allegations of 'illegal arms dealings', and to stress that the UDA was a legal organisation at that time:

> Mr. Davison said his UDR commanders were aware of his loyalist links but that having served a year in the regiment he was suddenly asked to leave. He says he was never given an explanation but now believes his superiors may have acted after he was identified in the 'subversion' document. Significantly, he says that he was never questioned on the allegation that he sold guns to loyalists ... within months of his UDR dismissal he joined the RUC, serving as a reserve constable for five years.

The Irish News piece said that his experience 'confirmed one of the document's central themes – that at the height of the Troubles it was all too easy to move from the ranks of loyalism into the ranks of the army and police'.[12]

The report also records Belfast-based UDR members involved in various instances of suspicious or subversive activity (the UDR in Belfast would prove to be particularly problematic, as we shall see later). Six members were discovered in full uniform drinking in a UDA club when they were supposed to be guarding a key installation. Others were found to have collaborated with Parachute Regiment soldiers in the theft of rifles from Palace Barracks in December 1971. Others were involved in smuggling guns from abroad and the theft of weapons from a UDR guard at a polling station.

The matter of weapons thefts is dealt with under the heading, 'Loss of Arms and Ammunition'. In this section, the authors of the Subversion report admit, 'Since the beginning of the current campaign the best single source of weapons, and the only significant source of modern weapons, for Protestant extremist groups has been the UDR.'

To illustrate this, the report sets out details of UDR arms losses for 1972–3. Over the course of 1972, almost 190 semi-automatic rifles, SMGs and pistols were lost by, or stolen from, the UDR. By comparison, it is noted that 'Regular Army weapons losses in Northern Ireland in 1972 were six SLRs, one SMG and nine pistols.' Over the first seven months of 1973 (up to the report's compilation), the UDR had 'lost' a total of twenty-eight semi-automatic rifles, SMGs and pistols, all of which remained unaccounted for. The authors noted, 'By comparison Regular Army weapons losses in Northern Ireland in the same period were two SLRs, nil SMGs and six pistols.' Most of the rifles and machine guns were 'lost/stolen' at UDR armouries or from soldiers on duty. The majority of the pistols, however, were said to have been lost or stolen from UDR soldiers at home or on their way to work.

The authors of 'Subversion in the UDR' baldly state their belief that 'the vast majority of weapons stolen from the UDR during this period are in the hands of Protestant extremists

... [and] there is a substantial body of intelligence to support the view.'

The report examines the weapons thefts from UDR armouries and from UDR guard detachments in 1972 and 1973, and notes, 'The question of whether there was collusion by UDR members in these thefts is a difficult one. In no case is there proof positive of collusion: but in every case there is considerable suspicion, which in some instances is strong enough to lead to a judgment that an element of collusion was present.'

The report then gives detailed accounts of three such raids. The first, a raid on the headquarters of 10 UDR (Belfast Battalion) in October 1972, saw '14 self-loading rifles and a quantity of ammunition ... stolen from this location, when armed men "overpowered" the Camp Guard'. The raid was clearly carried out by someone with 'prior knowledge of the unit layout and details of guard arrangements'. Indeed, the Subversion report notes, 'the initial security report into the incident concluded that it was probably carried out with "inside help" and that it was possible that "one or more members of the guard had prior knowledge of the intended raid and actively assisted in its prosecution".'

According to the Subversion report:

> it subsequently transpired that the guard commander on the night of the raid had nine previous convictions for deception and had spent a period in jail. He had been arrested in September 1972 for riotous behaviour outside Tennant Street RUC station following the shooting of two men by security forces in the Shankill and the arrest of a UDA leader. He had one UDA trace and three separate reliable reports subsequently indicated that he was a member of the UVF.

This is a reminder, if one were needed, that the discovery of members of extremist organisations in the UDR was not, and had not been, 'a major intelligence target'.

Similarly, in the second major raid (on the UDR-TAVR centre at Lurgan in October 1972 which we have previously discussed), soldiers on guard were 'overpowered' by a number of armed men, and a large quantity of weapons was stolen. The authors of the Subversion report note the conclusion to the Military Police investigation of the incident, which said:

> It is quite apparent that the offenders knew exactly what time to carry out the raid. Had they arrived earlier they may have been surprised by returning patrols and had they arrived later they may have been intercepted by the Tandragee power station guard returning from duty. The very fact that all the guard weapons had been centralised and there was only one man on the gate, a contravention of unit guard orders, was conducive to the whole operation. The possibility of collusion is therefore highly probable.

Of the third incident detailed – the theft of UDR weapons from Claudy RUC station in October 1972 – the Subversion report notes that those investigating the incident were 'unable to discount the possibility of collusion by a member of the UDR or the RUC'.

Similarly, the Subversion document says 'the possibility of UDR collusion in arms raids by Protestant extremist groups exist in at least two further cases'. It cites the theft of rifles and ammunition from a UDR guard at a polling station in east Belfast in March 1973, and more from a UDR guard by men 'themselves armed with self-loading rifles'. Shortly before the polling station incident, 'two men had strolled past the sentry and told him that they would return in a couple of hours "to steal your guns"'.

The report concludes, on the basis of these incidents, that the weapons thefts were the work of 'well briefed gangs who knew what they were doing, without a shot being fired in anger, or any significant attempt made to resist. It is difficult to resist the conclusion that members of the UDR were party to these incidents.' Similarly, 'the circumstances in which some weapons have been stolen from UDR soldiers at home or on the way to work has also aroused suspicion and it is likely that a number of these raids or hold-ups were carried out with the foreknowledge of the subject.'

The Subversion report continues: 'There can be little doubt that subversion in the UDR has added significantly to the weapons and ammunition stocks of Protestant extremist groups. In many cases ex-UDR weapons are the only automatic and semi-automatic weapons in their possession.'

It goes on to warn, 'Neither the British army, nor the minority community has yet experienced the full force of these weapons, for many are in store. Several have, however, been used and there is strong evidence that they have been in the hands of the most violent of the criminal sectarian groups in the Protestant community.'

In fact:

> One of the Sterling SMGs stolen from the Lurgan UDR/TAVR centre was recovered in the Shankill on 21 July 1973 in the possession of three men, two of whom were known members of the Shankill UFF/UVF group: they had just robbed a bar. Research at the data reference centre has subsequently indicated that this weapon has been used in at least 12 terrorist outrages,

including the murder of a Catholic, and seven other attempted murders.[13]

The sudden and large-scale arming of loyalist paramilitaries led the British to be cautious. The 'Subversion in the UDR' report states that 'It is a statement of the obvious that circumstances may well arise in which all the weapons stolen from the UDR may well be used, perhaps against the British army. They would form a most significant part of the armoury of the Protestant extremists.'[14]

The report then considers the circumstances under which the UDR might become 'unreliable':

> The ability of the UDR to carry out its duties has been compromised on only a very few occasions to date by the activities of disloyal or subversive soldiers. It does not require great mental agility, however, to conceive of circumstances in which subversion in the UDR might become a much greater problem. There are two possible situations in which elements of the UDR might well cease to be reliable:
>
> a) Should the Assembly fail and future Westminster plans also meet with no success, it is possible that the future leader of a 'Loyalist' political party might well declare a 'UDI'[15] for Ulster in an attempt to return power to 'Loyalist' hands. In these circumstances the loyalty of UDR members to HMG would be sorely tried, particularly if required to play any part in military activity against 'Loyalist' groups.
>
> b) If at any time it became a feature of HMG policy, perhaps under a Labour government,[16] to encourage

early and substantial progress towards the setting up of a powerful Council of Ireland, or towards the achievement of a United Ireland, the reliability of elements of the UDR would be brought into serious question. If the latter policy objective were to be undertaken by HMG it is conceivable that a large number of UDR soldiers would desert taking their weapons with them.

The Subversion report concludes with some stark warnings of the dangers inherent in the UDR. Comparing the UDR to other British army regiments, the authors say 'the regiment is wide open to subversion and potential subversion' because of 'the nature of its being, and the circumstances in which it operates'.[17] They conclude:

It goes without saying that the first loyalties of many of its members are to a concept of 'Ulster' rather than to HMG, and that where a perceived conflict in these loyalties occur, HMG will come off second best. So far this division of loyalties has not been seriously tested but already disquieting evidence of subversion is available ...

It is likely that there remain within the UDR significant numbers of men (perhaps 5–15%) who are, or have been, members of Protestant extremist organisations.

Subversion in the UDR has almost certainly led to arms losses to Protestant extremist groups on a significant scale ... Subversion in the UDR may well have been responsible for materially adding to the reservoir of military skills amongst Protestant extremists and it is likely that there remain in the regiment men who would be willing to engage in further arms raids should it be thought necessary ...

Except in limited circumstances subversion in the UDR has not compromised its ability to carry out its duties. There are, however, a number of predictable political circumstances in which the regiment might not only suffer a much higher level of subversion than at present, but in which elements of it might cease to be reliable.

It is interesting to note that in a secret paper from November 1973, on Op CHANTRY ('The reinforcement of Northern Ireland by up to six bns [battalions] in the event of a serious outbreak of Protestant extremist violence'),[18] British officials repeat this language when gauging the reliability of the UDR. Here, officials warn, 'Our assessment of subversion in the UDR has been "by the nature of its being, and the circumstances in which it operates, the Regiment is wide open to subversion and potential subversion". Although considerable co-membership of Protestant extremist organisations and the UDR exists it is likely that a majority of these men have joined extremist organisations for the "Doomsday" situation.'[19] State papers released in 2005 revealed the prime minister had discussed a secret 'Doomsday' plan in readiness for a 'panic' British withdrawal in May 1974. It is interesting to see this term applied here, by the British army, in November 1973.[20]

Returning to the 'Subversion in the UDR' document, it finishes with a stark warning: 'Any effort to remove men who in foreseeable political circumstances might well operate against the interests of the UDR could well result in a very small regiment indeed.'

The 'Subversion in the UDR' document is accompanied on the file by four letters of response from very senior officials. And although the document is described as a draft, it is significant that none of the letter writers disagree with its contents. One response, penned by a senior MoD civil servant – the head of DS10, no less – reads, 'I wish I could say that its contents come as a surprise, but I am afraid they do not.'

Just two years later, a 'Secret UK Eyes only' briefing was sent to the secretary of state. The briefing on the subject of UDR security – again from DS10 (with a security classification which meant that this document was not to be shared with local security forces) – appears to be an attempt to minimise the issue of loyalist subversion of the UDR, perhaps to reassure the political class that the matter was in hand. According to the document, an investigation had shown that 'a small number, around 200 spread between the 11 Battalions of the Regiment, are thought to have connections however slight with extremist organisations'.[21] As we shall see, subsequent events (particularly in Belfast, and the investigations into 10 UDR in 1978) suggest that this estimate was the tip of the iceberg.

CHAPTER SIX

A Question of Loyalty

The 'Subversion in the UDR' report closed with dire warnings from the British army about the regiment, including that the loyalties of many UDR personnel was towards their own concept of 'Ulster' rather than to the British government and, if these loyalties were tested, that there was a real threat of UDR guns being turned on regular British troops.

In a letter we have looked at previously, from June 1972, a senior official (MacDonald) in the Ministry of Defence wrote to Howe, the civilian adviser to the GOC in Northern Ireland, about the possibility of extending the UDR's range of duties.[1] The army was at pains to keep the UDR away from interface areas, and even the centre of Belfast, where their presence could lead to what MacDonald termed 'escalation violence'. Perhaps of most importance in the letter is the following: 'the implications of possible confrontation between members of the UDR and UDA are also considerable, and in some circumstances a heavy strain could well be placed on UDR loyalties'.

The UDA, in fact, came into direct and lethal confrontation with the British army in the latter half of 1972. The circumstances are worth setting out here.

Tim Pat Coogan has written that 'the outline of a concerted loyalist backlash against what were perceived as Catholic gains could be clearly discerned from the early summer of 1972'.[2] Over the spring of 1972, the UDA had grown in strength and had reorganised along more formal military lines. Emboldened, the UDA leadership decided to confront the government and the British army on the issue of the 'no-go' areas that the IRA controlled in West Belfast and Derry. Loyalists saw the continued existence of these areas as appeasement of the IRA and were determined to force the government to move against them. The UDA therefore erected its own 'no-go' areas and declared they would not remove them until the IRA was forced to remove theirs.

On 14 May the UDA organised a 'no-go' area in the Woodvale area of east Belfast, hijacking trucks and blocking off local streets, guarding the barricades with dozens of men in paramilitary uniform. When the army moved in to tear down the barricades, on the weekend of 20–21 May, serious rioting broke out across the city. Negotiations between the UDA and the army over the weekend restored temporary calm, however, and the barriers began to be taken down.

On 26 June 1972, UDA member John Black died, having been shot by soldiers at a barricade on the Woodvale Road five weeks previously, and received a huge set-piece UDA funeral.[3] In February 2021, PFC/JFF staff uncovered a report on the violence that resulted in John Black's death; in it, the army indicates that the incident was orchestrated by Sammy Doyle. Doyle was a well-known spokesperson for the UDA,[4] but it was only through the discovery in the files of this report that we now know he was also a member of the UDR.[5]

At several stages over the following weeks (June and July 1972), the UDA were allowed to march unimpeded, hooded and uniformed, through the centre of Belfast, though the wearing of such uniforms had been banned under the Public Order Act. The UDA were also allowed to retain their barricades, and to extend them at the end of June.[6] Behind those barricades there was widespread harassment, beatings and intimidation of Catholics.

By August 1972, loyalist paramilitaries were killing three Catholics for every Protestant, the same ratio as during the pogroms of the early 1920s. But then 'a tougher attitude on the part of the army began to manifest itself towards the Loyalists'.[7]

On the evening of 7 September 1972, two men were gunned down on the Shankill Road by British paratroopers. While there had been rioting earlier, relative calm had been restored – though paratroopers remained on the streets. The events of 6–8 September 1972 were to become known for a time locally as 'The Shankill Disturbances'. The UDA even compiled a document – 'The Shankill Disturbances: A Series of Eye-Witness Accounts' – which challenged the army's account of the disturbances in the area during this time, including the deaths of the two men.

On the night of 17 October 1972, an off-duty UDR private named John Todd was shot dead. Again, British paratroopers were responsible – they claimed to have come under fire whilst removing barricades in the Shankill area. A soldier told the inquest he had seen a gunman near John Todd's body but that he had not seen the latter armed. No weapon was recovered. A witness said he and John Todd had their hands raised when the shooting took place.[8]

John Todd was a member of the UDA, and armed UDA men fired shots over his coffin. He was also a private in the UDR,[9] however, having joined the regiment ten months before he was killed. The UDR did not acknowledge him as a member, nor did they list his name on its roll of honour.[10]

A week later, however, UDR commander Brigadier Ormerod was on television saying that if one of his soldiers belonged to the UDA, he would take no action (unless that soldier's UDA membership led to military misconduct).[11]

On 18 October 1972, loyalist leaders met with the General Tuzo, the GOC in Northern Ireland, to complain about the conduct of British troops in loyalist areas. A piece in *Fortnight* in November 1972 highlighted the absurdity of the UDR's tolerance of joint UDR–UDA membership:

> It was only two weeks ago that the UDA itself fired 500 bullets at the British Army. The fact that they were so poorly aimed that they didn't achieve anything is not really relevant. They were five hundred shots with intent. With the UDR playing a greater back-up role to the Army it is ludicrous to suggest that a man prepared to partake in treasonable acts (which is what firing at your own army is, I suppose) can still remain a member of the UDR. And what will the UDR/UDA men do when the UDA next confront the forces of HMG? Clearly the only solution open to UDA/UDR Jekyll and Hyders next time the UDA declare war on the army is to open fire on themselves in the name of either law and order or lawlessness.[12]

The army remained watchful for conflict between British troops (regular and UDR) on opposing sides, and the top levels of government were also aware of this possibility. On 15 March 1974, *The Times* ran an article titled 'Ulstermen Establish Subversive Group'. The article alleged that a group of men within the UDR and the RUC had established a subversive organisation, 'For Ulster', and had taken an oath threatening mutiny if the British government moved against loyalists. The paper reported of the group that 'for the past six months its members have infiltrated strategically important positions within the security forces'; it quoted 'a former UDR man' who said plans had been drawn up to capture army weapons, vehicles and equipment. The article continued, stating that the British army had 'acknowledged privately its concern at this development for some time, and there has been a suspicion that a mutinous group was being formed'.[13]

The loyalties of the UDR were about to be tested before an increasingly nervous British military establishment. The 'Subversion in the UDR' report concluded by considering the 'circumstances in which subversion might render the UDR (or elements within it) unreliable'. One of two political scenarios war-gamed in the report was a hypothesised wholesale rebellion within the regiment in the event that the government proposed a Council of Ireland or anything perceived to move in the direction of a United Ireland. A nervous British establishment was about to see if UDR loyalties would hold when their military and loyalist principles clashed.

The Ulster Worker's Council (UWC) was established in late 1973 to oppose power-sharing with the nationalist community and any consultative role for the Republic of Ireland in the running of the north. It comprised unionist politicians, loyalist paramilitaries, the Ulster Special Constabulary Association, the Ulster Army Council, and key workers from the Harland & Wolff shipyard and the power stations. The UWC decided to call a strike in May 1974, to overthrow the power-sharing executive and to scupper the proposed Council of Ireland – a key part of the Sunningdale Agreement, which underpinned the cross-community power-sharing arrangements. The strike began on Wednesday, 15 May. The story of the first few days was one of massive intimidation, as workers were threatened by loyalist paramilitaries.[14]

While loyalists enforced the strike by blocking roads and intimidating workers, they also killed thirty-nine civilians during its two-week duration, thirty-four of whom died in the Dublin and Monaghan bombings. On 28 May the strike succeeded in bringing down the power-sharing Northern Ireland Assembly – the first serious attempt since 1922 to allow any nationalist participation in government in Northern Ireland – and brought about the re-introduction of direct rule from Westminster. Ironically, despite British government pronouncements on the IRA threat to the state, it was loyalists who caused the apparatus of government to fail.

Throughout the crisis, the UDR was never called out. Why? Writing in 1994, Merlyn Rees, who had been secretary of state for Northern Ireland during the strike, said: 'Much nonsense had been written about the role of the Army in that strike. It is for Northern Ireland to deal with the paramilitaries. The Army's role is not to put down civil insurrection.'[15] This will come as a surprise to many readers.

Potter's account of the conduct of UDR members in *A Testimony to Courage* stands or falls on the reader's credulity:

> Despite the absence of any call-out of the UDR the soldiers flocked in to do duty. It was not just a matter of having nothing else to do, there was a growing feeling of frustration that they were not allowed to take more positive action. 'Stand back and observe' were the orders. Where possible, and it was usually possible, since the people manning the barricades regarded them as 'their' soldiers, they talked their way through ... 'Talking through' led to accusations of the

UDR fraternizing with the strikers. That was unjust. It was surely better to persuade than to use the heavy hand and, in any case, how could one use the heavy hand against the mothers pushing prams that 7UDR encountered blocking the main Bangor–Belfast road? Better to find another way …

Naturally there were soldiers who supported the aims of the UWC and there were reports that some had been seen helping to man the barricades. For those who lived in the UDA-dominated estates, in East Belfast for instance, the only way they could get out to do duties was to agree to take a turn on the barricades …

There were just two instances of attempts being made to subvert the loyalty of the soldiers, a platoon in 8UDR and a company in 3UDR. Both failed …

For the UDR the UWC strike was to prove a turning point …

'During the strike the UDR came of age,' Baxter [the UDR Brigadier] said. 'After that there was a great all-round improvement in the attitude of the Army and the Police.' He received a congratulatory signal from Major General Peter Leng, Commander Land Forces: 'My profound and sincere thanks for the extra hard work and long hours which the UDR have put in so willingly on behalf of law and order in the recent troubled days. I congratulate all ranks on their very high standards which is now so much the pattern of UDR affairs. Well done indeed.' …

It was a just reward for the loyalty of the soldiers to their battalions and their steadfastness under the most difficult conditions. Any doubts that remained about the Regiment's essential role in the security of the Province were resolved.

Ryder, for his part, is equally laudatory: 'It is to the UDR's general credit that it did not mutiny in this fundamental test of its loyalty, despite the ripples of revolution that ran through the community and the Regiment at that time.'

Look elsewhere, though, and it is possible to see that this is not the full story. A briefing note found among declassified files details the army's readiness for an SDLP delegation's complaints on the behaviour of UDR men during the UWC stoppage. It says, 'Since the UDR is 97% Protestant there are bound to be fears that the Regiment's impartiality is at least to some extent in question in the face of a conflict of loyalties between Westminster and Protestant Ulster.' The note continues, 'Complaints of the behaviour of UDR members during the strike have been numerous ... [including] that UDR patrols, (on duty) planted evidence on innocent Catholics; ... that UDR members (off duty) manned barricades and UWC picket lines; ... that UDR men interfered with attempts to clear barricades and actually helped fell trees to block roads.'[16]

The army's sole response to this was that 'the UDR was not used as such in clearing barricades or any other special duties connected with the strike.' The note's author continues, 'It would be naïve to believe that every single UDR member is blameless. There are undoubtedly many with extreme loyalist views who sympathised with the strike, and some who actually did join in.'[17]

Addressing SDLP assembly member Hugh Logue's specific concern regarding '26 UDR men in a picket line during the strike at the Hoechst Fibres Factory in Limavady', the note's author claims that all the men alleged to have been involved had been questioned and 'appear either to have been at the factory to enquire about the work situation, or as interested by-standers'. Wryly, he adds, 'Needless to say, this explanation is not likely to satisfy Mr. Logue.'[18]

Why was firmer action not taken against loyalists during the UWC strike? After all, British Prime Minister Harold Wilson had memorably described the strikers as 'people who spend their lives sponging on Westminster and British democracy and then systematically assault democratic methods'.[19]

An examination of the contemporary papers yields some telling answers. On 23 May a meeting had been held at Stormont Castle to review the security situation. Among those in attendance were the secretary of state, the GOC, the chief constable, and senior NIO and MI5 officials. The GOC advised that the army 'should maintain its low profile'. He warned that 'any attempt to force the issue [the UWC strike] would provoke an ugly situation'. The chief constable agreed with the GOC's analysis and added that 'a policy of confrontation would only provoke a greater reaction'. He said there had been shots fired at the police, 'which indicated the preparedness of the loyalists to use force'.[20]

The government continued to hold talks with members of the UWC. One such meeting, in 1974, gives a strong indication of the full extent of the UWC's influence over the UDR, and the British government's eagerness to appease them. According to the minutes of the meeting, which took place in August 1974 – just three months after the UVF car bombs had killed dozens of civilians in Dublin and Monaghan – representatives of the UDA, UVF, Red Hand Commando and Orange Volunteers attended.[21]

At the meeting, the UWC delegation proposed that two full-time UDR battalions be established, since 'the Army was tied down by Westminster politicians ... the UDR was weak with its wings clipped and ... loyalists had been forced to take arms at Westminster's failure to combat terrorism effectively'.[22] A handwritten message at the top of the note –

presumably by a senior official, though it is difficult to read – appears to say, 'The UWC appear to have made some valid points. This meeting might with advantage have taken place two months ago.'[23] A subsequent MoD study recommended against the UWC delegation's proposed two full-time UDR battalions because (a) there was 'insufficient manpower', and (b) 'full-time units could well turn into "strong arm" groups and do irreparable harm to the Regiment's image'.[24] Nevertheless, that this proposal was even considered – to the extent that it was explored as a legal (the Ulster Defence Act 1969 specifically provided for a part-time force) and military possibility by MoD bureaucrats – created the bizarre situation wherein loyalist extremists were dictating British military policy.

When a British minister was later asked to approve the creation of full-time battalions and asked where this proposal had come from, his officials freely admitted that the proposal emanated from the August 1974 meeting with the UWC.[25] No one in Whitehall, even at ministerial level, appeared to find it odd that loyalist paramilitaries would propose a significant expansion of a British army regiment that they were infiltrating, or that their proposal would be acted upon by the MoD.

In August 1975, after the murders of the Miami Showband and the GAA fans at faux-UDR roadblocks, press reports showed the UVF boasting of some of their number's dual membership of the UVF and UDR. This *Sunday News* piece includes the 'sympathies' message from members of 9 UDR for the deaths of Boyle and Somerville, who blew themselves up in the Miami Showband attack.[26]

On 10 September 1975, a meeting took place between Prime Minister Harold Wilson and Margaret Thatcher (then leader of the Conservative opposition) to discuss the deteriorating situation in the north, at which the secretary of state declared, 'The Army's judgement was that the UDR were heavily infiltrated by extremist Protestants, and that in a crisis situation they could not be relied upon to be loyal.'[27]

The Irish government was also aware of the risks of the UDR's divided loyalties. A declassified file contains an official assessment of the 'minority's position in a breakdown situation'. This fascinating document showed that the Irish government was aware of the need for advance planning, for areas where the catholic-nationalist population ('R.C.s') would be most in danger, should the crisis deteriorate further and loyalists take arms en masse in defiance of British rule.[28] Key to all of this, in the view of the Irish government, would be the disposition of the UDR:

> The major factor in the scale and type of attack will be the attitude and/or the presence of the British Army ... in any withdrawal situation, it is the opinion of all the SDLP members that I have spoken to, that the UDR and RUC Reserve would undoubtedly fight for the loyalist cause and the equipment available to the UDR (armoured cars, heavy machine guns) would allow them to wage war on a large and decisive scale ...[29]

After the Miami Showband killings in July 1975 and, a month later, the murders of Seán Farmer and Colm McCartney, a delegation from the SDLP met with the secretary of state to discuss their concerns over the UDR. Of particular concern was the issue of fake army checkpoints, at which Catholics were being attacked and killed. Both the Miami attack and the murder of the GAA fans took place at fake checkpoints manned by loyalist gunmen who included serving members of the UDR.[30]

An internal letter dated 9 September 1975[31] proposed some solutions to this problem, including:

1. Make membership of UDR contingent on a declaration that the man in question does not belong to any proscribed organisation. This of course would involve the re-proscription of the UVF [in fact the UVF was proscribed on 3 October 1975.[32] The UDA, by contrast, remained legal right up until 1992.[33]] ...

2. A strict screening procedure for new applicants – and for existing members chosen at random? The choice could in fact be rather less random than it might appear.

3. UDR arms and ammunition to be checked and controlled by regular army. Perhaps we could introduce a rule ... that every bullet fired must be satisfactorily accounted for. The current rule about firearms is that they may only be held when the member is on duty and must be surrendered when he goes off duty: but there is reason to believe (according to MOD) that this rule has not been strictly observed ...

4. UDR to be transferred from active to static policing duties. That is, rather than patrolling and setting up VCPs (and thus inevitably coming into contact with Catholics) they should have an essentially defensive function, guarding power stations, radio transmitters and the like.

Tellingly, however, the author adds, 'not armouries'. Presumably, then, by this stage, the British army was telling itself (if not the public) that the UDR could not be trusted to guard armouries. The secret letter concludes: 'This would have to be a gradual and covert process, and in a "Protestant crunch" situation we would have to be very careful about precisely who guarded key installations.'

So what was the British government's true position regarding loyalists, particularly those within the UDR? The truth was that while they were usefully allied with them, in reality they held them as carefully as you might a snake by the tail. And yet, within months, it was decided to increase the role of the UDR in intelligence gathering. The public were not to be told.

* * *

In 2019, Sam Thompson – a retired RUC and PSNI officer – gave an interview in which he recalled his experiences in those two forces, including during the conflict.[34] In this extract, when asked what the RUC thought of the UDR, Thompson had the following to say about UDR loyalties:

> Sam Thompson (S.T.): Well all I can do is speak about my own experiences … In Armagh around about '82 there was a local UVF Unit sort of sprung up. Let's just say there was a fair overlap between some of the UDR and the UVF. You know, if you had a nice Venn Diagram, you would have had a group that was coming to both.

> Interviewer (INT): The mid-Ulster triangle.

> S.T.: Well it was way after that. I'm not saying anything that can't be verified. There were people convicted in courts and so on for these things. So I'm not making this up. I'll just give you a little story. One night there was a sort of a row outside a bar that police got called

to and it was a couple of these young lads which were in this local UVF Unit. So it got a bit argy-bargy, you know, with police pulling batons out and swinging around these UVF guys and this UDR foot patrol came along. They actually started helping the UVF guys.

INT: So a UDR foot patrol started helping the UVF guys against the RUC?

S.T.: Against the police, yes. The inspector was there and had to tell them in no uncertain terms that if they didn't back off there were going to be very serious consequences.

INT: While, obviously, I believe it but for anybody living in America or wherever listening to this, would find it nearly unbelievable.

S.T.: They weren't swinging rifle butts at us or anything like that but they were trying to get these guys off side and stuff so they obviously knew each other.

INT: So this is a paid force within the British Army, helping loyalist paramilitaries against the RUC?

S.T.: Well the four of them that came down that street certainly were.

INT: And what year was this just for clarification?

S.T.: That was '82. You know, I don't want to start bashing them. As I say, I didn't have any great intimate knowledge of them. You know it would be totally wrong to say everyone in it was like that because I've heard very broad-brush statements against the RUC [the police service in which Sam served] 'oh they're all this, they're all that, they're all the other' and I can tell you they certainly weren't. But that did happen.

INT: There was certainly a perception, as you will agree with it, within the Nationalist community, that there were, I suppose, whether they were trained or not, they certainly weren't disciplined and they were pretty heavy handed and I suppose sectarian, which was a word that was justifiably used from the Nationalist community.

S.T.: I heard from some Catholics that they were always more frightened if they were stopped by the UDR rather than the police at a road stop.

INT: I remember people telling me that if they were stopped by the UDR they were praying that there was an RUC man with them.

S.T.: Yes, because while they mightn't have particularly liked us, I would still say that ordinary people going about their business at a road stop, you know, hadn't anything to fear from the RUC. I wouldn't say we were particularly well liked but I don't think that we were disliked in the way that the regular army or the UDR would have been.

CHAPTER SEVEN

The Roadblock Killings

In his work analysing policing around the world, John Brewer drew attention to the UDR's 'reputation for the harassment of Catholics in the course of routine duties' and, 'in rural areas especially, the behaviour of members of the UDR at roadblocks towards ordinary members of the public'.[1] This behaviour led the SDLP's John Hume to memorably describe the UDR as 'a group of Rangers supporters put in uniforms, supplied with weapons and given the job of policing the area where Celtic supporters live'.[2]

Many UDR members ruled their local areas with a swaggering entitlement. The PFC has on file an affidavit by a young (at the time) farmer about an incident in 1974 in which he and a friend were abused and tortured by a UDR patrol. The torture included prolonged beatings and a mock execution of one of the men. The farmer stated, 'I then recognised Oliver Gibson who was in uniform and carrying a revolver, a wee short gun, in his hand. There were other UDR men there who I could not see clearly enough to identify. Oliver Gibson spoke to the UDR men and said "Take them over the road" ... We were walked four or five hundred yards from the house down the road and then stopped.' Gibson then questioned the farmer at length about a property the farmer was negotiating to buy. He then shone a light into the man's eyes and said, 'Even though you know me you'll not be living to tell any tales ... We're not worried about doctors or anything. We have ways of making boys like you talk.'

Oliver Gibson, a UDR officer, was a founding member of the Democratic Unionist Party, or DUP. Gibson would later serve as MLA for West Tyrone from 1998 to 2003; he also had a seat on Omagh District Council for a number of years. By 2003, Gibson's name was being linked to the 1974 murder of Patsy Kelly, an unaligned nationalist councillor involved in the civil rights movement.[3]

Cllr Patsy Kelly is widely believed to have been the victim of 'an abduction and killing ... carried out by members of the Ulster Defence Regiment in uniform' at a UDR vehicle check point (VCP). Solicitor for the Kelly family Pat Fahy wrote of the 'massive cover-up' that, immediately after the murder, 'swung into action and has remained in place to this day'.[4] Significant forensic evidence has been found among declassified files by Ciarán Mac Áirt, a legacy investigator with *Paper Trail*,[5] which supports the theory of UDR culpability for the murder: two days after Cllr Kelly's body was found weighted down in Lough Eyes, the British army found ninety-seven bullets in the same lake; among these bullets were a number matching the calibre of those used in the killing of Cllr Kelly.

Not only did the police investigation not follow up on this important evidence, they withheld it from the Kelly family. This, and other forensic evidence of a footprint matching army issue boots found at the spot where Cllr Kelly was abducted, was buried by police at the time. Pat Fahy was adamant that, 'indisputably, various forces of the state have collaborated in ensuring that those who killed

Councillor Kelly would escape justice'.[6] At the time of writing, the case was the subject of a Police Ombudsman's investigation.

A recently declassified NIO report of a 1990 visit by Minister of State for Northern Ireland John Cope to Strabane and Castlederg records that one RUC superintendent, along with a 'vigorously assenting' RUC divisional commander, told Cope that 'it was essential for all [underlined in original] UDR patrols to be accompanied to keep soldiers in line. Some had very bad records indeed; some were an absolute "dream". It all depended on the attitude of the Major ... and ultimately on the Commanding Officer.' The note records that the superintendent then 'spoke of a company whose stay in Strabane had led to 5 prosecutions for criminal assault, including of a mentally handicapped boy'.[7]

There is abundant evidence of the frequent ill-treatment meted out to Catholics at UDR checkpoints. One surprising source is the Reverend Dr Empey, Church of Ireland Bishop of Meath and Kildare, who described his experience in a meeting with then Taoiseach Charles Haughey in January 1986: 'He mentioned that he had personally had an extremely unpleasant experience at a UDR roadblock some time ago (when the UDR had mistaken him for a Catholic priest and he had allowed this misunderstanding to continue for a few minutes in order to see how they behaved).'[8]

The files repeatedly show examples of the Irish government and the SDLP making direct complaints regarding UDR brutality at vehicle checkpoints. On one occasion in 1976, an Irish government official, Donlon, raised with his NIO counterpart his own mistreatment at a UDR VCP; however, he did not go so far as to make a formal complaint. Donlon reported that he had been stopped at a UDR VCP; while he was there, the UDR patrol 'saw that his car had a Southern number plate [and] they proceeded to take it and its contents apart'.[9]

Donlon recalled that some of the patrol 'were clearly under the influence of drink and they did so much damage to his car that it had cost him £100 to have it made good when he got back to Dublin'. Donlon asserted that the UDR 'had a bad record of misbehaviour' and 'there had been too many cases for [the NIO] to explain them away with ... "bad apple stories"'. This was an opinion that Donlon would certainly have made known to the southern government.[10]

In December 1985, the SDLP's Seamus Mallon himself fell foul of a UDR VCP in Portadown, where he was held for nearly an hour at around midnight. An internal memo on the incident claimed that the part-time UDR soldiers didn't recognise Mallon and that he had given his name as James. The memo's author writes, 'I suppose we should in a way be relieved that the UDR patrol did not recognise Mr Mallon (assuming this to be true) and were therefore not deliberately singling him out for special treatment. At the same time, one of the Regiment's operational advantages is supposed to be its local knowledge!'[11]

Earlier in 1985, a note of a meeting between the secretary of state for Northern Ireland and senior officials, convened to discuss the UDR, recorded that the secretary of state 'was wary of using local knowledge as an argument for using locally recruited UDR men in their own areas; it could mean that, in recognising people at VCPs and on patrols, it would be *more difficult for them to be evenhanded* in their approach [emphasis added]'.[12]

By 1972 the issue of roadblocks, both legal and illegal, was of real concern. An advice note from the Ministry of Defence provided Orwellian legal advice on UDA roadblocks, which were frequent throughout Belfast and elsewhere in the summer of 1972.[13]

The advice note stated that 'members of the UDA who create an obstruction are ... generally speaking committing an offence'; it then went on to outline some possible defences open to UDA members found operating them. As ever, it is important to remember that the UDA was a *legal* organisation, and would not be proscribed until August 1992.[14]

One suggested defence is that 'there appears to be nothing to prevent an ordinary citizen "flagging down" a driver'. Once the vehicle is stopped, a UDA member 'has no power to search a vehicle, though presumably he may carry out a search if the person in charge of the vehicle authorises him to do so'.

The document goes on helpfully to offer that 'the UDA might claim that their patrols were on the look out for terrorists and they might, therefore, want to invoke s.2 (3) of the Criminal Justice Act (NI) 1967 ... Thus if a car were seen to be driving at speed from the scene of an explosion, a member of the UDA might be justified in stopping it.'[15]

At this time the UDA were stopping cars in Belfast and questioning occupants to ascertain their religion. Those with 'Catholic names' were often taken away and tortured, and sometimes murdered. Two such victims were James McGerty and James Corr, who were stopped by UDA roadblocks on 26 July 1972 – tortured and murdered less than a month before the above 'advice' was issued. The report by the HET on James McGerty, on file at the PFC, states that the roadblock was in place over many hours.

Others taken from their vehicles at UDA roadblocks in the summer of 1972 and subsequently murdered included Francis Arthurs, Patrick O'Neill and Rose McCartney.

The authorities were aware that Catholic civilians were being abducted and murdered at these roadblocks but chose to tolerate their existence. In August 1972, Bernadette Devlin MP raised the issue of reports of illegal roadblocks in the areas surrounding Coagh (in Co. Tyrone) and Desertmartin (Co. Derry), and asked whether investigations had implicated members of the UDR in the operation of these roadblocks.

In a briefing document dated October 1972, it is revealed that the RUC chief constable had written to state that an incident had occurred at Desertmartin, 'where a UDR and an illegal UDA roadblock were operating a quarter of a mile apart. Police and military investigation of the UDA roadblock clearly established there was no collusion with the UDR.'[16] The ministerial reply to Ms Devlin repeated this assertion.

It may seem curious that a regiment of the British army and loyalist paramilitaries could operate their own roadblocks within a few hundred yards, apparently with no co-operation, but this question does not appear to have troubled the military authorities.

Later tragic events would confirm that some of those involved in illegal roadblocks were indeed members of the UDR.

The Miami Showband

In the early hours of 31 July 1975, five members of the popular Miami Showband, which had members and a passionate fanbase from north and south of the border, and from both Protestant and Catholic communities, were stopped by an apparent military checkpoint at Buskhill, County Down, as they travelled home to Dublin from a gig in nearby Banbridge. In fact, the roadblock was operated by members of the UVF, some of whom were also serving members of the UDR; it was a pre-planned ambush of the band members' vehicle. At that time, the UVF was a fully legal organisation, as it had been de-proscribed the previous year, in May 1974.[17]

The minibus – carrying the Miami's lead singer and frontman, Fran O'Toole; singer and trumpet player, Brian McCoy; lead guitarist, Tony Geraghty; bass guitarist, Stephen Travers; and singer and saxophonist, Des McAlea – was flagged down by a man in uniform waving a red lamp. The minibus halted at the junction of the main Belfast–Newry Road and Buskhill Road (the latter a minor road that led to Donaghmore village).[18] The band members were ordered out and told to stand in line with their backs to the main road. Several other soldiers emerged out of the darkness.

Band member Des McAlea remembered a man wearing dark-framed glasses giving an order to obtain the band members' names and addresses.[19] At the same time, two of the UVF gang – Wesley Somerville and Harris Boyle – were busy planting a bomb in the band's minibus. It exploded almost immediately, killing them both.[20]

The shockwave hurled the band's five members through a hedge, which went on fire. They were uninjured by the explosion and began running away across a field, but they were shot down by high-velocity weapons as they ran. One of the perpetrators paid particular attention to Fran O'Toole. He was shot between eighteen and twenty-two times at close range in the face, head, neck, shoulder and chest. Des McAlea, in the light of the flames, saw Brian McCoy and realised he was dead. He also noted that Stephen Travers was badly injured. He called out to Stephen, telling him he was going to get help. He bravely ran up the road, past the burning minibus, and hailed a car, which took him to Newry RUC station. The emergency services soon arrived at the scene and found the five bodies – three band members and two UVF men – and the other survivor, Stephen Travers.[21]

The next morning, the UVF issued a hurriedly defensive statement, claiming that a UVF patrol led by Harris Boyle had become suspicious of two vehicles – a minibus and a car – which, it said, were parked near the border. They claimed Boyle had ordered his men to apprehend the occupants for questioning. As Boyle and Somerville began searching the minibus, a bomb was detonated, killing both men outright. Simultaneously, the patrol, it was claimed, came under fire from the occupants of the car. The UVF said its patrol returned fire, killing three of their attackers and wounding another.[22]

The statement was blatantly untrue, and demonstrably so. Far from firing, the band members were savagely mown down. The following week, *Combat*, the UVF newsletter, brazenly carried sympathy notices from various loyalist extremist groups and 'the loyalist members of "A" Company 9 UDR (Co. Antrim)', who wished to convey 'their deepest heartfelt sympathies to the families and friends of Harris Boyle and Wesley Somerville (Mid-Ulster UVF) who were killed-in-action on Thursday, 31st July 1975.'

Immediately after the attack, the RUC investigation began. Exhibits were gathered, the scene was photographed and witnesses were interviewed. A recently discovered document reveals that one of the weapons used in the attack and recovered from the scene belonged to the B Specials, one, as the army document says, 'not handed in on disbandment of the B Specials'.[23] The notorious Robin Jackson was arrested on 5 August but was released without charge two days later.[24] The Miami Showband attack had taken place close to Jackson's home patch in Donaghmore, indicating his likely involvement.[25]

The Convicted Perpetrators

Lance Corporal Thomas Raymond Crozier, of 11 UDR based in Lurgan, was arrested on 7 August 1975 under Section 10 of the Northern Ireland (Emergency Provisions) Act 1973. A bag containing an army tunic, trousers and belt had been found in his bedroom during his arrest search. He was interviewed over the following two days, and eventually admitted his involvement in the murders and his membership of the UVF. Nonetheless, he sought to minimise his involvement and knowledge of the other perpetrators. Crozier suggested that he had passively taken part in what was a pre-planned operation with UVF members he didn't actually know. However, he made a statement to police on 8 August and was charged with the Miami murders the following day.

Minutes of a meeting between Irish ambassador, Donal O'Sullivan, and Douglas Janes (a senior NIO official in London), which took place within weeks of the atrocity, show that the British government was by then aware of the involvement of at least one UDR member in the attack. Janes told the ambassador that the man charged with murder – Crozier – was a serving member of the UDR. This was 'unfortunate', Janes says, but there was always a risk of a 'bad hat' in any large organisation.[26] Janes informed the ambassador that, in regard to the Miami Showband massacre, police were pretty certain they knew all the people involved, 'but that there seems no prospect of charging any others for murder'.[27]

One month later the UDR sympathy notice in *Combat* came to the attention of government officials in Dublin. Based on the notice, the Irish ambassador again raised his concerns with Janes as to the role of the British army and the UDR in the massacre. Janes replied that, 'naturally', enquiries had already been made, 'and there was no reason to believe that it was genuine'. An anonymous official, however, had later written in the margin of the note, 'We must look into this.'[28]

James Roderick Shane McDowell was an optical worker from Lurgan and a sergeant in the same UDR battalion as Crozier. He escaped the round-up of suspects in August; it wasn't until 23 October that he was found in the home of Robin Jackson in Lurgan, when police came to search the property after the murders of Peter and Jane McKearney earlier that evening. Jackson was absent, but they discovered McDowell, who refused to provide his personal details. He was taken into custody for screening, upon which his identity and membership of the UDR was established. He was soon released but was required to resign from the UDR because of his association with Jackson.[29]

Among the evidence recovered from the Miami murder scene was a pair of broken spectacles, which proved to be a vital clue. One hundred thousand optical files belonging to opticians in Portadown, Lurgan, Newry and Dungannon were inspected, until it was ascertained by detectives that only seven people in the infamous 'Murder Triangle' area used lenses like those found at the scene. McDowell was one of them. He was arrested on 12 January 1976 under Section 7 of the Prevention of Terrorism Act 1975. Having first denied involvement, he agreed to make a statement during his second interview by Newry CID. Like Crozier, he tried to minimise his role in the operation.[30]

On 26 June 1976, while on remand awaiting trial, McDowell wrote a letter to Robin Jackson outlining the strength of the evidence against him. He concluded the letter with the phrase, 'Robin, there is very little hope for us but I hope the rest of the lads will learn from our mistakes.' This evidence was later produced at the trial to prove that McDowell was more actively involved than he had admitted.[31] This, and the scientific evidence against him, led McDowell to change his 'not guilty' plea to 'guilty' when the trial opened in October 1976.[32]

Both Crozier and McDowell were convicted at Belfast City Commission on 15 October 1976 and sentenced to life imprisonment.

John James Somerville – a brother of Wesley Somerville – was arrested on 18 August 1975 but was quickly released. He was, however, rearrested on 23 September 1980, and was initially interviewed about UVF activity in Dungannon, Portadown and Newry. He was interviewed a total of eleven times over a period of four days; following what had developed into a lengthy theological discussion with a detective, he admitted that he had been involved in the Miami Showband murders. Like Crozier and McDowell, he too minimised his role.

Both John and Wesley Somerville were well known to the security forces prior to the attack on the Miami. They had been arrested, along with another accomplice, for kidnapping two men, planting a bomb in the men's van and driving it into the middle of a Catholic housing estate in Coalisland, County Tyrone, on 5 March 1974. The bomb exploded, seriously injuring a number of people, including a baby. The Somervilles' accomplice, Trevor Barnard, was (along with others unknown) charged with unlawfully imprisoning the two men in their own van. In November 1974, Barnard was sentenced to two years for the kidnapping case. Two days after Barnard was charged, the Somerville brothers appeared at Belfast Magistrates' Court, also on charges of assaulting and kidnapping the two men.

Thereafter, however, no more was heard of the case against the Somervilles. Anne Cadwallader has written that no explanation can be found for 'the mysterious evaporation' of the charges against the brothers; she argues that had they been convicted on this charge, many lives might have been saved.[33]

John Somerville was convicted of the Miami Showband murders on 9 November 1981. Despite the court's recommendation that each should serve a minimum of thirty-five years for the Miami Showband murders, Crozier was released on 5 March 1992, having served sixteen years of his life sentence, McDowell was released on 29 September 1993, having served seventeen years of his life sentence,[34] while Somerville was released under the terms of the Good Friday Agreement in November 1998, having served seventeen years of his life sentence.[35]

The Involvement of Robin Jackson

Robin Jackson was one the most notorious figures of the conflict. He was born in 1947, in the townland of Donaghmore, County Down – very close to where the Miami Showband attack took place. His first known foray into loyalist activities was when he, and other members of his UVF gang, took part in a raid on the 11 UDR armoury in Portadown on 23 October 1973; however, he may have been involved in the murder of Seán McDonnell in Mayobridge, County Down, on 22 August 1973. At that time, Jackson was – as a declassified army log sheet shows[36] – a serving member of 11 UDR.

John Weir said in his written affidavit that Robin Jackson was not only involved in murdering the O'Dowds, but had also planned the co-ordinated attacks on them and the Reaveys, on 4 January 1976, with RUC Reservist James Mitchell at the Glenanne farmhouse.[37] A Sterling submachine gun used in the Miami Showband attack was later used to kill the O'Dowds.[38] Barney O'Dowd was able to describe one to the RUC one of the gunmen who attacked his family – a detective thought the description closely matched Robin Jackson. There is, however, no record of Jackson being questioned.

Many observers believe that Jackson benefited from an element of official protection and alleged immunity against prosecution throughout his murderous criminal career, that he benefited from 'a corrupt and indefensible relationship with enough RUC officers to protect him from ever facing a murder charge'.[39] At one point Jackson was said to have told UVF colleagues of 'someone looking after me'.[40] In 1980, two RUC officers were convicted of the murder of a Catholic shopkeeper, William Strathern, in 1977. Yet one of the convicted men named Jackson as the gunman. The RUC said that Jackson did not appear before the court for 'reasons of operational strategy'. In his report into the Dublin and Monaghan bombings, Judge Barron wrote, 'it is hardly surprising that this oblique phrase has been taken by some to indicate that Jackson [was] ... working for or with the RUC Special Branch.' But Barron said it might also have meant that the RUC had no evidence on which to prosecute, 'but did not wish to admit this in public'.[41] In the context of all that has been presented here, the reader may weigh which is more likely. Jackson's involvement in many murders, including the 1974 Dublin and Monaghan bombings, is recounted in detail in Anne Cadwallader's ground-breaking *Lethal Allies*.

Jackson was arrested in the week after the Miami Showband attack but was released without charge two days later. Decades later, the HET found that there had been an opportunity, in May 1976, to rearrest and interview Jackson about the Miami Showband. On 18 May, Edward Tate Sinclair, a dairy farmer, was arrested at his farm near Dungannon following the recovery of firearms, ammunition, explosives and bomb components. The following day, Sinclair was allowed to return to his farm, under the supervision of Detective Chief Inspector Frank Murray, ostensibly to work. While there, Murray discovered a 9mm Luger pistol secreted behind a wall fan. The pistol was intact with its magazine, which contained four bullets.

With the Luger was a homemade silencer – a long metal tube with black adhesive insulating tape wrapped around it. A forensic examination of the gun, silencer and tape revealed two fingerprints, matching Jackson's, on the silencer's metal barrel. Critically, the exhibit was then mistakenly labelled, indicating that the prints had been found on the tape (not the barrel). Jackson was arrested on 31 May.[42]

The same day, Detective Superintendent Drew received categorical confirmation that Jackson's fingerprints had been found on the barrel of the silencer before the tape had been wrapped around it. Jackson was interviewed by Drew on 1 June, when the former made a statement denying he had ever been to Sinclair's farm. He admitted, however, that he knew him through a loyalist club in Portadown. Drew placed the Luger, silencer and magazine (but not the tape) on the interview table. Jackson denied handling them. He was asked if he could offer an explanation, should his fingerprints be found on either the pistol or the silencer (or both). Jackson again denied he had handled the items but then volunteered the following information: one night at the Portadown loyalist club, Sinclair had asked him for some tape and he gave him 'part of the roll I was using in the bar'.[43]

In his statement, Jackson said he got to know about his

fingerprints on the tape (which Drew had not mentioned) when he was warned by a detective sergeant and a detective superintendent on 24 May that he should clear off, as 'there was a wee job up the country he would be done for and there was no way out of it for him.'

On 2 June, Jackson was charged with possession of a firearm, a magazine, four rounds of ammunition and a silencer, with intent to endanger life. The Luger pistol had been used in the attack on the Miami Showband, and also in the murder of John Francis Green in County Monaghan. Despite this significant new evidence, Jackson was not questioned about the Miami Showband attack, nor were the Gardaí (the Irish police force) informed regarding the connection to the J.F. Green murder in their jurisdiction. There is no evidence, either, that the Miami investigation team was informed of these developments, which could have provided reasonable grounds to justify Jackson's rearrest.

Detective Superintendent Drew's prosecution report stated that Jackson knew before his arrest that his fingerprints had been found; that Jackson claimed a senior RUC officer had tipped him off about a week before his arrest. The report stated that if Jackson's allegations about the police officers were true, it was 'a grave breach of discipline and police confidentiality on the part of the officers concerned'. Drew reported that aspect of the case to the Complaints and Discipline Department for investigation. There is, however, no evidence that any criminal or disciplinary investigation was initiated by RUC headquarters.[44]

When Jackson stood trial on 11 November 1976, the only charge he faced was possession of the silencer. The trial judge rejected Jackson's defence that his fingerprints were only on the tape and had been transferred onto the silencer. He did, however, accept that the finding of Jackson's fingerprints on the silencer was not evidence that it had been in his possession. The judge stated that for a case of possession to be proved, it had to be established that the accused had knowledge, assent and control. Incredibly, Jackson was acquitted.[45]

The HET concluded in relation to Jackson, the security forces and the Miami murders, 'To the objective, impartial observer, disturbing questions about collusive and corrupt behaviour are raised. The HET review has found no means to assuage or rebut these concerns and that is a deeply troubling matter.'[46] Jackson was on the security forces' radar from an early stage but yet was able to walk free and continue his reign of murder for many years afterwards.

On 13 December 2021 the survivors of the Miami Showband attack, and the families of two of their murdered bandmates, agreed to a total of £1.5m in damages in settlement of a civil case against the Ministry of Defence and the PSNI over state collusion in the attack. The civil case accused the MoD and PSNI of assault, trespass, conspiracy to injure, negligence, and misfeasance in public office. The settlement was made without admission of liability. Des McAlea told *The Irish Times* afterwards, 'I was glad to see that it did come out that it was collusion' and the fact that the case lasted only one day was 'like admitting liability'. He said that he believes the British government was afraid of what might have become public knowledge during a trial, and that 'on the night of the Miami massacre there was at least six more men there who were never traced, never found, never charged and never will be'.[47]

Seán Farmer and Colm McCartney

On 24 August 1975, less than a month after the attack on the Miami Showband, two friends, Seán Farmer and Colm

McCartney, were driving back home to Derry after attending a football match at Croke Park, in Dublin. While they were travelling, an RUC patrol discovered a fake UDR VCP, near Newtownhamilton in County Armagh, 'probably set up to ambush GAA supporters – just like them – returning home from Croke Park'[48] – the occasion of Derry playing in the All-Ireland Football Semi-Final was significant and the route home for Derry supporters was evidently a tempting target. According to the RUC man in charge of the patrol, they had been immediately suspicious of the checkpoint as they did not recognise any of the uniformed men, and they also knew there were no planned checkpoints in the area. A recently discovered army file confirmed that there were no army or UDR VCPs out at the time.[49]

The RUC patrol – three RUC men in a single car, wearing civilian jackets over their own uniforms – were stopped by the checkpoint. One of the apparent UDR men, a man with long hair and an 'unusual accent',[50] asked to see a driving licence. He shone a flashlight into the RUC car and saw the officers' weapons, upon which he jumped back, saying, 'It's you! Police!'[51]

The RUC officers drove away at speed and confirmed with their base by radio that there were no scheduled patrols in the area. Apparently, however, they chose not to investigate any further and returned to their base. The only steps they took were to tell the British army duty officer of their encounter, and to warn Gardaí that an apparent fake VCP was operating just inside the border.

Many years later the HET interviewed the RUC officer who led this patrol, Frederick Bartholomew, who told the HET that he was certain that the men operating the fake VCP wore standard British army-issue uniforms and carried regulation issue weapons and equipment. He was also certain that the men were not from Newtownhamilton UDR. Despite this, after his encounter with a suspicious group of heavily armed men, neither his patrol nor the British soldiers in Newtownhamilton raised the alarm or left their base to investigate further.

Shortly after the RUC had fled from the fake VCP, Seán Farmer and Colm McCartney arrived and were shot dead by the men there. After the killers had dispersed, other travellers, all of whom had come from the same match as Seán and Colm, including cousins of Colm, arrived upon the scene. Upon seeing the victims, they drove together to the nearby Keady to raise the alarm. None of these eyewitnesses was ever contacted again by police, until the PFC sought them out over thirty years later. At the time, the witnesses had even offered to return to the location of the bodies, but that was declined by police in Keady (who said the scene might be booby-trapped).[52]

Three weapons were used to murder Seán and Colm: a .455 Webley Mark VI revolver, a 9 mm Luger pistol and a .45 Colt automatic pistol. Both the Webley and the Luger were used four months later to kill the three Reavey brothers, on 4 January 1976. The Luger was also used, in June 1976, in the attack on the Rock Bar (in which all the assailants were serving RUC officers).[53]

An RUC intelligence report, received immediately after Seán and Colm were killed, named one of their killers as Philip Silcock. Then, in December 1978, the RUC officers directly involved in the attack on the Rock Bar were being investigated by police. During their interviews they admitted that two serving UDR men – Robert McConnell and another whose name is known to the PFC – were among those manning the fake VCP where Seán and Colm were murdered (both UDR men were subsequently killed by the IRA).

McConnell and Philip Silcock had been involved together in the attack at Donnelly's Bar, where Sterling sub-machine gun UF57A30490 (see chapter four) was used. The December 1978 investigation also revealed that a serving RUC officer named Laurence McClure had been involved in the killing of Seán and Colm (McClure was also a suspect in the fatal Dublin and Monaghan bombings in 1974). The net was apparently closing in on the killers of Seán McCartney and Colm Farmer.

However, although RUC intelligence reports (both in 1975 and, again, after the arrests of the RUC officers in 1978) suggested that Silcock was involved in killing Seán and Colm, the RUC made no effort to question him and he was never charged with involvement in these murders. Laurence McClure denied involvement in the murders of Seán and Colm, and was likewise never charged in relation to them. Meanwhile, both of the UDR men were dead – McConnell was killed on 5 April 1976; his partner-in-crime was shot by the IRA in 1975.

The HET's report into the killing of Seán and Colm is a stark illustration of the RUC's failure of the two men and their families. Even taking into account the huge pressures of work at the time, it says, there was intelligence naming two people in the Mid-Ulster UVF as being responsible, and yet 'No action was taken ... and there is no record that it was made available to investigators [that is, Special Branch intelligence was not passed to CID investigators].' Furthermore, 'The use of UDR uniforms (mentioned in intelligence, described by Sergeant Bartholomew and his police colleagues) would surely have caused immense concern if this were an isolated incident. However it was not.'[54]

The murders of Seán Farmer and Colm McCartney had taken place just three weeks after the Miami Showband massacre, in almost identical circumstances, and yet there was an utter failure by the RUC to investigate. Here were murders at two faked UDR VCPs, within one month of each other – and at both bogus VCPs, serving UDR officers were involved. The HET concluded, 'relatives of the victims in cases such as these, are convinced that investigations were not rigorously conducted, in a deliberate effort to conceal security forces' involvement ... The HET is unable to rebut or allay these suspicions.'[55]

Seán and Colm were random and easy targets, identifiably Catholic because of the journey they were taking, travelling home after watching their county play a Gaelic football match. Colm's cousin Seamus Heaney later wrote, in memory of Colm, 'The Strand at Lough Beg', imagining the circumstances of his death. On 28 August 1975, four days after Seán and Colm were killed, Secretary of State for Northern Ireland Merlyn Rees sent a memo to British Prime Minister Harold Wilson, penning a far more prosaic epitaph for the two men: 'Assassination squads masquerading as VCPs create new problems and also make necessary some reappraisal of the activities of the UDR.'[56]

CHAPTER EIGHT

Life and Death in the UDR

The UDR evolved across the 1970s, expanding in numbers and deployments, having greater responsibility, even allowing women to join the ranks of 'male citizens of good character', and crucially, assuming intelligence duties.

On 11 March 1971, the under-secretary of state for defence, Ian Gilmour announced that, just shy of a year since its formation, the UDR was 'now a firmly-established part of the security forces in Northern Ireland', with a strength 'over 4,000' and on target to reach the full figure of 6,000 troops set out in Hunt's White Paper of November 1969.[1]

In September 1971, General Ford, the Commander of Land Forces in Northern Ireland, announced a rapid expansion of the UDR that would increase this staffing ceiling from 6,000, then 8,000, then up to 10,000,[2] with three additional battalions formed. In December 1971, 8 UDR was formed, followed by 9 UDR and 10 UDR in January 1972.

In June 1972, Headquarters Northern Ireland was mulling over the UDR's development – hamstrung, however, by the 'unsettled situation' that prevented the army planning 'beyond the medium term future'. Contributing to this were the 'volatile and unpredictable' attitudes of the local population.

In the same memo, the army had an eye on possible Protestant 'disappointment' if the UDR was not to be allowed to outgrow its then 10,000-man recruitment limit. Such disappointment might only swell the ranks of the UDA.[3]

In June 1972 the chief of the general staff recommended greater use of the UDR to 'relieve some of the burden on the Regular forces' to cope with an 'imminent growth in demands on troops during the marching season'.[4] This was despite the fact that the British command knew the UDR was itself part of the problem. The chief of the general staff admitted that an 'Increase in the UDR's visible presence might help mollify Protestant opinion, but at the expense of increased Catholic mistrust. It would be unwise to expect the UDR to have to confront militant Protestants.' In September 1972, 11 UDR was formed, bringing UDR strength up to an all-time peak of more than 9,000, making it 'the largest infantry regiment in the British army'.[5]

Intelligence Role

As the UDR expanded in numbers, so too did its operational remit. A March 1974 army paper on the UDR referenced the 'number of members ... associated with Protestant paramilitary organisations'. Yet the same document mentions that proposals for enhancing the UDR's intelligence-gathering capability were being prepared for submission to ministers.[6]

According to an April 1974 document, 'The UDR and Intelligence', senior military figures, including the chief of the general staff, discussed an intelligence-gathering role for the UDR. While this was 'primarily the task of the Regular Army and RUC ... intelligence gathering is already practised to some extent [by the UDR] ... especially in the country areas where the local knowledge of its members is strong'.[7]

Time and again, reference can be found to the usefulness of the local knowledge of UDR members – an inevitable result of UDR personnel living among the communities they were policing. Ryder noted that local UDR personnel played a vital role: 'helping to identify those in the community who played an active terrorist role or provided support networks. The tradesmen: postmen, milkmen, meter readers, who populated its ranks part-time were ideally placed to provide such information, gleaned on their daily rounds.'[8]

In Dingley's 'Combating Terrorism in Northern Ireland', the author writes that 'There was never a shortage of recruits to join the local UDR ... The UDR was an important addition to the anti-terrorist armoury (one reason why it was always so heavily vilified by Republicans). Being local the UDR had good knowledge not only of the territory but of individuals and activists.'[9]

Tommy McKearney, a former senior member of the Provisional IRA in Tyrone, expressed how well aware republicans were of this particular strength of locally raised security forces:

> Both the UDR and the RUC Reserve were recruited locally and had, therefore, a comprehensive and detailed knowledge of their areas of operation. As local men, they were able to distinguish between various accents that are so distinctive to a Northern Irish ear, but would not resonate with regular soldiers reared in Britain ... some UDR members were even able to recognise young republicans by family resemblances to older relatives. They had, too, the ability to differentiate between families sharing similar names ... In closely mixed rural areas, members of the UDR or RUC Reserve were intimately familiar with the rhythm and pattern of life

in their district ... The Provisional IRA would have been incredibly naïve, not to say extraordinarily stupid, had it failed to recognise the threat these forces posed.[10]

In fact, the war being waged by the British army depended increasingly on support from the UDR, though army commanders worried in April 1974 that care needed to be taken, 'if it [the UDR] were seen too ostentatiously to possess and operate in an intelligence gathering role' – and 'lest the UDR become drawn into malicious neighbour-watching'. Accordingly, 'any extension of the UDR's intelligence-gathering role would need to be carefully controlled'.[11]

Needless to say, despite this proposal being aimed at gathering 'intelligence on terrorist activities', there was 'no intention of recruiting or encouraging members of the UDR to become informers on subversive elements within the UDR although, as you know, subversion in the UDR is a cause for concern'.[12]

The move to expand the UDR's role into intelligence gathering was given the go-ahead in October 1974 by the secretary of state for Northern Ireland, Merlyn Rees, on the proviso that the changes be made 'as discreetly as possible'.[13]

If it seems outrageous that the British state would even contemplate using such a force – many of whose members had sympathies with loyalist paramilitaries – in an intelligence-gathering role, bear in mind that this aspect of the UDR was never publicly disclosed. By 1975, it must be recalled, both the contemporary prime minister and a future prime minister of the United Kingdom, a Western parliamentary democracy, were aware that the largest regiment in its armed forces was 'heavily infiltrated' by members of illegal paramilitary groups. By then, the UDR had become an essential element in the long-term security strategy.

'Ulsterisation' and 'The Way Ahead'

The British government's security strategy shifted during the course of the Troubles. A significant change began in 1974, when Secretary of State for Northern Ireland Merlyn Rees announced that full responsibility for law and order was going to be transferred from the British army to the RUC. This was 'Ulsterisation'.

A deliberate reference to the US government's policy of Vietnamization (whereby primary military responsibility towards the end of the Vietnam War began to be abdicated and placed in the hands of the South Vietnamese regime), it was 'a policy according to which British Army soldiers from the "mainland" (that is, England, Scotland, and Wales) were gradually replaced with members of the locally recruited security forces, thus transferring the responsibility (as well as the human cost) for law enforcement to the local population'.[14] As Peter Taylor put it, 'the price was to be paid in *Protestant* blood ... This suited the British government since (with occasional, dramatic exceptions) fewer soldiers were carried back to Britain in coffins.'[15]

This was to be rather callously reflected by the prime minister herself, Margaret Thatcher, who is reported to have announced at a reception at Hillsborough in 1987 'that all she cared about was British soldiers being killed in Northern Ireland and their bodies being returned to Britain'. A note reported that 'One particular man to whom she said this has two sons in the UDR, one of whom has been wounded, turned on his heels when she finished and walked away. This was given as a typical example of her insensitivity.'[16]

Similarly insensitive, but no less instructive, were comments by Lord Richard Dannett, the former head of the British Armed Forces, in September 2021. Dannett was speaking from his home in Norfolk in a live TV programme examining the radical and illegal plans of the British government of the day to deal with legacy (under which all legal proceedings regarding conflict-related killings would be halted). Dannett complained that the broadcast 'didn't focus on any soldiers [or] soldiers' families, over 700 of whom lost their lives in the province'.[17] In fact, the broadcast had carried stories of five victims – told by their families – two of whom had been UDR soldiers. So, rather damningly, it seemed in the eyes of the ex-Head of the Armed Forces that UDR personnel were not British soldiers at all.

Ulsterisation had three convenient 'wins' for the British government. Firstly, it 'constituted an effective distortion of the situation, especially for foreign consumption, projecting the irrational image of a war of religion'[18] – between Irish Catholics and Irish Protestants (the latter wanting to be British). This, alongside a policy of 'criminalisation' of Republicans, was about 'concealing the real causes and consequences of the Anglo-Irish conflict'.[19] Internationally, of course, the British did not want to be seen 'as a colonial army in an occupied territory'.[20]

Secondly, as John McGarry and Brendan O'Leary described the situation: 'What the British public regarded as Irish people [the UDR and RUC] were doing most of the ... policing of Irish people. British policy-makers were therefore not constrained by large losses of "real British" lives (i.e., Great British soldiers)'.[21]

Thirdly, it enabled the British army to train its focus elsewhere, for 'without their loyal volunteer service, battalions would not be able to fulfil their operational commitments'.[22] As early as 1970, the secretary of state for defence was worrying that 'the maintenance of the garrison of Northern Ireland at its present level involved heavy expenditure and imposed a serious strain on the Army'.[23] By 1976, there were concerns for Britain's position in NATO from British over-extension in Ireland. According to an internal memo, the British Army on the Rhine (BAOR) had not been able to take part in major NATO exercises between 1971 and 1976 because of its Irish commitments.[24]

An NIO official of the time told the academic Peter R. Neumann[25] that the British were 'taking the view that the job of the British army was to defend the North German plain from the Red Army, not chasing around the backstreets of Belfast'.[26] Loyalists in the backstreets of Belfast took a different view: in a 1980 letter to a colleague in the NIO, Richard Jackson, civil adviser to the GOC, wrote, 'Whilst there is undoubtedly a Loyalist willingness to contribute to security (anti-terrorism), by putting on a uniform and patrolling the border, I am not so sure there is much enthusiasm for contributing by training to deal with the odd Russian parachutist.'[27]

Hugo Arnold described the unfortunate result for everyone on the island of Ireland:

> As the regular army presence was scaled down (and with it the politically less acceptable level of English, Scottish and Welsh casualties), the number of UDR and RUC members killed rose sharply. Since Protestants made up over 95% of these forces, they increasingly became targets of the IRA and INLA [Irish National Liberation Army]. Northern Irish Protestants understandably felt that such attacks were aimed specifically against their community, and as a result the whole politico-security problem became more sectarian and politically intractable.[28]

But back to 1976, at which time Rees established a ministerial working party to progress Ulsterisation under the leadership of John Bourn (a senior civil servant seconded from the Home Office).[29] The Bourn Committee's proposals were outlined in an unpublished document entitled 'The Way Ahead'.

Under this new strategy, the UDR was given an expanded role: to be 'remoulded into a more effective force, with better training and greater responsibility … Instead of having the UDR as support for the regular army, the regiment was to be trained up to carry some of the army's workload – but not riot control.'[30]

It was now, however, formally tasked with intelligence gathering: 'each UDR unit formed an intelligence cell, both to receive and disseminate incoming intelligence and to process material for issue to patrols on the ground'.[31]

Declassified files suggest that as early as February 1976, the UDR were conducting covert intelligence operations using unmarked vehicles. An entry in a file containing the commander's diary for 3 UDR in County Down records, 'This week we have introduced a new variation in our night operations by using covert vans to deploy recce patrols, a variation that did not go unnoticed by critics of the Security Forces for long.'[32]

By the end of 1977, we see the UDR conducting intelligence operations in plain clothes: 'Brigade has authorised the Battalion to carry out plain clothes patrols in Bangor and Newtownards in an attempt to prevent incendiaries being placed in shops during busy afternoons. The soldiers and greenfinches are given photographs of the suspect bombers from Belfast, and mingle with the crowds along the pavements and in shops.'[33] By 1981, the files show, they were using unmarked vans to move around – as in this entry for 1 March:

> The Battalion has adopted a new 'Concept of Operations 81', drafted by the CO … From now on within

this area, with certain in-escapable exceptions the great majority of our patrols will deploy in covert vans. This creates problems, as there is only one van per Company, and if they are used to deploy patrols by day as well as by night, it is inevitable that they become known, and there is considerable increase [*sic*, possibly 'unease'] in the Battalion that one of our patrols will be shot up whilst tightly packed into the back of a van.[34]

One has to wonder at the effectiveness of the UDR's intelligence operations, particularly noting them as described above. The files show that such doubts existed in the minds of the British too. In a draft minute responding to a 1984 paper by Lord Lyell (parliamentary under secretary of state at the NIO) on the role of the UDR, an official writes frankly that:

> Local UDR commanders certainly believe that their units are a source of irreplaceable intelligence on republicans; so they would of course fear that any disappearance of the UDR from the ground would lead to a gap in knowledge. The view is emphatically not shared by those responsible for intelligence in the RUC or the army. It is not contested that the UDR know, or think they know, who all the local republicans are; but this is a large part of the problem of the UDR (and a further reason why HQNI like sending UDR elements on tasks in other parts of the Province). UDR knowledge is in short not intelligence, as understood today.[35]

A handwritten note by another official accompanying this minute says, 'I have not seen the local knowledge point put better.'[36] A further scathing review in the same file says 'the UDR has only a limited intelligence collection and collation system which does not enjoy the full confidence of RUC Special Branch. This is unlikely to change.'[37]

Ryder has written that:

> Doubts about the reliability of many members of the UDR were now widely held within the RUC ... Those on the inside knew that the vetting system, designed to keep undesirables out of the UDR, was largely a veneer ... The RUC knew, too, of the close links, especially in Belfast, between certain members of the regiment and loyalist terrorist groups ... UDR officers pleaded, almost fought, according to one, to be allowed access to intelligence material, but without success ... The reasons were all too apparent ...
>
> In this context, the politically pragmatic decision to involve the UDR in the sensitivities of intelligence work, both by giving them a role in obtaining it and providing them with access to existing material, was to have important consequences for its longer term reputation and, as later events showed, many of the misgivings expressed turned out to be very well-founded indeed.[38]

We have seen how unsubstantiated rumours, malicious gossip and sectarian bias within the UDR found its way into 'intelligence reports' and eventually led to the targeting and murder of the individuals named. Nevertheless, regular army units relied upon the local knowledge of UDR members, also often with lethal results. A notable example was the killing in 1972, by soldiers of the Argyll and Sutherland Highlanders, of Michael Naan and Andrew Murray, while the two men were at work on Naan's farm.[39] According to Edward Burke's analysis, in *An Army of Tribes*, Naan was killed because of his neighbours' false denunciation of him as 'a known IRA man', which revealed 'the occasional excessive reliance of regular British army units' on local part-time UDR soldiers.[40] It seems the British army was sometimes 'ready to accept UDR labelling of local men as "known IRA" without question'.[41]

In 1990, then Alderman Peter Robinson of the DUP, later to be first minister of Northern Ireland from 2008 until 2016, wrote a pamphlet called *Hands Off The UDR*. In this, he succinctly captured the UDR's use in intelligence gathering, unashamedly reflecting the brutal military traditions of recent British colonial military figures such as Templer and Kitson: 'One of the long list of eminent Ulster born soldiers, Field Marshal Sir Gerald Templar [*sic*] said "local insurgency forces can only be defeated by locally-recruited counter-insurgency forces". Now can you see the vital role of the locally recruited UDR? They know the terrorists and they know the terrain.'[42]

In rural areas especially, the UDR was seen as the local eyes and ears for British regiments that were on four-month emergency secondments in areas as hostile and unfamiliar as would be the valleys of Helmand or the streets of Basra for later generations of British soldiers.

Life in the UDR

UDR members undoubtedly suffered as a result of the conflict in Northern Ireland, and many UDR members and their families paid the highest price for living in the community. Nevertheless, this was an asset which the British army couldn't resist exploiting.

It is difficult to find consensus on the numbers of UDR casualties across the conflict. According to one author, an ex-soldier himself and an oral historian of British soldiers' experiences, '203 serving members of the UDR were killed during the Regiment's lifetime. 40 of these brave men and women were killed on duty.'[43] An academic study into the 'place-memories' of UDR survivors says that 206 members of the UDR lost their lives,[44] as does the 2001 edition of the authoritative *Lost Lives*. In 2010, Mervyn Storey, an elected representative of the DUP, said in the Northern Ireland Assembly that by the time of the UDR's dissolution, '197 members and 47 former members had been murdered'.[45] According to 'The Regimental Association of The Ulster Defence Regiment', 197 UDR members were killed, and 'a further 62 UDR veterans were killed after they had resigned/ retired from the Regiment'.[46]

Whatever the true figure may be, it is a terrible toll. Most were killed by the IRA, and many while off duty and in the presence of family members, including young children. A military psychologist who worked with UDR personnel from 1987 to 1994 has written that UDR soldiers were:

> constantly under threat, not only in operations, but also at home and while going about family business in the community where members lived and worked ... the great majority were killed off duty. Many served 10 years or more, including some who served throughout the full twenty-two years of the regiment's existence. Even after leaving the regiment they remained at risk ... Those who live in rural areas, such as farmers, and anybody working in a fixed routine – bus drivers, tanker drivers, postmen – were especially vulnerable. It is hardly surprising that combat stress has some 400 ex members of the UDR on its books.[47]

One former UDR soldier wrote that the main difference between the mainstream British soldier and those in the UDR was 'the permanence of the latter's predicament':

> Both the emergency (4–6 months) or resident battalion tour (18 months) ended eventually; that of the UDR didn't ... The UDR men and women lived, ate and drank in the communities they had to patrol; they had to shop and relax amongst the very people they might have arrested or questioned or were actively seeking ... knowing that their every move was being observed by the enemy within.[48]

Another recalled:

> I was warned by my superiors that my life would be in danger and to take care of my personal security ... I saw a helicopter hovering over ... my friend's house who was also a member of the UDR. A police car came along and they told me that my friend had been shot and that he was gone to Enniskillen in the ambulance ...
>
> It was an awful experience and something I will remember 'til the day I die. After that experience, I had no other choice but to leave my land and way of life ... At the time, I couldn't find a job and I had to go and sign-on full time with the Ulster Defence Regiment. And I can tell you, I wasn't a soldier – I was a farmer and I missed my land very much.[49]

Elsewhere, Margaret Urwin has written about the dreadful case of the Graham family:

Their father had served in the B-Specials for many years. When the UDR was formed in 1970, he joined, along with three of his sons. Hilary, one of his daughters, joined in March 1974. Hilary sustained severe injuries when a car crashed through a UDR checkpoint. She never recovered and died some weeks later. The IRA killed Ronnie, aged 39, in June 1981 as he delivered coal to a house near Lisnaskea. Cecil, aged 32, was killed five months later, while he was visiting his Catholic wife and 5-week-old baby. They were staying with her parents in the nationalist village of Donagh ... They attempted to kill Jimmy, aged 39, on two or three occasions before they finally succeeded, in February 1985, when they shot him as he sat in his school bus in Derrylin.[50]

Urwin then recounts the memories of journalist, author and former priest Michael Harding, who was the curate in Derrylin at the time of the attack on Jimmy Graham. Harding recalls:

One morning in February, I was having porridge in the kitchen when I heard gunshots outside. I went to the front door and saw a van drive away from the school bus on the other side of the street. Masked men with guns were in the back of the van, and they shot and cheered and yahoo-ed as they drove away from the bus. The bus driver was lying dead on the floor of the bus in a pool of his own blood. By mid-afternoon journalists had arrived. When they asked me questions, I told them what I had seen. I described the men roaring in the back of the van. That night on the news it was the main headline ... the story was personal. It revealed something about the killers. They weren't disciplined. They were full of vengeful, sweaty lust and, as they went away, were as delighted as football fans when a goal had been scored.[51]

The Grahams were described by a Church of Ireland clergyman as 'traditional border Protestants, typical of the rank-and-file members of the UDR'. The Grahams, and people like them, were 'strongly loyalist; lived in isolated rural areas, worked as labourers, factory workers and drivers, playing in local football and tug-o'-war teams, occasionally still went out with Catholic girls, and died because they lived – not as soldiers under siege – but as not particularly bright, and sometimes indiscreet, young men in a bitterly divided community'.[52]

As is so often the case in conflict-torn societies, women carried a heavy burden. On 6 July 1973, the under-secretary of state for defence for the army, Peter Blaker, announced the recruitment of women to the UDR. Blaker said, 'In these enlightened days it may seem odd that a Bill is needed to remove this measure of apparent discrimination, but in the very different circumstances of 1969 the Ulster Defence Regiment Act, which set up the regiment following the Hunt Inquiry, specially excluded women.'[53]

But this was no emancipatory act – Blaker admitted as much himself, saying that 'it is now clear that the exclusion of women from the regiment is a disadvantage'. That disadvantage was:

> the immediate need ... for women searchers to help the Ulster Defence Regiment battalions when conducting checks on people who might be carrying explosives or other arms. Since only women should search women,

and we do not have enough members of the Women's Royal Army Corps or the RUC, there is a gap in our security arrangements. The object of the Bill is to enable us to close the gap.[54]

As Ryder puts it, there was a 'pressing operational requirement for women members of the security forces to counter the increasing involvement of women'[55] in the ranks of the IRA. Recruitment of women into the UDR opened officially on 16 August 1973. Potter reports that the first enlistments were carried out by 2 UDR at Gough Barracks on 16 September, when the Women's UDR (WUDR) – soon to become known informally as 'Greenfinches' – was formed.[56] Within a year, 500 of the 700 vacancies in the WUDR were filled.[57] According to Potter:

> Many of the early recruits came from those executive and professional classes whose males were signally reluctant to enlist – Senior Civil Servants, a former barrister, school teachers, the headmistress of a primary school, laboratory technicians, an assistant air traffic controller ... Women with infants were required to furnish a certificate stating that they had someone to look after their offspring while they were on duty.[58]

So much for Under-Secretary Blaker's enlightened days.

In language strikingly at odds with the fact that he was writing in the twenty-first century, Potter described the skill set of UDR women:

> They made good searchers ... With their higher-pitched voices they made excellent signallers and, in time, as the UDR assumed greater responsibility, many

of the operations rooms were manned by Greenfinches. By nature they were better than the men at First Aid. Before long some of the 10UDR girls were dealing with the aftermath of a shooting incident, a passenger on a bus hit by rifle fire, and in doing so finally won over their CSM [Company Sergeant Major], an old soldier who had deplored the incursion of women into a male preserve and had wanted nothing to do with them.[59]

UDR women were integrated into their battalions from 1973 onward – this was not practice anywhere else in the British army until 1992 – however, they were not allowed to be armed. Potter says this was because 'most had no wish to carry a weapon. As they saw it, their role was to take on as many other tasks as possible and leave the men to get on with the fighting.'[60] One doubts that women in the UDR were as meek as Potter suggests. Elsewhere he reports that seventy-eight UDR women had taken action against the MoD for work practices which, the European Court in 1990 ruled, contravened accepted European standards.[61]

In May 1974, seven months after they had started undertaking operational duties, the first UDR woman was killed. Private Eva Martin was hit by fragments of a rocket fired by the IRA in an attack on the British army base at Clogher, County Tyrone. Private Martin had been one of the first women to join the UDR.[62] Three other UDR women were later killed during the conflict, two of them on patrol.

On 6 April 1976, Lance Corporal Gillian Leggett was shot and killed in an ambush. A colleague, another UDR woman, was wounded. The wounded soldier was awarded a medal, according to a regular British soldier seconded to the UDR, 'for good work in looking after Gillian before she died at the scene, and for maintaining good communications during the incident ... Some of the UDR girls were much more versatile and quite often more use than some of the men, this was a well-known spoken fact amongst the regulars attached to the UDR.'[63]

One of the most notorious murders of a UDR woman – one which shook people across all communities here – took place in October 1977, in Middletown, County Armagh. Margaret Hearst, a UDR part-timer and a single mother of a three-year-old-girl, was shot multiple times at her home by an IRA unit. One of the rounds fired narrowly missed her sleeping child. Margaret's father, Ross Hearst, was also killed by the IRA in 1980.

In Ken Wharton's *A Long Long War* – one of Wharton's oral histories of the conflict, and a valuable resource for voices of the security forces – an ex-UDR soldier identified as 'Cpl Brownlow, E Coy 5 UDR' says, 'UDR personnel were phenomenally brave ... Throughout the 22 years of the UDR's existence only three percent of those eligible to join ever made the effort. It would be wrong to condemn outright the 97 per cent eligible people for their failure to join the UDR.'[64]

Perhaps it would be wrong to condemn those who didn't join up 'outright', but Brownlow clearly resented this long afterwards. In this, he was echoing remarks made by Brigadier Ormerod in October 1972, when he complained that only 2.7 per cent of eligible men had the 'determination and guts' to join the UDR. He repeated these sentiments in April 1973, shortly before his departure from command of the UDR, when he said, 'Far too many people in Northern Ireland are leaving the dirty work to far too few people ... It is time other people took a turn.'[65] Perhaps this explains Ormerod's willingness to recruit men who would otherwise join 'a paramilitary organisation such as the UDA as an alternative to the UDR'.[66]

Similarly, Urwin reports comments by Viscount Brooke-borough – a UDR officer – who 'criticised the business classes for their failure to support the security forces actively. He noted that the UDR was drawn largely from farming and working-class communities, "by and large the business classes, while they supported peace, didn't support the fight against terrorism".'[67]

Urwin also reports the views of Brigadier John Oborne, defence attaché in the British embassy in Dublin, after a visit to Northern Ireland in September 1984. He 'noted a view expressed to him that the unionist middle-class were ducking out of their responsibilities, believing that, whatever happened, their own lifestyle would survive or, alternatively, that they would be able to leave Ireland. He was told that "the backbone of the UDR was the farmers, mechanics and, indeed, the unemployed".'[68]

One organisation dedicated to helping former UDR personnel estimated, in 2005, that 'there were 58,000 Ulster Defence Regiment ex-service personnel, along with what must be another 250,000 family members', amounting to, they say, 'approximately 300,000 people abandoned'.[69]

In 2006, at a talk hosted by the Meath Peace Group entitled 'The Legacy of War – Experiences of UDR Families', findings were presented of research into the effects the conflict had had on UDR personnel and their families.

Martin Snoddon (Director of the Conflict Trauma Resource Centre in Belfast) said:

> There was little heard of any research that had been done with former members of the Ulster Defence Regiment, with respect to their needs as a legacy of the conflict … we were very conscious that they were suffering in silence. Because the reality was everybody else was

ignoring those needs: from the British Government who employed, encouraged and sanctioned the operations of the Ulster Defence Regiment – not one of the people that I engaged with in that research had a kind word to say or even in fact had anything to say with regards to support received from the government after service.[70]

In 2006, eight years after the signing of the Good Friday Agreement – and fifteen years after the dissolution of the UDR – these legacy issues included 'security, employment, welfare, financial and psychological support, family impact, social interaction, memories, and of course acknowledgement and recognition for sacrifice and service'.[71]

Mr Snoddon told the meeting that 'there is evidence that young people from those families have a huge seething resentment with regard to the British forces and how they have been treated'. One female UDR veteran present, named Rosemary, told the meeting, 'I do feel a bit grieved the way we have been treated by the British Government and the Northern Ireland Office, but I don't feel bitter because I took a great sense of pride in the time that I served and that pride overshadows any bitterness I feel.'

One cannot help but feel some sympathy for their predicament, but the British government's neglect of this particular legacy issue – one which we mightn't often think about – is that, as Snoddon warned:

There is a danger there, where that can actually lead young people. I spoke to young people along the border corridor whose parents were members of the security forces and they swore that if things erupted again, that they would never join the state forces. They would join the paramilitary groups, because that is where they felt that they would get support after ... within that unionist community, they had normally been very much married to law and order, but if the same type of problem was to arise today, the dangers are that they would gravitate towards forces other than the state forces.[72]

In January 2021, a Belfast newspaper carried an interview with family members of a part-time UDR officer, Ivan Toombs, who was killed by the IRA at his place of work on 16 January 1981. Mr Toombs had survived a previous attempt on his life in 1976. The interview showed clearly the transgenerational impact of Mr Toombs's death upon the family forty years later, his son Paul saying, 'You think you live in times of peace but sometimes people forget the lasting effect it has on the second generation and even, to an extent, the third generation.'

Paul Toombs also said that while many would 'try to demonise the UDR', his father 'felt that for normal, good society for everybody, somebody had to stand in the void and keep the peace, and for the vast majority of people that I speak to within the security forces, that was also their main drive'.[73]

Both Potter's *A Testimony to Courage* and Ryder's *The Ulster Defence Regiment: An Instrument of Peace?* are recommended reading for a full account of the heavy price paid by UDR troops, and their families, in the conflict. It is not our contention that all who served in the UDR did so with malice or hatred for the Catholic or nationalist community. It is possible to acknowledge the human beings who lived and died wearing the uniform of the British army in Ireland while at the same time holding the regiment to account for its failings and its crimes.

Ken Maginnis has said of his time in the UDR that he never came across a 'bad apple, only bruised apples. There are those whose level of tolerance is breached and make a mistake and we deplore it.'[74] But the problem with the UDR is that their subversive actions were not the misdeeds of a few bad apples, or (as some suggested) the odd 'bad hat'. A victims' advocacy group that works with and for ex-members of the security forces in Northern Ireland has, as recently as January 2021, euphemistically described a full-time member of the UDR who murdered an elderly man, Samuel Millar, in 1976 on behalf of the UDA as merely one of the UDR who 'saluted a different code'.[75]

It should be borne in mind that the dichotomy of perspectives regarding the UDR – the difference between minimising the harm they did and those who would (in the words of Paul Toombs) 'try to demonise the UDR' – to this day poisons the debate and understanding around legacy and dealing with the past in this part of the world.

CHAPTER NINE

Criminality in the UDR

Between 1985 and 1989, UDR members were twice as likely to commit a crime as the general public. The UDR crime rate was ten times that of the RUC and about four times the British army rate. By the early 1990s, around 120 members/ex-members of the regiment were serving prison sentences for serious crimes, and seventeen had been convicted of murder.[1]

These are shocking figures. Yet there has been public anxiety about the extent, and tolerance, of criminality within the ranks of the UDR almost since its inception. As mentioned previously, by October 1972 such was the 'disturbing rise in the number of cases involving UDR men in the courts' that *Fortnight* magazine warned that the UDR could shortly become 'discredited'.[2] In 1976, *Hibernia* magazine catalogued the regiment's 'Roll-Call of Disgrace', a list of more than 100 UDR men charged with crimes since the regiment's formation. The list prompted calls from the SDLP for disbandment of the regiment.[3]

Staff at the PFC have amassed a large volume of evidence, from press reports of court appearances alone, which shows that these concerns were valid. As Ryder states, 'The true extent of subversion and criminal indiscipline with the UDR is a carefully protected official secret ... Ever since the formation of the UDR and the emergence of the first concerns about Loyalist infiltration, the army, the Ministry of Defence and the government itself have gone to considerable lengths to shield the Regiment from embarrassment.'[4]

Perhaps nothing illustrates this better than the material that the PFC uncovered revealing a series of highly secret meetings, beginning in February 1978, held in Belfast – between HQNI, Intelligence and Security Company at 39 Brigade (which covered Belfast), the director of security in London and, eventually, the secretary of state.[5]

These meetings concerned an internal investigation for fraud, corruption and subversion into 10 UDR – the Belfast city battalion of the regiment, based at Girdwood Park in Belfast. In fact, two separate investigations were launched – one by the Special Investigations Branch of the Royal Military Police (RMP/SIB) after a routine audit of 10 UDR's accounts uncovered evidence of major fraud; the other by 120 Security Section (military intelligence) after a UDR weapon went missing.

The minutes of a meeting held on 1 February 1978 to discuss crime and security in 10 UDR provide a synopsis of the SIB and Security Section reports into the incidents. It was discovered that up to seventy members of the battalion had links to loyalist paramilitary groups at some level, while it was also suspected that up to thirty members of the battalion had engaged in large-scale fraud, claiming an estimated £30,000–£47,000 for duties not carried out. This money was strongly suspected of being passed to the local UVF.[6]

The minutes show that SIB reported, 'In respect of the theft of stores and equipment, irregularities of stores accounting and the control of keys have revealed the ease with which these items have passed to paramilitary organisations.' There had been significant thefts from the battalion's stores, and 'the general impression gained' was that two specific companies of 10 UDR ('D and G Coys') were 'the supply and financial support elements for local paramilitary organisations'.

A 'minor' investigation by 120 Security Section 'revealed that certain SNCOs [senior non-commissioned officers] had been involved or were involved in para-military activities'. It found that seventy members had paramilitary traces, and 'This figure has since grown'. It also showed the brazenly open relationships between UDR members and loyalist gangs, finding that 'known members of para-military [sic] organisations' – who had no legitimate connection to the UDR – were allowed to socialise in the UDR messes and clubs inside the army base.[7]

The assessment by 10 UDR themselves was that the 'full situation was not known due to the inability to get a steady supply of good information'. This was perhaps because, according to UDR chiefs, there was some kind of noble motive – in other words, 'There was a clear tendency for the loyal members of the bn [battalion] to "cover-up" in an attempt to preserve the name of the UDR.'[8]

With good reason, the minutes add that both investigating agencies agreed 'There was cause for alarm that the practices so far revealed at Girdwood Park would be repeated in some degree at other locations.'[9]

A note dated 24 February 1978 shows army command getting nervous as UDR personnel became aware they were being closely examined: 'The knowledge that the investigations are being conducted is now down to platoon level ... it is apparent that it has provoked a reaction ... it is natural that any person or grouping who feels threatened will seek to relieve the pressure by any means available.'[10]

On the same date this note was written, a high-level meeting took place at which, according to the minutes, the CO of 10 UDR warned that soldiers under his direct command could 'leak' to the press, 'if the investigations were continued at the same intensity as the previous few weeks'.[11]

It was agreed at this meeting that while the SIB investigation (the financial fraud aspect) may continue, 'the intensity of the security investigation should be reduced by decreasing the rate at which individuals were being interviewed and by concentrating only on those individuals on whom suspicion of paramilitary involvement was most strong'.[12]

The question of 'test-firing' 10 UDR's weapons was raised (by the Northern Ireland Office) in order to forestall media queries. However, the idea that the companies most under suspicion should be singled out for testing was 'invidious'. It was agreed that 'HQ UDR and SIB should consult to find a more equitable method of organising test firing should the need arise'.[13]

Abruptly, on 27 February, a decision was taken regarding the Security Section investigation – the investigation into the fact that 10 UDR formed part of a supply chain to the UVF – which was to suspend it 'temporarily'. Why? Because 'the investigations may affect morale in the battalion'.[14] The reader may make their own mind up, but it seems apparent that the British government was more afraid of 'UDR members leaking the investigations to the media' – in which case, all of a sudden, the investigations would have 'political importance'. Of course, 'the criminal investigation, which is politically less contentious, was to proceed at its former pace'.[15]

The situation could not be written more starkly. At least fifteen members of 10 UDR based at Girdwood Barracks in north Belfast, who had been in the battalion over a period of years, were also members of the UVF. UDR by day, UVF by night.

In this period, the Belfast UVF included a particular gang of sadistic, sectarian killers, the Shankill Butchers, who went down in infamy, even in the context of the terrible thirty-year conflict. They kidnapped, tortured and murdered Catholic civilians, usually using butcher's knives and axes in the so-called 'romper rooms' attached to some Loyalist drinking clubs.[16] Eight members of this UVF gang received a total of forty-two life sentences for their litany of crimes, including at least twenty-four murders, which they committed between October 1975 and May 1977. It is significant that most of these gruesome murders took place within one square mile of Girdwood Barracks, the base of 10 UDR.[17] One of the gang, Edward McIlwaine, was a UDR soldier.

While there were fears that the, apparently more serious, 120 Security Section investigation into subversion in 10 UDR 'may affect morale in the battalion', ways were being found to protect the sensibilities of the battalion's troops. When it was proposed that firearms tests be carried out on the personal protection weapons of 10 UDR members (as requested repeatedly by members of the SDLP), so concerned were the powers that be to avoid the 'invidious' scenario of the battalion feeling itself to be under suspicion that an excuse was sought to carry out the ballistic assessment without annoying its members.

The minutes of a follow-up meeting on 7 March 1978 note, 'A suitable reason, ie the selection of weapons for the Bisley Shoot, was available to explain the test firing.'[18] Bisley, in Surrey, is home to the British National Rifle Association; it is also the location for the Operational Shooting Competition, in which members of the British armed forces compete for the Queen's Medal for Shooting Excellence.

It's interesting to consider here that only a couple of years previously (1975), a senior British official was moved to note about the testing of UDR personal protection weapons that 'surely the main point about such testing would be the protection of the UDR from damaging slurs cast against them by opponents?' A fair point, one might think. After all, 'in at least one case a UDR unit asked to have their weapons tested to refute allegations made by an SDLP politician'.[19]

Also of interest is that the official suggests that personal protection weapons could 'be used secretly and illegitimately' – a euphemism surely for 'illegally' (of which, more later). What the military leadership feared was that some 'UDR disaster' would occur and the British would find themselves 'under heavy and embarrassing pressure as a result to do something about testing weapons'.[20]

That disaster arrived in 1978. By 2 March 1978, we learn, 'investigations currently being conducted within 10 UDR are revealing evidence of serious penetration of the battalion by paramilitary organisations',[21] and that it was 'likely that the Battalion [10 UDR] has been infiltrated by the UVF'.[22] The importance the British attached to these investigations was such that reports were circulated to ministerial level and officials were being asked to 'regrade' relevant material as 'SECRET UK EYES'.[23]

Of course, as the British feared, the press got hold of the story – but crucially, only of the lesser investigation, the one into fraud. The declassified file entitled 'UDR Irregularities' contains a copy of a report by *The Guardian's* Anne McHardy, published on 13 March 1978, which says that detectives were investigating allegations of 'fraudulent pay claims' within the UDR.[24] In mid-March this investigation was subject to a 'temporary halt ... to allow the situation to stabilise'[25] (amid some discomfort and fears of agitation within 10 UDR's ranks);

however, in a confidential document dated 14 November 1978, the conclusions of the two investigations into 10 UDR are outlined. Captain W. Guthrie, writing on behalf of the GOC, states that the Security Section investigation recommended that seven men should be discharged from the UDR. It was agreed that three men should be discharged for 'administrative or disciplinary reasons, or by non-renewal of service'. One man was 'allowed to continue serving after representations by the CO to Commander UDR and Commander Land Forces'. One was discharged 'for reasons not connected with security'. Security grounds were used to dismiss only two.[26]

A further fourteen men were made the subject of 'Local Reporting Procedure', whereby, for one year, the individual was the subject of quarterly reports from his commanding officer. Regarding the fraud case, in which it was believed that money may have been passed to the UVF, Guthrie reports that the allegation was 'never substantiated' and that the completed case had been handed to the Director of Public Prosecutions.[27]

So we have a significant and deadly breach in the security and integrity of 10 UDR in which:

- The army feared that seventy soldiers in 10 UDR were linked to the UVF in Belfast, including one member of the psychopathic Shankill Butchers killers;
- UDR personnel were suspected of defrauding the UDR to the tune of £47,000 and redirecting that money to the illegal loyalist UVF, while UDR equipment was regularly stolen, and for use by that same group;
- UVF members regularly and openly fraternised with UDR personnel at the UDR's Girdwood Barracks social club;

- The army were forced to consider secret methods of test firing UDR soldiers' weapons – to check whether they had been used in sectarian murders – and the collusion investigation was then suspended after a senior UDR officer claimed it was damaging morale within the regiment.

By 1978, in other words, subversion was still widespread. Given that at least seventy members of the Belfast battalion had subversive links, the estimate provided by Defence Secretariat 10 in 1975 (a 'small number, around 200 spread between the 11 Battalions of the Regiment are thought to have connections however slight with extremist organisations')[28] was clearly an underestimation.

Despite concerns of 'serious penetration' of the battalion by the UVF this information was withheld from the public and parliament after a deliberate decision by army commanders to cover up evidence. As will be shown, however, this did not mark the end of 10 UDR members' involvement in collusion. The battalion would be implicated in some of the worst and most blatant incidents of collusion in the Troubles.

Even at that, given the level of loyalist infiltration of 10 UDR, it is chilling to note that a special arrangement had existed whereby UDR battalions could volunteer for extra duties in different areas of Northern Ireland: the Province Reserve UDR Force, or PRUDR system, allowed a UDR battalion to detach a company for a tour of duty outside of their own area each weekend.

This must give rise to questions – and particularly in the context of the Shankill Butchers – as to who volunteered to serve where, and why and when they served. Is it a coincidence that this PRUDR scheme was formally ended in 1978, just one month before it was learned that investigations were being conducted within 10 UDR, and these inquiries were finding 'evidence of serious penetration of the battalion by paramilitary organisations'?

After the scheme was ended, UDR battalions were free to arrange 'similar cross-exchanges amongst themselves' – with the exception of 10 UDR, which could nevertheless arrange 'occasional deployments' to the rural stomping grounds of 3 UDR (in south Down) and 8 UDR (east Tyrone), 'to which they [10 UDR] attach importance'.[29]

Covering up the UDR members' criminality was done, as Chris Ryder expressed it, 'with a regularity that implies that it is standard practice'.[30] When UDR personnel faced charges in court, the fact of their UDR connections was routinely suppressed. UDR personnel charged with crimes tended to be hurriedly and quietly pushed out of the regiment so that, 'if the UDR connection comes to light, the offender can be distanced as a "former" member'.[31]

Take, for example, the case of UDR soldier Edward McIlwaine. He was arrested as a member of the Shankill Butchers, for that gang's activities on 13 June 1977, and was charged within a week with kidnapping and wounding offences. He was discharged from the UDR on 1 August 1977 (before the case was heard in court) for 'poor attendance'. Following extensive research into the Shankill Butchers, Martin Dillon says that McIlwaine's 'dismissal came about as a result of a communication from the police that he would shortly be questioned about serious crimes'.[32] While the UDR insisted that McIlwaine's discharge was already in progress before his arrest, in fact McIlwaine was on a police suspect list for some time before his arrest and, as Ryder says, 'it is inconceivable that the UDR was not aware of his wanted status'.[33]

As was common practice, McIlwaine's UDR membership was not disclosed in court and was only publicly admitted by the UDR after the SDLP's law and order spokesman Michael Canavan publicly questioned Secretary of State Roy Mason on it. A secret memo in recently discovered files betrays the anxiety this revelation provoked among the authorities. Here, an official suggests that the secretary of state 'will wish to have some amplification' to the revelation of one of the Shankill Butchers having been in the UDR.

A second official is requested to 'put up a note' (prepare an explanatory note) in time for the secretary of state's arrival that afternoon – 'after probing as necessary with HQNI' – especially about whether there was any failure on the UDR's part 'to take action' or to 'suspend immediately after he [McIlwaine] had been charged, as alleged by M [Michael] Canavan'.[34]

A subsequent note on the file reports the view of 'Deputy Commander UDR' that 'even had circumstances come to light, he [McIlwaine] would not necessarily have been discharged automatically. The gravity of the charges *may have resulted in a suspension from duty* [emphasis added], but since he was still at that stage innocent under law there would have been no justification for any further action until the trial result was known.' The note's author, an NIO official named Pope, records that the SDLP's Michael Canavan had asked if the trial judge was made aware of the fact that McIlwaine was a member of the UDR, as it 'would have been both relevant and pertinent'. Pope records the deputy commander's view that the judge was not made aware, since 'It is difficult to see how the individuals [*sic*] membership of the UDR could be construed as having any direct relevance to the facts or conduct of the case.'[35]

Just as bizarrely, although Roderick Shane McDowell and Thomas Crozier (convicted in October 1976 of the Miami Showband massacre) were members of the UDR –

and in UDR uniforms at the time of the murders – this was not mentioned at their initial court appearance.

In March 1984, *Phoenix* magazine published a list of almost one hundred cases where members of the UDR had been charged with serious offences, mostly involving firearms or explosives. The authors made the claim that 'It is a directory of Dishonourable Discharge that is unmatched in the "security forces" of any country in Europe and probably not even in South America. And even this list does not claim to be exhaustive.'[36]

The authors also noted the 'standard practice for any UDR member charged with a serious offence to be required to resign from the Regiment before appearing in court', and that they may therefore be described in court 'as a "former" UDR member. Or the fact of UDR membership is not mentioned at all.'[37]

Ciaran MacAirt of *Paper Trail* has done great work in uncovering significant instances of this. In one instance from 1975, we note that the secretary of state and senior army officers were kept apprised of a court case against a UDR man on charges of conspiracy to manufacture explosives and possession of explosives. A member of DS10 assured all that the man's 'membership of the UDR did not come out in court and the case so far has not attracted any publicity.'[38]

In another instance, PFC/JFF uncovered the case of a serving part-time UDR man who was arrested for his role in the armed robbery of a building society in County Antrim. According to this report to the secretary of state from G.W. Davies of the NIO's 'Law and Order Division', 'The robbers demanded cash and forced an assistant to write a cheque which they took to a nearby bank to cash.' Somewhat inevitably, this buffoonish robbery ended with the arrest of the UDR soldier and his accomplice. The soldier 'later admitted taking part in seven separate armed robberies'. Davies, of the ironically named Law and Order Division, then reports that the soldier had resigned before being charged and that 'the Police will not be referring to his membership of the security forces'.[39]

The above letter strongly implies that the NIO, the RUC and the prosecution service were all party to perverting the course of justice. There was a consistent policy of withholding the UDR identity of criminals. It was not just a kind of ad hoc, case-by-case decision, taken at a junior level, which one might expect to result from the odd 'bad apple' in the ranks.

Compounding this, a 'Note for the Record' dated 11 May 1988 – after a parliamentary question was tabled by Kevin McNamara MP – revealed that the prevailing policy in respect to convicted security force members included that records were 'not kept in respect of persons who resigned the service before their case came to trial'.[40]

In 2016 PFC/JFF uncovered the UDR identity of a sectarian killer, William McClelland; he was personally responsible for at least two murders, and his membership of the UDR had been intentionally obscured during his prosecution and conviction.

In June 1980 the UDA killed John Turnly, a former British army officer who came from a landowning unionist background. By the time of his death, however, he was an avowed republican, a member of the Irish Independence Party and an elected councillor. He was killed on 4 June while being dropped off by his wife to a meeting in Carnlough, County Antrim. Three men were arrested in the aftermath of this murder, one of them McClelland, yet the available police statements in the court papers make no reference to alibis being checked or swabs taken to check for firearms residue, nor is there any mention of fingerprints being taken. As it turned out, these were the killers, and because they were not identified as such, they killed again. On 24 August they were lying in wait for Rodney McCormick, a former prisoner, as he returned home with his wife; he was shot dead as he was about to enter his home.[41]

In September 1980, twenty-nine men were arrested and charged with various crimes, including murder, attempted murder, robbery, possession of firearms and causing explosions. The twenty-nine included two serving members of the UDR, as well as McClelland. It was while reading the notes from the RUC's McClelland interview that PFC/JFF staff noticed an unusual statement. McClelland said he 'would be pleading guilty at the court'. But then McClelland remarked 'that the shoe was now on the other foot' as he had done duty previously in the Crumlin Road Court and now he was the prisoner.[42]

This discovery prompted PFC/JFF staff to investigate McClelland's background further. The PSNI had previously told PFC/JFF that it held no information to indicate that McClelland was a member of the armed forces, UDR or the Prison Service. After PFC/JFF dug deeper, it emerged that McClelland had been a prison officer while Rodney McCormick served a sentence for armed robbery in the 1970s. Under questioning, McClelland later claimed McCormick was killed because 'he had done time and become a Provie [an IRA member]'. The McCormick family denies that Rodney had any involvement with republican groups.

A HET report into the murder showed that a gun used to kill Rodney McCormick was also linked to the attempted murder of a Catholic prison officer in May 1980; the officer was shot six times in the back but survived. That same weapon was also connected to the murder of another Catholic man in Newtownabbey in September 1979. In January 2016, the

MoD admitted that William McClelland had been a member of the UDR; however, as was the practice, this was never mentioned in court.

Did McClelland's past as both a prison officer and a UDR member protect him from proper police investigation? Years after his father's murder, Rory McCormick expressed his certainty that if the murder of John Turnly had been properly investigated with any integrity, his father would not have been subsequently killed.[43]

The discovery of evidence revealing how UDR criminality has been obscured is ongoing. As recently as January 2021, PFC/JFF found new evidence relevant to the investigation of the Glenanne series of killings. (The UVF's Glenanne Gang is believed to have killed over one hundred Catholics and nationalists in the 1970s; it was responsible for some of the worst atrocities of the Troubles, including the 1974 Dublin and Monaghan bombings, which resulted in the deaths of thirty-four people, including a pregnant woman and her unborn, full-term baby.[44])

On 23 October 1973, the UVF raided Fort Seagoe, the armoury of E Company, 11 UDR Portadown (inevitably a declassified army document suggests that the raiders had assistance from members of 11 UDR). According to Anne Cadwallader's *Lethal Allies*, 'Searches were carried out for the missing weapons and, among others, the home of Winston Buchanan outside Portadown was searched. Nothing from the Fort Seagoe raid was found, but police did find 140 pounds (64 kg) of explosives, two grenades, bomb-making equipment, two radios and 5,000 rounds of assorted ammunition.'

Buchanan told police he had been forced to store the weaponry by Robin Jackson (a notorious murderer, a key figure in the Glenanne Gang's activities and a UDR man). As

Anne Cadwallader puts it, 'This did him [Buchanan] no harm when it came to sentencing. For this massive haul, Buchanan received just one year in jail.'

Recently discovered archive files show that Buchanan was a member of the UDR, a fact that has never before been uncovered. The records of 3rd Infantry Brigade show both the arms find on his property[45] and reports, seven months prior to this, of suspicious incidents at Buchanan's filling station: 'Armed robbery at Winstons Buchanans [sic] filling sta. ... Owner Prot and a member of 11 UDR ...'[46]

And most damningly:

> At 2330 hrs on 16 Apr the Buchanan Filling Station ... Gilford was held up and robbed by three armed men with an SMG and two revolvers. During the attack the owner's pistol, an German Arminus [sic], 22 revolver ... was taken by the raiders. A small bomb was left on the premises and exploded causing extensive damage.
>
> Comment: This is the second time that a bomb has been left at this Filling Station. Previously the SOCO [Scene of Crime Officer] rendered the bomb harmless. Buchanan, a Pte in the UDR, alleges that he has been threatened by letter on several occasions stating that he would be shot and his premises bombed. Buchanan is known to be in financial trouble and it is strongly suspected that this may have been his own work with probable UDA help. Buchanan's possible involvement in subversive activity cannot be overlooked.[47]

Buchanan's name – and membership of the UDR – may now be added to the list of security force members linked to the Glenanne Gang.

The Fermanagh UVF unit, which engaged in serious cross-border attacks in the early 1970s, consisted of about ten men. These included Robert Bridge, George Farrell, George Ramsey, Billy Spence, all from Enniskillen; Drew Thompson and John Smith, from Kilskeery; and David Johnston, from Tullyhommon (the part of Pettigo that is in Co. Fermanagh). Between them they were responsible for bomb attacks in Clones (16 October 1972); Clones [again], Belturbet and Pettigo (28 December 1972); Carrickode Parish Hall (22 June 1974); Blacklion, County Cavan (11 September 1974); and multiple bomb attacks on the town of Swanlinbar (between May 1974 and May 1976).[48]

One of the gang, George Farrell, was arrested on 16 May 1976 as he crossed the border at Cloughore Bridge near Ballyshannon, County Donegal. He was charged in the Special Criminal Court two days later – with causing an explosion and with having firearms and ammunition with intent to endanger life at Pettigo on 28 September 1973, and with causing an explosion and being in possession of a Sterling revolver at Carrickode on 22 June 1974.

In a memo dated 18 May 1976, T.C. Barker of the NIO wrote to the permanent under-secretary of state for Northern Ireland; he refers to Farrell's arrest, of which he had been apprised by British army HQ in Northern Ireland. He stated that Farrell was likely to be charged with firearms offences. He noted that HQNI also had a report suggesting that Farrell might have confessed to bombings in Belturbet and Pettigo.[49]

Barker was concerned that it would be revealed in court that Farrell had been a member of the UDR from November 1970 until 29 April 1976. In fact, it appears that Farrell was discharged from the UDR only after his arrest on 16 May – an *Irish Times* article from 1976 reports that he told a garda inspector in May 1976, 'he had been a member of the UDR since 1970'.[50] Once again, we see the practice of obscuring the truth of UDR membership when criminality was exposed. In a second memo dated 25 May 1976, Barker states that Farrell 'may have implicated two other known members of the UDR, and possibly a third, in unlawful activity in the Republic'.[51] Farrell was convicted on 4 November 1976 and sentenced to fifteen years' imprisonment. On appeal, however, his conviction was overturned on a technicality.

Papers recently discovered among the declassified files reveal the anxiety that the UDR's criminality was causing among British officials and commanders. Here, we see officials discussing, in 1979, public relations efforts – a damage limitation exercise – required after the sentencing of the Shankill Butchers and the revelation that McIlwaine was a serving UDR soldier: 'The Press release aimed to show that the criminals were a mere drop in the bucket of around 20,000 men overall ... I doubt whether the line makes sense even on a straight statistical basis, and I have told MOD that it is anyway not a helpful line to peddle at present.'[52]

Pressure was mounting on the British over the flagrant criminality of significant numbers of UDR personnel. In December 1983 the SDLP's Paschal O'Hare wrote to British Prime Minister Margaret Thatcher expressing alarm 'at the increasing numbers of members of the UDR appearing in the Courts on some of the most serious charges'. O'Hare, drawing on his personal experience as a solicitor in the criminal courts, referenced 'the long litany or catalogue of charges which have brought over the years against members [of the UDR] who, all of a sudden, become "ex-members" once they appear in the Dock'. O'Hare's conclusion was, 'It is quite clear that this regiment has been infiltrated by paramilitary organisations and is doing nothing to bring about the peace which we all so ardently desire.'[53]

An *Irish News* article in 1985 – '"Axe the UDR" Angry

Mallon Replies to Hurd' – carried remarks by Seamus Mallon castigating the secretary of state for defence, Douglas Hurd, for the behaviour of the UDR and Hurd's recent call for Catholics to support and join the regiment. Mallon said that, since its formation, 'the UDR has acted as a paramilitary wing of unionism', motivated by sectarianism. Their involvement in 'sectarian murder' – including the murders of Seán Farmer and Colm McCartney at a fake army road check in 1975 – and 'common criminality' had been referred to as 'occasional mistakes' by Hurd.

This gave rise to some seriously ruffled feathers; a legal adviser in the NIO, Coulson, wrote a lengthy response for the benefit of his colleagues, which is worth examining here in detail. On 4 February 1985, Coulson wrote:

> In a recent diatribe ... Mr. Mallon cited a number of criminal acts which had been committed by UDR members as proof of the Regiment's undisciplined and bigotted [sic] nature. He went on to claim that the regiment was anti-Catholic and would have no role to play in the creation of a just and stable solution.[54]

Coulson had apparently asked army HQ in Northern Ireland to provide him with figures 'about the crimes known to have been committed by UDR personnel', and it was upon this material that he based his note. Coulson cautioned, however, that:

> this list may not be exhaustive. For example, I believe that one of the 'Shankill butchers' was a serving member of the UDR when he committed the offences, but had left the force by the time he was caught and tried. It is possible also that some UDR members

could have been involved, as Mr. Mallon claims, in
unsolved crimes claimed by the Protestant Action
Force, such as the murder of Farmer and McCartney[55]
in Newtownhamilton in August 1975.

It should be noted here that the suspicion, held by Whitehall,
the MoD and NIO in 1985, of UDR involvement in the
murders of Seán Farmer and Colm McCartney in 1975 has
only recently been uncovered.

Coulson's note was accompanied by an annex: a list of
convictions of UDR personnel supplied to him by HQNI. It
appears not to have been the army's first attempt to track
UDR criminality. One previous memo on the subject has the
handwritten caveat, 'A useful summary, but there are plenty
of other incidents not yet the subject of criminal proceedings!'[56] Once the figures were in hand, perhaps the British
would release them? It seems not. A handwritten note on an
accompanying paper on the file suggests they might not have
been ready to be so forthcoming: 'Yes we must get the figures.
Then we need to decide what to do with them.'[57]

Coulson's annex of UDR criminality ranges wildly in
its coverage. It includes numerous instances of assault, but
also 'Manslaughter of Mr. Paisley's milkman', 'Shot cousin
with PPW [personal protection weapon]', 'Shot daughter
with PPW' and 'Fatal shooting incident against another SF
[security force] member'.[58]

The list, produced by the army themselves, is a useful
aide-mémoire to counter the claims that complaints about the
UDR – who were supposed to be, lest we forget, 'citizens of
good character' – were nationalist or republican propaganda.

In a letter dated 30 January 1985 in which HQNI
seemingly supplied Coulson with his initial figures, an official
wrote, 'I mentioned to you the possibility of a background

note showing UDR personnel charged (including those with cases completed) over the past 18 months or so ... this might now amount to about twenty men – *a figure that would cause alarm if it occurred in a British police force or regiment in GB* [emphasis added].'[59]

Faced with this litany, Coulson suggests that 'these crimes could be put into some form of perspective; however without some further information this would not be easy to do'. The difficulty was that:

> at least one of the convictions for murder and six for manslaughter were for 'domestic' crimes with no sectarian connotations: but it is not possible without a great deal more research to determine either the nature of the assaults which are listed in the annex or whether these offences were committed whilst on duty. Whether such research would be useful must be doubtful. It is sufficient for Mr. Mallon's propaganda purposes that UDR men should have committed any offences against Catholics over the past one and a half decades and the precise number is immaterial.

An aside here on the chilling term 'domestic' as it relates to crimes – a term used, as we see, again and again: 'At least one of the murders, 5 of the manslaughter cases and the majority of the assault cases were offences of a domestic nature.'[60]

The term is used similarly here:

> Since 1969 1 soldier has been convicted of murder in the course of his duties.
>
> 8 UDR members, 2 RUC officers and 2 soldiers have been convicted of murder as a result of the security situation but other than in the course of their duties.

In addition there will have been a number of 'domestic murders'.[61]

What might the term mean? Apparently this meant crimes 'with no sectarian connotations', or not 'committed whilst on duty'. Such crimes included murder, manslaughter, rape, assault and child abuse.[62]

The sad fact is that then, as now, domestic violence in Northern Ireland was 'epidemic'. In 1997 Monica McWilliams analysed 'the implications for abused women and children living in a society dominated by a high level of social disruption and ... the various responses to domestic violence when it occurs in the midst of political violence'. McWilliams wrote that 'In Northern Ireland, as elsewhere, there is a kind of continuum that ranges from the least to the most acceptable type of murders.' The widespread possession of personal protection weapons has had a devastating impact in Northern Ireland: 'A significant feature of the incidents in which guns had been used in homicide or assault cases was that the majority of victims have been married to members of the security forces.'[63]

The sheer volume of personal protection weapons held by members of the UDR may be gauged by a note from 1981. It was occasioned by Lord Brookeborough weighing in to the question of UDR members holding such weapons and suggesting that SMGs be considered for issue. From the note, it seems that – at that time – about 400 men in 4 UDR held SLRs, which they kept at home, and about eighteen held SMGs. The unit was about 600 strong.[64]

McWilliams argued that the increased availability of guns 'meant that more dangerous forms of violence were used against women within the context of their own home'.[65] Nonetheless, she was clear on the most important factor in UDR members' 'domestic crimes':

One further dimension to the Northern Ireland conflict is the problem that women face when they live in … an 'armed patriarchy'.

The interaction of militarism and masculinism in Northern Ireland means that there is a much wider tendency to use, or to threaten to use, guns in the control and abuse of women within the context of domestic violence. For a proportion of women within these households, the guns have provided the additional fear that they or their children could be shot in conflicts involving domestic violence.[66]

One can only wonder at the nature of the drama behind the following incident, 'of two UDR men shooting it out', found among the files of 3rd Infantry Brigade (a HQ element for the security forces, including several UDR battalions). It is obvious, however, that it was the ready availability of guns that made such scenes – so redolent of the Wild West – possible:

Cpl Smith, 124 Int. Section [3rd Infantry Brigade] was driving a female passenger from Newcastle to Lisburn when he was overtaken by a car which had been behind him for some time. The car pulled up in front of him so that he had to stop. The driver of the car came towards Cpl Smith and pointed a pistol at him through the window. Cpl Smith left the car drawing his pistol as he did so. Smith then fired 9 x 9mm rds at the man hitting him in leg and arm. The man returned 2 shots with out [sic] hitting Cpl Smith. Cpl Smith then drove the injured man to Lagan Valley Hospital, Lisburn. The wounded man is Cpl Allen Clerk, 'B' Coy, 9 UDR. He is not seriously injured.[67]

In October 2020, Ryan Miller reported for SCOPE NI that almost one in five recorded crimes in Northern Ireland are crimes of domestic violence.[68] Susan McKay reported in December 2021 that Northern Ireland is the only region in the UK and Ireland without a strategy to tackle gender-based violence, and that it has the highest rate of domestic murder in Europe. Needless to say domestic violence is not confined to the homes of UDR personnel but is a blight on the entirety of society. As McKay writes, 'Northern Ireland was well described as an "armed patriarchy" during the Troubles, but while the guns have long since been decommissioned, the mindsets of the patriarchs have not.'[69]

Returning, however, to 'Mr Mallon's propaganda' that UDR men should have committed 'any offences against Catholics', this prompted in Coulson the following extraordinary statement about Mallon:

> that does not mean that we should not attempt to counter the effects of Mr Mallon's propaganda attacks upon the UDR. It must be clearly recognised that, although his methods may differ, *his aims are complementary to those of the IRA* [emphasis added]. On the one hand the IRA are carrying out attacks on members of the UDR, and particularly off-duty members, with the intention of provoking a loss of morale and discipline in the Force and also creating an anti-nationalist reaction which at best might manifest itself as an overt antagonism towards the nationalist community and at worst in crimes being committed against that community.

The SDLP, by this logic, was causing the very overt antagonism about which they had the cheek to complain:

Mr Mallon, by exploiting any overt signs of this reaction and any lapses from discipline in the UDR, is complementing and assisting this process of alienation, and there can be little doubt that he and his political colleagues are fully aware of this. In combatting this political offensive, we must of course do all that we can to prevent the UDR's critics from obtaining more grist for their propaganda mills ... if our only response to this propaganda assault is to clamp down on the UDR we would be in danger of exacerbating rather than diffusing the anti-nationalist reactions in the regiment.

Coulson could personally testify to the deep-feeling complaints about the UDR, having recently attended the funeral of a UDR soldier killed by the IRA:

Having attended Private Graham's funeral this weekend I was nearly overwhelmed by the deep bitterness which the majority of responsible (and hitherto very moderate) members of the UDR felt towards the SDLP, and particularly Mr Mallon. Although they accepted that members of the Regiment had on occasions misbehaved and indeed committed criminal acts – which they deplored as much as anyone – they felt that it was irresponsible to use these isolated incidents as grounds for criticising the Regiment as a whole. In their view the SDLP were creating a moral climate which went a long way towards justifying the IRA's campaign of murder.[70]

At the top of his own diatribe, Coulson referred to the challenges that the unavailability of statistics posed for those seeking to defend the UDR. Coulson suggested that more research was needed but also wondered if it would be of any assistance in the end. ('Whether such research would be useful must be doubtful.') In March 1985, the MoD wrote about this thorny issue to the NIO:

1. One of your people spoke to me earlier in the week about what could be said to the Irish about criminal offences by the UDR.
2. I should say straightaway that it is very difficult to provide information of this nature, not because we have anything to hide (indeed the story we have to tell is a good one – you might say surprisingly so) but because we did not make a practice of recording this information in the year following the formation of the Regiment, and much of it is now lost forever.[71]

Indeed, the Irish government furnished the British embassy in Dublin with its own compilation of UDR criminality, which was the subject of an embassy report in August 1985. The incidents outlined ranged from murder, attempted murder, possession, robbery and UVF membership, to gross indecency with underaged children.[72] The list also includes the murder of Tony Harker, an unarmed twenty-one-year-old who was shot in the back, in disputed circumstances, on 24 January 1982 in Armagh. His killers were members of 7 UDR (Belfast), who were on weekend border duties. No one was ever charged or convicted for this. It is interesting to note that the Irish government was keeping track of UDR criminality alleged by the nationalist community, as well as crimes for which there had been convictions.

British Ambassador Alan Goodison remarked of this litany that 'the list is worth circulating as evidence of the kind of thing which the Irish Government think about when someone mentions the Ulster Defence Regiment'.[73] The reaction from the NIO was characteristically defensive:

> The list does appear to bear a loose resemblance to the lists of UDR crimes that we have had at one time or another from the army ... Since it is highly improbable that their list is completely askew ... the problem becomes one of persuading the Irish to stop obsessing themselves with the past (ie UDR men who have done bad things and are not in the UDR any longer) and concentrate on the future.[74]

This should be read alongside the following cautionary note. In Ryder's biography of the UDR, he refers to Minister of State for the Armed Forces Archie Hamilton's attempts, in 1989, to sidestep questioning by Seamus Mallon on the UDR's record-keeping:

> The minister sidestepped Mallon's attempt to explore the pre-1985 position because the information could only be obtained at disproportionate cost – (a) parliamentary euphemism which really means that the government is not prepared to disclose the information. These sanitised figures are not much help in measuring the actual scale of criminalities and subversion in the UDR and *it has to be assumed that the government's consistent refusal to publish the information, which, given the implications of the problem, is almost certainly compiled, conceals a worrying situation* [emphasis added].[75]

CHAPTER TEN

'An Aspiration Unlikely to be Fulfilled'

In 1979, British Prime Minister Margaret Thatcher was musing on events in Northern Ireland, urging praise for, in a handwritten note, the *'volunteer Ulster Defence Regiment (? Is that the name) [sic]'*. Her officials clearly had difficulty reading her handwriting; their typed-up version of her comment reads: 'The Prime Minister would also like to see some reference to the valiant work being carried out by the Ulster Volunteer Force.'[1]

Apparently, Thatcher's officials didn't realise the difference between the UDR, the largest regiment in the British army, and the UVF, a loyalist paramilitary group. An accident, maybe, but they would have been surprised to find themselves in agreement with many in the nationalist community in Northern Ireland, who saw no difference either. The 1980s would see more of such official ignominy heaped upon the UDR.

For example, in 1983 a row had developed because the Executive Council of the Isle of Man did not want the UDR on its territory (the regiment was looking to attend adventure training on the island). It was clear the Isle of Man authorities didn't want to be associated with the UDR. Despite the agonies this evidently provoked in Whitehall – 'we would not wish to see the UDR being treated differently'; 'problems caused by the Executive Council's spurning of the UDR'; 'we should not allow the Council to discriminate against the UDR' – the British weren't going to put up too much of a fight for the regiment's honour ('I would not advise the Secretary of State to die in the ditch on this point').[2]

In 1984, British Caledonian Airways sent a request to the MoD to 'borrow 9 Ulster Defence Regiment Pipers and drummers for a promotional tour in Texas (there being no Scots regiments free at that time)'. The response of the FCO to this approach – recorded as a part of an official's discussion with his MoD counterpart – is revealing: 'I have spoken to him on the telephone to say that I thought the proposal potentially disastrous ... it would be bad for us, for the UDR – and fairly hopeless promotion for British Caledonian, I would imagine.'[3]

The problem of the UDR's credibility was raised by the secretary of state for Northern Ireland, Douglas Hurd, who requested 'an in-house discussion with Ministers about the UDR' in November 1984. Ahead of this, an official in the NIO produced a paper about the present and future role of the UDR in which it was admitted that 'the UDR has become a symbol of sectarian division'.

This really quite damning note continues to say that 'the regiment is mistrusted, even hated, in much of the Catholic community, and by many Catholic politicians ... More significantly, it is not held in the highest regard by the RUC itself (including the Chief Constable ...) even amongst regular soldiers it is not universally popular.'[4] In support of this, the note makes reference to a case raised by James

Molyneaux of the Ulster Unionist Party, who had reportedly voiced his concerns privately with the NIO 'about the way in which some UDR patrols abused their position in relation to members of the Catholic community'.[5]

In October 1984, the NIO had found themselves fire-fighting following speculation that the UDR was to be disbanded. Chris Ryder, then of *The Sunday Times*, had contacted the NIO, having been 'alerted to this topic by private comments from two NIO Ministers and by a point of view being actively promoted by the RUC'. An internal memo recorded the following: 'He [Ryder] understands the RUC Special Branch in particular have reservations about the UDR and spoke of their "disgraceful catalogue" of behaviour. He also believes the security effort put into the protection of a minority of UDR soldiers in border areas far outweighs the contribution those soldiers are able to make to security overall.'[6]

We have previously seen reference made by the NIO to the fact of loyalist 'sensitivity at any prospect of its [the UDR's] role being diminished.[7] No wonder, then, there was such 'Loyalist sensitivity'. The UDR was self-evidently theirs and theirs alone. In fact, in 1978 the UDR was criticised by Ian Paisley for an order mobilising 2 UDR (in Armagh) 'to protect the Catholic population'. The main issue for the NIO was evidently not the criticism that the UDR was protecting the minority population but rather 'the question of how Mr. Paisley got hold of it [the mobilisation order]'. This is a stark illustration of the ownership, by one side of the community only, of the UDR.[8]

A 1984 document – a letter from an official in the MoD to a colleague in the Cabinet Office – shows the British view of any possible UDR impartiality. The official wrote, 'It is important that the UDR is seen to be impartial and not to favour this or that sectional interest. Clearly with almost exclusively Protestant membership this is an aspiration unlikely to be fulfilled.'[9]

In 1986, an FCO official gave his opinion of the UDR to a colleague in the MoD, writing, 'I am afraid my own personal view is that for all its courage and dedication (which I certainly do not underestimate), and despite its incorporation into the British Army, the UDR is an inescapably sectarian body and an obstacle to reconciliation between the two communities in Northern Ireland.'[10] Illustrative of exactly this, a note by an NIO official written after a visit to 4 UDR in Enniskillen speaks of 'the Battalion (and the Protestant community they represent)' – so much for notions of serving the whole community.[11]

So what were the views of the UDR's own constituency – Protestants and loyalists? In 1979, a paper produced by Major P.H.S. Newel and Major A.F. Roberts of 10 UDR, a 'Civil Affairs Report',[12] purported to be a survey of the Belfast population. Rather hopefully, the report says, 'while the statements made cannot be claimed to have had the authenticity of a public opinion poll through sheer numbers interviewed, we feel that the research and work put into it must give a fair opinion of how John Citizen is thinking'.

The report by 10 UDR in fact finds interesting detail on broader attitudes among the Protestant population, identifying 'a small but growing trend among some Unionists towards becoming Anti-British'. The authors report:

> It is quite alarming to note the growth of this attitude in the business and professional classes. The result of this is a highly confused Ulster Protestant who is unable to comprehend his apparent rejection by the mainland ... the Ulster Protestant rejects his Irishism

but has nothing to take its place. This situation may be in part one of the reasons that there is a distinct reluctance on the part of some of the rugby or golf club types to serve in the UDR.

As we have seen already, others have commented similarly – among them, Viscount Brookeborough ('by and large the business classes, while they supported peace, didn't support the fight against terrorism') and Brigadier Oborne ('the unionist middle-class were ducking out of their responsibilities'). To date, perhaps not enough attention has been paid to Protestant attitudes to the UDR. The vox pop by 10 UDR reports that:

> in the early days of the 'Troubles', the UDR was regarded by most of the Protestant population as a partisan ally in uniform. Two things appear to have changed this. The first was the last 'Workers' Strike'[13] where the UDR was seen to come of age in its impartial treatment or, as one Protestant put it, 'We always thought you were our mates.' The second factor has probably been the emergence of the daytime Ops Platoons consisting of full-time members ie a different species of UDR man.

The report went on to say that as far as the Protestant population was concerned, there appeared to be 'a diminishing image of the friendly neighbourhood UDR man'.

Being in the UDR carried with it a mass of contradictions. Someone could, for example, be refused a firearms certificate by the police and yet still be considered suitable for the UDR. This is contained in the note of a meeting on 12 March 1985, which included the secretary of state for Northern Ireland, the GOC and the UDR commander: 'Where the RUC refused a firearms certificate in respect of a serving UDR soldier, the case would be examined carefully by the CO. However where the person concerned had a good record in the Regiment, it would be wrong to discharge him merely on the grounds that he had been refused a firearms certificate.'[14]

In fact, the number of cases 'where people had been refused firearms certificates and yet were considered suitable for the UDR' was concerning enough to prompt a reinvigoration of the UDR's screening procedure. A note of a meeting on 13 February 1985 between the secretary of state and his officials, at which this was discussed, records that the procedure, as it stood, was not 'an adequate safeguard against the recruitment of irresponsible people and hot-heads'.[15]

Of course weeding out the undesirables, who couldn't be trusted by the RUC to hold a firearm, had its own complications. A note on a meeting between the Secretaries of State for Northern Ireland and for Defence, Douglas Hurd and Michael Heseltine, saw ministers and officials wrestling with concerns 'about the procedures for vetting and re-vetting members of the UDR', since a 'case had come to light in which a man who had been refused a fire-arms certificate by the RUC continued to serve in the UDR; HQ Northern Ireland seemed to see no difficulty in this.'

Tellingly, at a ministerial meeting in the MoD on 15 July 1985, Under-Secretary of State for the Armed Forces Lord Trefgarne said that 'it must be borne in mind that the UDR had been formed as a replacement for the disbanded B Specials; it was natural that certain patterns in their way of thinking had been carried forward into the UDR.' An NIO official remarked that 'one problem in weeding out undesirable elements in the UDR was that the process might involve compromising delicate Northern Ireland Special Branch sources.'[16] *Plus ça change*, one might reasonably think.

Another oddity of UDR membership was that someone could be in the UDR and at the same time in the UDA, but they could not be a UDR soldier and an MP: 'The reason for excluding UDR members from the House of Commons and any Northern Ireland Assembly is that they might otherwise get drawn into partisan or sectarian argument over Northern Ireland issues, which would be inappropriate for a member of a non-sectarian force.'[17]

Nevertheless, in September 1977 we find Enoch Powell – he of anti-immigrant 'rivers of blood'[18] notoriety, and by then the Ulster Unionist MP for South Down – 'on patrol in Newry with a C Company [of 3 UDR] patrol'. The British army log describes Powell as 'dressed in combat kit and with face blackened'; he 'obviously enjoyed the experience of being a soldier again'.[19]

The UDR's ignominious reputation is continually highlighted by extracts from recently discovered files. In July 1982, 3 UDR's 'Historical Diary and Record' discusses the creation of the UDR Medal and the UDR Long Service and Good Conduct Medal, both recently announced by the British prime minister. Unfortunately, it turned out that it was difficult to establish who was entitled to these medals, owing to poor record-keeping – and further, because 'the conditions have been made so difficult to achieve that it seems unlikely many people will qualify anyway'.[20] Worse, 3 UDR's record admits, 'at the moment we know of only two men in the battalion who definitely qualify, both of them unworthy'.[21] Which surely begs the question, why were they still there?

Further correspondence on the UDR Medal shows that the British were very much aware of how it would look to be making this award while members were in court for murder and other offences. In 1986 Secretary of State for Northern Ireland Tom King wrote that 'it is time to move ahead on the proposals put forward last year to enhance the rules of eligibility for the Ulster Defence Regiment Medal. Not that this is an ideal time for the Government to be seen to be giving enhanced recognition to service in the UDR, with one trial in progress involving serious charges against members of the Regiment, and others in the offing.'[22] By this time, four UDR members were facing trial for the murder of Adrian Carroll in Armagh in 1983. King continued, 'But, for just that reason, there is little likelihood of a significantly more favourable moment for doing so in the foreseeable future.'[23] King's pessimism was not misjudged; just two months after his remarks all four UDR men were convicted of Carroll's murder.[24]

In 1984 the loss of a list of names of members of 10 UDR gave rise to discussions about what was required 'to safeguard 36 UDR officers and men who have been put at risk by this breach of security'.[25] This is of course deeply ironic given what we now know of the supply chain of targeting information from the UDR to loyalist extremists. That the loss was the fault of an English training major – a file of the members' personal details was lost when his car was stolen – exposed some of the fault lines between the UDR and their British *overseers*. Following the incident, articles in the tabloid media – including one which criticised the English hierarchy of the UDR – alleged that 'morale was being hit by the "cocktail circuit" image of some of its regular officers'.[26] At this time, local unionist politicians were pushing for more local senior officers in the UDR. Readers may recall that the decision to appoint regular army COs to each battalion was not universally popular (see p. 23).

In November 1985 the army conducted a 'UDR Study Period', desperate no doubt to curtail the UDR's plummeting reputation. The first day was spent examining 'the credibility of the UDR'. Alas, if one had hoped to find that a period of reflection might have been of benefit here, a note of the meeting by the civil adviser to the GOC records that 'it was disheartening to be reminded that in the UDR's eyes, the problem could be alleviated, if not eradicated, by an increased PR effort'. It is apparent from this note that at least the army's top brass in the north knew 'all too well that in the eyes of the media, the various sectarian crimes committed by UDR soldiers and the allegations of harassment cannot simply be dismissed as the work of "a few rotten apples"'. Nevertheless, among UDR officers, 'There was a disappointing reluctance to accept the view of at least one police officer present, viz that the best PR resulted from actions and attitudes in dealing with members of the public.'[27]

It is noteworthy that the GOC, Robert Pascoe, attended the 'Study Period' if only to record his remarks on the 'credibility' of the UDR. Referring to forthcoming trials of UDR personnel for serious crimes, he said that 'it was no longer good enough to talk in terms of "a few bad apples"'. Instead the UDR 'must ensure that its record improved'.[28]

All quite ridiculous, especially when one considers the view prevailing in the NIO in London. In a note for use by ministers in answer to questions, prepared by the NIO's Security and International Division, the author comments on the UDR's sectarian image that 'It is true that the Regiment is largely recruited from one part of the community and that less than 3% are Roman Catholics. The Regiment would like to increase this percentage. It is not, however, true that the Regiment acts in a sectarian manner.'[29]

There is an inked x beside this last statement and 'come off it!' handwritten in the margin. It would seem from the files that this comment was by a Foreign Office official named David Barrie (in the FCO's Republic of Ireland Department), who in a cover note for the document wrote, 'x is fairly preposterous'.[30]

Declassified files clearly show that the FCO had a less-than-admiring view of the NIO at the time. Earlier on the same file, Barrie remarks upon a draft document received from the NIO that apparently had been the subject of some rewrites between the two offices. He has noted in the margin, 'we had difficulty interpreting the NIO draft which was opaque to the point of incomprehensibility. Obviously we didn't improve it enough!'[31]

Aside from these quirks and oddities, legitimate concerns and warnings about the UDR continued to be made by Sinn Féin, the SDLP, the Irish government and a variety of journalists. Book-ending the 1980s were two devastating critiques: the first by Mary Holland in the *New Statesman*; the second was Sinn Féin's pamphlet 'The Ulster Defence Regiment – The Loyalist Militia'.

Holland's piece – a critical article to mark the 10th anniversary of the UDR's establishment – included the SDLP's law and order spokesman Michael Canavan's campaigning against serious sectarian crime by members of the regiment. It also refers to the routine passage of large numbers of loyalists 'who join the UDR, stay in it for a short time during which they receive sophisticated training in the use of weapons and explosives, and then drop out'. She concluded that, in 1980, 'for better or worse the British Government is now regarded as having quite deliberately trained 21,000 people, almost all Protestants, in the use of sophisticated weapons. That fact and, as important, the fear of what it could mean in an atmosphere of sectarian conflict, must now constitute one of the major obstacles to British withdrawal from Northern Ireland.'[32]

By 1990 the Sinn Féin publicity department was able to look back over the two decades of the UDR's existence to date and provide compelling evidence – a litany of murder and crime based on news reports – that 'puts it in the category of an official death-squad, on a par with similar forces operating in Latin America ... while members of the UDR are regularly included on the British Queen's Honours List'.[33]

This comparison to death squads elsewhere is not fanciful, and it is not beyond the British to employ them. In April 2020 Jack Straw, who was both home secretary and foreign secretary in British governments between 1997 and 2006, was interviewed by the BBC about Iran's support of militias in Iraq and was discussing the effectiveness of such proxy forces. 'Proxy forces do work, it's not something that is confined to the Iranians,' he said. And then, with a laugh, 'I mean, we know that.'[34]

Professor Bill Rolston has written that 'there are many parallels in the Northern Ireland experience with that of death squads elsewhere ... The state's involvement in death squads in Northern Ireland emerged almost naturally from previous British colonial experience.'[35] According to Rolston, 'there is a continuum of death squad activity based on state control – from direct state initiation and management at one pole, to state attempts to co-opt vigilantism at the other'.[36]

Through its relationship with loyalist extremists, and perhaps its place in the lineage of British colonial militia, the UDR can be safely said to occupy a space on this continuum – a prime example of what Rolston calls 'the "public-private mix" in death squad activity',[37] and 'the tripartite pheno-menon of state death squad activity, loyalist death squads, and collusion between state agents and loyalist paramilitaries'.[38]

A word here on the legacy of colonialism with respect to the UDR. Dr Huw Bennett has written of 'the army's colonial practice of seeking "loyalist" elements in local society who could be co-opted in militia forces'.[39] Bennett argues that 'There's no doubt that the creation of the Ulster Defence Regiment was influenced, for the British Army, by the experience in the Empire. These kinds of locally raised regiments that were controlled and commanded by British officers, as an intrinsic part of the chain of command of the British Army, were common through all of the counterinsurgency campaigns.'[40]

It is interesting that while local men could be UDR battalion commanders, the Ulster Defence Regiment Act 1969 enshrined that 'the immediate commander of the UDR was to be a Regular Army brigadier'.[41] Didn't they trust a local commander for the regiment? Consider this from Ed Burke, in *The Journal of Imperial and Commonwealth History*:

> At the outset of Operation Banner the Catholic Bishop of Derry, Edward Daly, recalled a very 'colonial attitude' during his visits to 8 Infantry Brigade Headquarters in Ebrington, Londonderry. Some of the officers, he observed, knew more about India than Ireland. Later, he recalled, a very different, savvy and 'modern' officer would emerge but 1969 to 1976 was a time of flux.
>
> Senior Northern Irish civil servant Ken Bloomfield also recalled that civil servants posted to Belfast after the introduction of direct rule in March 1972 'approached their task like district commissioners sent out to administer a tribe of rather thick-headed savages'.
>
> A part-time officer from the Ulster Defence Regiment (UDR) complained that regular army officers 'look on us as friendly tribesmen'. Colonial attitudes died hard, it seemed – and the army's initial operations in Northern Ireland did rely upon some measures recently used in the colonies.[42]

In April 1972, the Earl of Enniskillen – an influential peer who had been a senior officer in the Kenya Police Reserve during the Mau Mau uprising, before returning to County Fermanagh and serving as a major in the UDR – wrote a memorandum for William Whitelaw. In it he congratulated the new secretary of state for Northern Ireland on his appointment, before urging him to look to colonial tactics, including allowing the RUC to take their place in 'the total war machine ... a system of integration such as we had abroad and which proved very efficient and effective'.[43]

It is worth noting the colonial adventures adorning the CVs of some of the UDR's commanding officers since its formation. The first commander of the UDR, Brigadier Logan Scott-Bowden, was a career army officer with a distinguished war record. He was heavily involved in the long planning process for D-Day, and helped pilot ashore a wave of amphibious tanks onto Omaha Beach on D-Day itself. A citation for one of his decorations stated that 'his individual feats of gallantry are almost too numerous to record'. Among his postings after the war were two years in Aden, service in Palestine, and a term as brigade major 'countering insurgency' in Burma. He was completing a course at the Indian National Defence College when he was recalled for the new post of commander of the newly formed Ulster Defence Regiment.

Succeeding Scott-Bowden in 1971, Brigadier Denis Ormerod was the first Catholic commander of the UDR. Ormerod joined the army in 1940 and was commissioned into the British Indian Army. He had served in Malaya and Palestine during internal security operations in the post-war period. Brigadier Harry Baxter commanded the UDR from 1973 to 1976. Baxter was an Irish-born fourth generation soldier and served as a second lieutenant in the Indian Army in the Second World War. He later operated in Burma, Palestine, Egypt, Greece and Malaya – where he was mentioned in dispatches. The height of the British counter-insurgency war upon the Malayan Chinese population saw the high commissioner, Henry Gurney, 'effectively absolve the security forces from their duty to act within the law [with] terrible results', including the notorious Batang Kali massacre of December 1948, when twenty-four unarmed prisoners were murdered by British troops.[44] It is unclear what Baxter did to merit a mention in dispatches in such a notoriously vicious context. Brigadier Baxter was the commander of the UDR at the time of the Miami Showband killings.

If, as Ed Burke has observed of such men, 'colonial attitudes died hard', what must the impact have been of all of that colonial experience and its attendant prejudices upon the policy and practices of the UDR's commanders?

Plastic Bullets

A feature of colonialism is the deployment of methods and weapons that, in the modern age, would not be contemplated 'at home'. Rubber and, later, plastic bullets have been fired by the security forces in Northern Ireland since 1970. Despite occasions of serious civil disorder in Britain, they have never once been used there. In 2012, the assistant commissioner of the Metropolitan Police said that while plastic bullets had been stockpiled there, 'they have never been deployed in a public order situation ... They have been authorised, but it's not a tactic we would want to use.'[45]

In Northern Ireland, seventeen people were killed during the conflict by members of the security forces firing plastic or rubber bullets – eight of the seventeen people were children, and all but one was Catholic. Despite their prolific use by the British army, the RUC, and then the PSNI, they were not made accessible to the UDR.

Since its foundation, the UDR had been 'precluded from being used for crowd control and riot duties in cities' – the usual scenarios in which the security forces tended to use plastic bullets. By 1988, however – by which time sixteen people had died from security forces firing the weapons – GOC NI was floating the case for equipping the UDR with baton round guns, 'to enable them to protect themselves without resorting to lethal force'. The rationale provided: that there were the occasions when UDR patrols 'found themselves subjected to severe harassment by terrorist sympathisers, with stones and sometimes petrol bombs being thrown, or when attempts have been made to seize weapons etc. Under such circumstances the only alternative to running away ... is to fire live rounds.'[46]

This proposal was circulated despite note being made that 'the baton round gun is a potentially lethal weapon, particularly when fired at close range'. The main disadvantage foreseen by the army for the proposal was the perception among 'the Irish' that the British government would be 'equipping a force, which they regard as sectarian, with the means to harass and injure the Nationalist community'.[47]

The proposal was greeted cautiously by the political class. Foreign Secretary Geoffrey Howe said, 'The Irish will need reasonable notice ... I would expect very severe criticism if baton round guns were used by the UDR in circumstances where there was no RUC presence.'[48] Following up, an FCO official expressed Howe's further view that 'while he would not argue against the UDR carrying equipment less lethal than that with which it is already armed, the ability of the UDR soldiers to stand their ground in circumstances where previously they might have decided to withdraw makes it all the more important that there should be an RUC presence on such occasions'.[49]

In due course, the weapons were issued to the UDR, albeit under strict conditions. Every UDR deployment with plastic bullets (the GOC in Northern Ireland told the secretary of state for Northern Ireland) had to have the personal authority of the commanding officer[50] – who was always a 'Regular', and therefore a 'British', soldier. It was, as the GOC described it, 'an emotive issue',[51] and so there would be no public notice about the decision.[52]

In June 1990, the British army gave a briefing to the joint offices of Irish and British officials in Belfast. Among the army delegation were the GOC NI, General John Waters, and the commander of the UDR, Brigadier Charles Ritchie. The Irish delegation said they had been 'appalled by the decision to issue plastic bullets to the UDR ... after twenty years of UDR existence' and 'deeply worried about the impact on community relations of any use of plastic bullets by the UDR'.[53]

General Waters said they were to be used only when 'the sole alternative would be to use live ammunition in defence of life or equipment'. The Irish side surmised this referred to radio equipment. The obvious counter to this, one might have thought, would be to query the emphasis given to radio equipment ahead of the right to life. The Irish 'were left with the impression that the possibility of loss of sensitive electronic equipment by UDR soldiers was an important factor in the decision to issue plastic bullets'.[54] Tellingly, the UDR never fired a plastic bullet. Given the torturous process by which issuing them had to be justified, it is questionable whether the weapon was ever in fact entrusted to a UDR patrol.

Legality of UDR Call-out

There were serious concerns among MoD legal advisers – which may have consequences today – about the very *legality* of the UDR on active duty. In May 1981 the secretary of state for defence was provided with potentially explosive legal advice on the matter of the UDR and the legality of its statutory call-out provisions.[55]

The memo raised concerns as to whether UDR soldiers were legally 'on duty', as the formal call-out procedures were not being followed, and had not been since the early 1970s. Legislation allowed for the UDR to be called out on an emergency basis or on a permanent basis, and the advice suggested that the original call-out in 1970 had been through the emergency procedure – and that this therefore created doubts as to the legality of UDR soldiers serving throughout the 1970s. Were soldiers operating on a 'voluntary' basis, and were their actions lawful?

As a result of this failure to 'call out' the UDR on a permanent basis before 1981, the officials were concerned about the legality of arrests, search operations and other actions carried out by members of the regiment.[56] Where the call-out procedures can be brought into question, it may be that a member of the UDR purporting to exercise legal powers was not entitled to do so.

At this remove, and with only limited access to official documents, it is difficult to judge the importance of this advice. It may be that, decades later, an individual might wish to challenge a pre-1981 arrest by the UDR through the Criminal Cases Review Commission, which has the statutory powers to search for documents pertaining to the issue. Convictions of persons for failing to answer a question or for resisting arrest might also be called into question. It is interesting to note, however, that the MoD successfully kept a lid on this advice until, in 2020, PFC/JFF staff discovered the memo.

CHAPTER ELEVEN

The Demise
of the UDR

A t the beginning of 1981, a working group involving the NIO, MoD and HQNI was ready to report its findings on a 'way ahead' for the UDR – in reality, an internal assessment of the future *need* for the UDR.[1] It was agreed that the UDR would be scaled back eventually to a 2,000-strong part-time force for Home Guard purposes. This development was felt to be sensitive – indeed, any public discussion was judged to be 'highly counter-productive and perhaps even dangerous at the moment'.[2] Therefore, this information was to be kept among a small number of people.

In fact, 'the appraisal would be conducted in the strictest secrecy ... neither UDR officers nor others in Northern Ireland would be given any cause to think that the future of the regiment was in any way under review'.[3] Evidently this was taken very seriously, with numerous officials noting the need to destroy, and confirm the destruction of, this volatile document, although this did provoke anxieties in some quarters. An official cautioned against 'being foolishly zealous' and complained:

> I do not think we can realistically expect all concerned
> in the office to destroy all their papers on the appraisal.
> I also question whether it would be right to try to
> expunge from the record in this way the record of
> the detailed work which went into the appraisal ...
> some of that work could prove important for our
> successors.[4]

The document says that 'a major ingredient in the decision
to create the UDR in 1969 was the political need to provide
full opportunity for the Loyalist community to make their
own contribution to the security of the Province following
the disbandment of the "B" Specials. They have, since
its inception, been strong supporters of the Regiment.'
Nonetheless, there was a strong case, it is recorded, 'for
not perpetuating a force which would continue to be seen
by the Catholic minority as retaining the sectarian stigma
of the USC and as, at best, unsympathetic to them. To do
so ['perpetuate' the UDR] could be a serious hindrance to
the development of a stable political and constitutional
settlement, and could harm the process of reconciliation
between the communities.'[5] One might reasonably ask what
chance there was of reconciliation, when one community had
for some time been armed, primed and aimed at the other by
the British government.

   In December 1980, an NIO official (named Burns)
outlined the process by which the appraisal team had arrived
at its conclusions: 'interrupted in July [1980] when the GOC,
apparently misunderstanding the situation, said ... that he
was opposed to any further consideration of the UDR'. But
by the end of August, they 'had overcome this hiccup' and
work on the paper progressed.[6] The draft report had three
main recommendations:

a) When the present emergency has ended there will be no requirement in Northern Ireland for a force on the lines of the Ulster Defence Regiment ...

b) It is premature (in both political and security terms) at this stage to take major steps to reduce the size of the UDR: but it must be left to the judgement of the GOC Northern Ireland ... to reduce unnecessary duties by the UDR, to reallocate UDR soldiers to other parts of Northern Ireland, and to trim the UDR in other operational ways.

c) It would be wrong to announce now any long term policy concerning the UDR, but the NIO, MOD and HQNI should ... review the possibility of making public the Government's policy in relation to the future of the UDR.[7]

It is clear that by 1980, senior officials in the NIO, MoD and army saw no future for the regiment: 'The kernel of this lies in the first recommendation, that there is no long term requirement for a force such as the UDR. The working party was unanimous on this point.'[8]

Burns concluded, 'it is quite possible that the GOC will take the view that the report having been completed should now be locked away'. He was right – the GOC, Richard Lawson, 'stated very firmly his view that it should not go to Ministers'.[9] The appraisal group pushed back, Burns writing again to his appraisal team colleagues about the GOC:

I do not think the GOC fully understands that ... a report such as this which advocates a significant development in our policy cannot be of any value at all unless it has been seen and approved by the relevant Ministers. If we accept the GOC's constraint, then we shall, in effect, be burying the report. I doubt very much whether the GOC would have the Ministry of Defence's support in taking this attitude.[10]

To which the NIO permanent under secretary replied, 'I think we must make it clear to the GOC that it is our duty to put this to Ministers ... We cannot and will not refuse to advise the Secretary of State when he asks for advice.'[11]

At a subsequent meeting between Burns and Lawson, the GOC's concerns were made explicit:

> [He] remained very worried at the prospect of the report being shown to Ministry of Defence Ministers. There had, he said, been a draft Army Board paper in November about the future of the UDR which he had succeeded in quashing only after discussion with the Secretary of State for Defence [Francis Pym] ...
>
> With Mr. Pym's departure the GOC doubted whether MOD Ministers would give adequate weight to Northern Ireland factors. He feared that if the present report were shown to MOD Ministers at the present time, it might be seen as a simple statement that in the long term the UDR was not required, and this statement might in turn be translated by MOD into a demand for immediate cost saving cutbacks ...
>
> The GOC said several times that his anxiety was that the report would 'set things in concrete' ...
>
> The GOC was not as certain as the authors of the report that there would indeed be a need for a 'third force' ... one interpretation of the GOC's view is that he may one day suggest that the UDR should be abolished altogether, without replacement. This may make excellent military logic [but] ... we may

nevertheless have a political need to retain some local part-time defence force.[12]

Nevertheless, the appraisal went ahead and was supplied to ministers. The finalised agreed appraisal (including the views of the GOC and the RUC chief constable) concluded, *inter alia*, that:

> the role of the UDR will diminish rather than increase in the medium term ...[13]
>
> If the UDR were disbanded without replacement we consider that Loyalist criticism would be overwhelming and would be very difficult for the Government to absorb politically ...
>
> Disbandment will be greeted with relief by the Catholic community, and with dismay if not actual anger by the Loyalists ... They will still seek an opportunity to train and prepare for a renewed terrorist campaign against Ulster, however remote this possibility may appear ...
>
> On our present assessment of political facts, the best chance of minimising both Loyalist and Catholic criticism seems thus to lie with the concept of a new force. The very creation of the UDR ... [has] shown that it is possible to move away from an entity with political and security disadvantages like the USC and at the same time to satisfy the Loyalist desire to contribute actively to maintaining security.[14]

The writing was on the wall for the UDR in 1980, but the public wasn't to know. The appraisal concluded, 'This Government has remained silent on the long-term future of the Ulster Defence Regiment, and we do not recommend that that silence should be broken now.'[15]

By 1985, in the negotiations of the Anglo-Irish Agreement, the future of the UDR was firmly on the table as one of the 'Associated Measures'. That year had barely begun when seventeen-year-old Paul 'Kelso' Kelly was shot dead at a UDR checkpoint. The vehicle he was in, along with four others, failed to stop at the checkpoint, which was set up on Kennedy Way, a main arterial route into nationalist west Belfast. Paul's inquest heard that he was found to have suffered around fifty wounds from bullet fragments.[16]

Paul's killing prompted the Irish minister for foreign affairs to express to the British ambassador the Irish government's 'grave concern' at the killing. A note on a Department of Foreign Affairs file records that:

> The Minister conveyed in the strongest terms the conviction of the Government that the UDR should not be deployed in nationalist areas in Northern Ireland ... The Minister said he was convinced that the UDR was seen by many loyalists in Northern Ireland as an armed militia of their own community ... Nationalists in Northern Ireland believe the UDR to be an armed instrument of domination of their community by the majority community. As such the UDR was a dangerous source of division in Northern Ireland. Its deployment in nationalist areas could result only in further alienation, confrontation and violence.[17]

The file also notes a catalogue of UDR crimes, including the then recent murder of Sinn Féin election worker Peter Corrigan, 'the murder of the Miami showband ... the involvement of a serving UDR member in the Shankill Butchers, the murder of Adrian Carroll in Armagh in 1983, and numerous serious sectarian offences'.[18] It notes the catalogue of criminality discussed elsewhere in this volume – including murder, death threats, wounding, false imprisonment, sectarian arson, assault, indecent assault, gross indecency and rape of a child.

The Irish government file concludes:

> the membership of the UDR is to all extents and purposes [*sic*] exclusively unionist and protestant [*sic*], their victims have almost exclusively been Catholic and nationalist. Their existence and their behaviour are a major element in the growing feeling of alienation within the minority community who find it impossible to identify with the UDR. It seems clear from the extent of the crimes committed by the UDR and from the extent of the manner in which they engage in the petty harassment of the minority community that there has been insufficient control over the manner in which they are recruited and insufficient control over UDR members once they become serving members of the Regiment.[19]

The file also records the resolution adopted at the SDLP annual conference in January 1985 calling for the disbandment of the UDR. It notes that none of the speakers who spoke to the motion dissented from the view that it should be disbanded.

The Anglo-Irish Agreement, signed in November 1985, provided the architecture for the Irish and British governments to consult regularly and formally on the administration of Northern Ireland. For the first time, the British conceded a role for the Dublin government in the running of the north, in return for co-operation on security. The British prime minister of the day, Thatcher, was famously of the view 'that the island of Ireland contained more terrorists than anywhere in the world, apart from the Lebanon'.[20]

Thatcher would later express regret at signing the agreement, for its perceived failure to deliver fully on security co-operation.[21] Before then, however, the British had to deal with the fallout among loyalists after giving Irish government influence in the north of Ireland. The loyalist backlash was led by unionist politicians, including the DUP's leader and firebrand street preacher Ian Paisley. Paisley bellowed, 'Never! Never! Never!' – a kind of catchphrase now forever associated with him – outside Belfast City Hall as he addressed a loyalist protest denouncing the agreement in November 1985. Later that month, inspired by Paisley, a UDR patrol reportedly pointed their weapons at the Irish army across the border in County Donegal, shouting, 'Never! Never! Never!' A declassified FCO note records the official Irish complaint about the episode, which 'provoked fears about UDR discipline of the kind which had been mentioned during Anglo-Irish Agreement negotiations'.[22]

Also that month, a regimental dinner fell victim to the UDR's high dudgeon about the agreement. Lord Lyell, a cabinet minister, was invited to a dinner by 8 UDR, but it then transpired that many UDR grandees said they wouldn't attend if Lyell was there. The MP, and former UDR major, Ken Maginnis, who had invited the minister, now found himself in the unfortunate position of being at odds with his comrades, who, 'feeling the betrayal by the Government and the NIO Ministers just as deeply as I do', said that to attend would be 'surrender of principle'. Eventually Lyell was asked by 8 UDR not to attend. Lyell's cause was not perhaps helped by his having previously lamented the loss, in the UDR, of 'an opportunity for a non-sectarian force ... due to the fact that many of the dreaded B Specials joined ... and secondly, by the intimidation of Catholics'.[23] As reported by historian Éamon Phoenix, this was in response to a request by the secretary of state for Northern Ireland, Douglas Hurd, for 'an in-house discussion with Ministers about the UDR' in November 1984.

Nevertheless, the UDR survived the Anglo-Irish Agreement intact. British–Irish negotiations had encompassed ways of reforming, or even merely modifying the regiment. Declassified papers show the British weighing their options – including the adoption of a 'Code of Conduct', the possibility of increased training for part-time members, and the secondment of more regular NCOs to the UDR.[24] Secretary of State for Defence Michael Heseltine said that there should be 'full liaison between the police and Army authorities in ensuring that the UDR was manned by the right quality of people'.[25] The GOC NI apparently accepted all of this as reasonable, and why wouldn't he accept such compromises when the SDLP's Seamus Mallon was urging that the UDR be dissolved entirely? According to former FCO official David Goodall, during the negotiations the Irish delegation warned the British that 'there was a risk of a split within the SDLP, where Seamus Mallon would not be satisfied with measures to reform the UDR ... but wanted to insist on its outright disbandment'.[26]

Secretary of State for Defence Douglas Hurd was said to be 'extremely pleased' at the GOC's response – as was Heseltine, since, 'if the UDR did not succeed in carrying out its security duties efficiently, the British Army might find itself having to undertake an even greater burden of security duty within the Province'.[27]

Meanwhile, of course, collusion between the security forces and loyalism carried on, helped by the accommodating 'blind eye' cast by officialdom. A declassified file shows notes for use by ministers in answer to questions on UDR recruiting and vetting/screening. One such note outlines a safeguard whereby, 'Should the local RUC have any reservations about the behaviour of a soldier within the community, these can be passed to the Commanding Officer and, where necessary, acted upon.' In the margin is the handwritten comment, 'not much of a safeguard'.[28]

Passing targeting information was, as we have seen, a particular problem within the UDR. In May 1988, Private Joanne Garvin, of the UDR, was detained by army HQ's 120 Security Section on suspicion of receiving targeting information from a regular army soldier, Corporal Cameron Hastie of the Royal Scots. This came to light, the file says quite opaquely, 'following allegations made by a woman UDR private'. Hastie, implicated by Garvin, was arrested on leave in Edinburgh. Both Garvin and Hastie received suspended sentences of eighteen months, despite the court hearing that the targeting information had been given to the UVF. This leniency was compounded by the army retaining Hastie in his regiment, since he 'had served 6 years, had a very good record of Service, was regarded as an able and professional Junior NCO with good potential'. The file shows that the judge sentencing Hastie 'had treated him leniently in the light of the CO's wish to retain him in service'.[29]

The notorious British army agent and UDA quartermaster Brian Nelson said in a statement to police investigators that, of the UDA's intelligence material, 'ninety nine percent involved the UDR'.[30] Compounding the gravity of this, in December 2012 Desmond de Silva QC, in his review of the 1989 murder of Pat Finucane, reported that the UDA tended to assume security force contacts were providing infallible and immediately 'actionable' information, leading to immediate killings; a Security Service assessment of the UDA noted that '[the] UDA recognises the need to corroborate intelligence, but if it comes from RUC or UDR sources, it tends to be taken as authoritative'.[31]

It should be noted that the punishment of Garvin and Hastie does not undermine our general thesis of collusion and impunity; de Silva reported that 'limited action does appear to have been taken with respect to some members of the UDR in the late 1980s. Several members of the UDR were convicted for criminal offences relating to loyalist terrorist activity during this period ... However, it must be said that, even with respect to the UDR, the action taken was minimal in view of the scale of the problem.'[32]

This case preceded, by a matter of weeks, the murder of Loughlin Maginn by 'the UFF' – a cover name for the UDA – on 25 August 1989. Following Maginn's murder, his killers claimed he had been a member of the IRA; stung by the revelation that Maginn had no connection to the IRA, the UDA showed a BBC reporter pictures of alleged IRA suspects acquired from security sources, including one taken of Loughlin Maginn in RUC custody. Forced to act in the wake of this episode, the British government appointed Metropolitan Police Commissioner John Stevens to head what would become a ten-year series of investigations into collusion between state forces and loyalist paramilitaries in numerous killings. This would amount to 9,256 statements taken, 10,391 documents recorded (totalling over 1 million pages) and 16,194 exhibits seized. Only the 'Overview and Recommendations' of this work has ever been released publicly.[33]

Stevens' investigations, he wrote, 'highlighted collusion, the wilful failure to keep records, the absence of account-ability, the withholding of intelligence and evidence, and the extreme of agents being involved in murder'[34] – including the murder of solicitor Pat Finucane in 1989.[35] The impact of his investigative work was seismic, and the reaction of the secu-rity forces was implacably hostile. His work was obstructed throughout – 'his obstruction was cultural in its nature and widespread'[36] – and his incident room was even destroyed in a fire, which Stevens believed 'was a deliberate act of arson'.[37]

Stevens' investigations gave rise to huge anxiety within the UDR. On 8 October 1989, his team arrested a total of twenty-eight full-time or part-time members of the UDR, all but one based in Belfast. The arrests were assisted by 300 RUC officers, and 'a number of photo montages and ammunition were seized'.[38] The arrests led to a defensive reaction by the army and officials; a brief was prepared that included the line, 'Totally reject the suggestion that joining the UDR is in any way comparable with joining any terrorist or extremist organisation'[39] – language that is very familiar in the context of contemporary British arguments for immunity for their former troops for illegal killings during the conflict. The brief was also used to assert that the future of the UDR was not in doubt.

The files show that both the Colonel Commandant of the UDR, David Young,[40] and the Honorary Representative Colonel Commandant, Dennis Faulkner,[41] wrote serial letters of complaint about Stevens' arrests of UDR personnel. These included letters to the chief of the general staff (the professional head of the army) and to the secretary of state for Northern Ireland. The arrests, the complaints and a pending Panorama television programme[42] on the regiment were exercising military minds. The secretary of state was by then looking at options whereby the commander of the UDR would have effective powers to discharge soldiers suspected of representing a security risk.[43] A fine case of 'locking the stable door after the horse has bolted' if ever there was one.

Despite these ongoing crises, mid-July 1989 saw military planners preparing an 'Operational Policy for the UDR in the 1990s'.[44] Among its conclusions was that the threat from republican violence was likely to continue, with particular high risk to part-time UDR personnel. Nevertheless, 'There is a long term requirement for the UDR, even after the present campaign, both to support the Police and for Home Defence.'[45]

A failure to read the room, perhaps, but by July 1992 the UDR was no more, having been amalgamated with a regular army regiment, the Royal Irish Rangers, to form the new Royal Irish Regiment. The pace of change was such that the first run of Chris Ryder's 1991 book, *The Ulster Defence Regiment: An Instrument of Peace?*, required a new edition the following year to supplant its last chapter, which was entitled 'The Future – An Instrument of Peace'.

The creation of the Royal Irish Regiment came in the context of the massive overhaul of Britain's armed force, called 'Options for Change', which resulted from the implosion of the Soviet Union and the end of the Cold War. But it surely was also influenced by what Ryder (in his second edition) referred to as 'long-running concerns about the conduct and integrity of the UDR ... the top secret and unpublished conclusions of the Stevens investigation ... doubts about the internal culture of the UDR ... [and] worries about the reputation of the UDR ... buried deep in the pending trays of the mandarins at Stormont Castle and in the vaults of the Ministry of Defence in London'.[46]

In February 1992, Prince Andrew, the British monarchy's Duke of York, was named incoming commander-in-chief of the Royal Irish Regiment. Perhaps fittingly, the Royal Irish Regiment revived an old name from Anglo-Irish relations – the original regiment, disbanded after the partition of Ireland in 1922, was the first element of the British army to attack the Irish rebels during the 1916 Easter Rising. A Royal Irish Regiment officer at the time said of his men, 'They regarded, not unreasonably, everyone they saw as an enemy, and fired at anything that moved.'[47]

CHAPTER TWELVE

Sinning Quietly

The UDR arose from the ashes of the discredited and disreputable B Specials, a force that James Craig, the UVF gunrunner of 1912 and first prime minister of Northern Ireland, once said proudly 'could substitute as Fascists'.[1] Before him, the British prime minister in 1921, Lloyd George, drew a direct parallel between 'the violence of the paramilitary Ulster Special Constabulary (USC) and that of Italian fascists'.[2]

It would of course be ridiculous to equate the UDR with fascism but it perhaps proved difficult for the regiment to escape the shadow[3] of such predecessors and tradition. As Dr Huw Bennett said:

> There was a real and genuine hope at the instigation of the regiment that it would be truly cross community and would be non-sectarian in character, but it became apparent very quickly that that was not going to be the case, and the British army was willing to live with the consequences which were that this would be in many ways a sectarian regiment.[4]

The UDR was created partly to salve unionist anger at the loss of their B Specials. That anger is encapsulated in an interview given by a former RUC constable quoted in Ellison and Smyth's *The Crowned Harp*, about policing in Northern Ireland. The former constable said:

> The B-force was disbanded to placate nationalists ... The one thing I'll always regret, and I'll tell you we would have a different situation now – was that the Specials weren't let loose on those Civil Rights ones. I'll tell you the whole thing would have been stopped dead ... it would have been stopped dead. There would be none of the problems you have today.[5]

A former B Special told the same authors of the disbandment of the B Specials:

> I remember feeling very angry at that time. We didn't do anything wrong, never as far as I was concerned. I remember there was a lot of talk in the platoon about ... well going over to a disreputable side of life [the UVF] but nothing ever came of it. We talked as well about handing in our guns in protest but decided to see what the new force [the UDR] would look like. A lot of the men joined that including myself.[6]

It is hard to see how such vitriol could have been excluded from the policy and practices of the Ulster Defence Regiment, not least when one considers the wholesale importation of B Special personnel into the nascent regiment in 1970. During the parliamentary debates on the formation of the UDR, Labour MP Kevin McNamara described the situation in this way: 'It was exactly the people going around at night on their patrols, putting up road blocks, stopping cars, knocking on doors and pushing rifles through windows who made my family and other relatives afraid of the B Specials. Those are the people who now [were] taken over completely into the new Ulster Defence Regiment.'

It is harder still to see how the regiment could have ever met the avowed expectations of the British government, to be representative of the community as a whole. Speaking at the launch of the Royal Irish Regiment, Lt General Sir John Wilsey lamented the UDR's legacy: 'now the UDR has not sought to be sectarian, one-sided or filled its ranks with Protestants, but that's the way it turned out'.[7]

An indication of just how full these ranks were came from the UDA themselves. In his history of the organisation, Ian S. Wood says that 'A 1984 issue of *Ulster* listed with pride the number of UDA life sentence prisoners in the Maze [Prison, outside Belfast] who had records of service with the security forces. Of the forty-one "lifers" [serving life sentences] in this article, nine, it was claimed, had served in the regular army, five in the UDR, six in the Territorial Army and four in the RUC'. Twenty-four out of forty-one UDA 'lifers' came from the security forces, five from the UDR.[8]

The problem was baked into the regiment upon its formation. The UDR was always presented as a legitimate element of the British army but it only ever operated in Northern Ireland. In addition, its battalions – organised on a local level, according to county (closely aligned to the old B Special companies) – were populated by men and women recruited locally, from within their own communities, with all the attendant benefits that brought to the army and hazards it brought to the UDR personnel. However, all senior officers came from the regular army – never from within the UDR itself. Dr Anne Mandeville, of the Faculty of Law and Political

Science at Toulouse University, has captured precisely the problems inherent in all of this – what she called 'the birth defects' of the UDR:

> The British government therefore created, although the expression in itself is rather paradoxical, a militia regiment ... [There is] a sort of curious paradox: a militia force is dissolved in general opprobrium. What do we choose to succeed it? Another militia force. In the sectarian context, this decision was to have fundamental consequences in terms of the political identity of the new force ...
>
> [It was at] the same time presented as an arm of the State but deeply in solidarity with the Protestant community, 'integrated' into the British army but separated from it organically, geographically and by its 'specificity', the UDR is a kind of monster.[9]

This was a monster of which the British military top ranks themselves were afraid. And why not? It could not be expected to be loyal to the Crown – it was arguably only ever loyal to a version of 'Ulster' – and up to 15 per cent of UDR personnel, according to British army estimates made in August 1973, were also likely members of armed loyalist organisations.[10] The odds were such that, if seven UDR colleagues were sitting together in a canteen, one of them was a loyalist extremist connected to a paramilitary group.

A March 1974 British army briefing document from DS7 at the MoD suggests the unease this provoked:

> If as seems likely [these numbers] disclose only the tip of an iceberg, they serve to remind us that the UDR is inevitably subject to the same strains as the rest of

the civil population in Northern Ireland, and that in a show-down the value of the Force against militant Protestants might be very limited.[11]

And yet we know, via the Tuzo plan, that the British army not only tolerated but also courted militant loyalists as a tool in its war in Northern Ireland. Recent remarks in a different context by General Nick Carter – who retired in 2021 as head of the British armed forces – are instructive in British military pragmatism regarding its choice of allies. Shortly after the Taliban had retaken Afghanistan, expelling NATO forces from the country in 2021, Carter described the Taliban as 'country boys' who had 'honour at the heart of what they do'.[12] Is that what the British thought of loyalist killers in the ranks of the UDR, too?

In the preceding pages we have shown that, from the very outset, London knew the UDR was bound to attract active loyalist recruits but pressed ahead to form the regiment anyway. One of its functions was to 'channel ... Protestant energies that might otherwise become disruptive'. In 1986, in an internal FCO memo, a senior official asserted that while some would like to disband the UDR, 'the MoD finds this part-time local militia essential for financial and manpower reasons'.[13] Thanks to a dysfunctional screening process for applicants, it was inevitable that this militia force would be vulnerable to penetration by loyalist paramilitaries and to 'subversion'.

As a result, the UDR functioned as a facility for loyalist groups within which paramilitaries had access to military training and equipment. Aside from the large amount of UDR weaponry entrusted to the personal care of UDR personnel in their homes, where it was available to any UDR member who doubled as a paramilitary targeting Catholic civilians, there was also a steady traffic of weaponry and intelligence data from UDR personnel and bases into the waiting arms of loyalist paramilitary groups.

This weaponry and intelligence was used repeatedly to kill Catholic civilians. In addition, Whitehall, the NIO, and the MoD knew there was collusion both in weapons thefts and in murderous attacks. Combating such collusion was never a priority, and so many people lost their lives. The British knew that the UDR was fatally penetrated by loyalist paramilitaries, with whom they had formed a tactical alliance to defeat the IRA. The decision to set up full time battalions of the UDR was made at the specific request of loyalist paramilitaries. At the same time, the British feared that the UDR could readily prove disloyal and turn their guns on British officers. They distrusted the regiment to the extent that there was a policy whereby only *regular* British soldiers could be in command. Despite such precautions, there was a disproportionate rate of criminality within the heavily-armed ranks of the UDR. This was so damaging as to require a policy of erasing the UDR membership of personnel appearing before the courts.

For the NIO, the MoD and Whitehall the priority was defeating the IRA, which meant turning a blind eye to loyalist violence. While the UDR's history is promoted as a noble tradition of defending the community, in the eyes of many in the Catholic, nationalist or republican communities, the priority for the UDR was maintaining the dominant position of the unionist community. For many people, the UDR was simply the B Specials with better weapons. What Michael Farrell once wrote of the B Specials could equally have been written about the UDR:

> the local security forces were ... as tainted by involve-
> ment in harsh repressive policies and association with

loyalist paramilitary groups as they had been in 1922, and they were as deeply distrusted by the Catholic minority as they had been then. The conclusion seemed clear that it was not so much the personnel of these forces who were at fault – they were, after all, the products and indeed, the victims of the situation in the North ... It was the attempt to establish and maintain a separate sectarian-defined state in the North of Ireland, in opposition to the wishes of the majority in the rest of the country and of a very substantial minority in the North itself, which was at the root of the problem.'[14]

Our assertions in these pages are made on the basis of evidence from declassified official files. Staff and volunteers at the Pat Finucane Centre and Justice for the Forgotten have spent years trawling through such files. On many occasions, documents have been found that unlocked closely guarded state secrets about the British 'dirty war' in Ireland. These have provided the basis for ground-breaking books such as *A State in Denial* (Margaret Urwin's exposé of the extent of the British government's collaboration with loyalist death squads), *Fermanagh: From Plantation to Peace Process* (Urwin's comprehensive history of County Fermanagh, including detailed analysis of all conflict-related deaths in the county) and *Lethal Allies* (Anne Cadwallader's body of evidence, which proved the role of British security forces in the Glenanne Gang's litany of killings in mid-Ulster), as well as the award-winning film *Unquiet Graves*, which also explored the murderous trail of the Glenanne Gang.

The work of exploring declassified files is ongoing, yet it is constantly met with opposition and obstruction. Many relevant files remain closed. It is an indictment of British security policy that important files remain inaccessible, including in the cruellest of circumstances. Files on two children killed with plastic bullets in the 1980s, Paul Whitters and Julie Livingstone, are to remain closed for decades (until 2059 and 2064, respectively). By then, of course, anyone who actually knew Paul or Julie will likely be dead.

It is a fact that when important documents have been found among declassified files, and the facts among them publicised by campaigners and victims' families, many have been swiftly 'reclassified' to prevent further exposure. Decisions to do so are taken by the National Archives 'Reclosure Panel', which removes any file that has been requested by a government department and considers whether or not it should remain at the National Archives. According to Ian Cobain in *The History Thieves*, 'it usually complies with the government department's request'.[15] Another body, the 'Takedown Panel' applies the same principles to official websites containing material from The National Archives.[16]

In *The History Thieves*, Ian Cobain lays out in meticulous detail the British government's policy of extreme secrecy, which has 'gone far beyond that which is required for the safe and secure business of government'.[17] Cobain quoted the former cabinet minister Richard Crossman, who observed in 1971 that 'secretiveness is the real English disease and in particular the chronic ailment of British government ... One result of this secrecy is to make the British electorate feel it is being deliberately kept in the dark and increasingly to suspect the very worst of its rulers; another is to ensure that the House of Commons is the worst informed legislature in the world.'[18]

In the colonial British genocide of the Kikuyu people (who the British called 'Mau Mau') in Kenya, official papers show that the colonial Attorney General, Eric Griffith-Jones, described the torture of Kikuyu detainees as 'distressingly reminiscent of conditions in Nazi Germany'. Nevertheless, in an official memo, the same man – a Queen's counsel – advised the British colonial governor in Kenya, 'If we are going to sin, we must sin quietly.'[19]

Indeed, such was the brutality of this quiet sinning that none other than notorious racist Tory MP Enoch Powell (who, we recall, would later undertake 'patrols' with the UDR) was moved to declare that a nation that behaved in this manner did not deserve an empire.[20] And yet it took a legal case brought by survivors of the genocide against the Kikuyu to uncover the truth of British colonial rule in Kenya. This was because of Operation Legacy, Britain's concealment or actual destruction of its colonial records – what Cobain calls 'an extraordinarily ambitious act of history theft, one that spanned the globe … intended to erase all trace of the darker deeds of Britain's colonial enterprise'.[21]

Anyone familiar with the conflict on the island of Ireland will find echoes of our recent past here. John Stevens has described how he became aware of undisclosed documents after conducting three inquiries into allegations of security force collusion with loyalist paramilitaries. He is on record as stating that though his team had accessed 'something like a million documents – tons and tons of paper … there was a large cache of intelligence and documentation elsewhere in Derbyshire which we had never seen. No one has ever told us about it.'[22] In 2013 *The Guardian* revealed that the MoD was holding an enormous cache of over 66,000 files at a depot at Swadlincote in England. The files should, by law, have been declassified and transferred to the National Archive under the thirty-year rule. This cache included documents about the conflict here:

> The hidden archive includes what is described as 'hundreds and hundreds of boxes', each containing

about 10 files, that were sent to the warehouse when the British army's Northern Ireland headquarters closed four years ago. One MoD archivist describes it as looking like 'the final scene from Raiders of the Lost Ark', in which box after box can be seen stretching into the distance.[23]

It is as imperative for the truth about British policy in Ireland to emerge as it has been for the evils of colonialism to be revealed around the world. It has been the same counter-insurgency policies in action, much as it has frequently been the same colonial personnel putting these polices to work.

For this work, in addition to acknowledging all these problems, it is important to note the context in which this present work was written. In July 2021, Brandon Lewis, the British secretary of state for Northern Ireland, set out controversial proposals for dealing with the legacy of the conflict in Northern Ireland. Crucially, these proposals included a statute of limitations that would end the prosecution of any Troubles-related offences. This was an unprecedented intervention in the criminal justice system and the policing arrangements that were central to the Good Friday Agreement.

It proposed an end to all inquests into killings that have been ordered by the Attorney General of Northern Ireland; all investigations by the Police Ombudsman for Northern Ireland, even those where 'grave and exceptional' new evidence of police misconduct has emerged; all civil actions being pursued through the courts by families seeking disclosure from the Ministry of Defence, and others, on evidence of collusion between state forces and paramilitaries; and all investigations being conducted by the Legacy Investigation Branch of the PSNI, which considers historical cases of killings.[24]

The proposals united legacy practitioners and victims and survivors of the conflict from across the spectrum in opposition. A former senior military legal advisor Lieutenant Colonel Nicholas Mercer said there was 'an overwhelming political, legal and moral case for abandoning this proposed amnesty'.[25]

A gathering of UDR veterans and families of UDR personnel killed in the conflict convened in October 2021 to outline their opposition to the plans. One UDR veteran said the proposals 'stabbed victims in the back'. A relative of a UDR man killed by the IRA called the proposals 'immoral and wrong'. The *Tyrone Courier*'s front-page coverage of the meeting had the headline 'United & Disgusted Relatives [UDR]'.[26]

What was apparent to many observers was that the British government's decision to end Troubles-era prosecutions was entirely motivated by ensuring that the brutal truth about the state's role in the conflict never sees the light of day. A joint statement from leading legal academics and human rights groups compared the plans to an amnesty declared by murderous Chilean dictator Augusto Pinochet and said that the proposals appeared 'designed to obscure and obfuscate truth recovery and access to justice'.[27]

The denial of access to history is a part of a continuum of British state efforts to obscure its colonial past – 'to protect the reputation of the British state of generations earlier, concealing and manipulating history – sculpting an official narrative – in a manner more associated with a dictatorship than with a mature and confident democracy'.[28] Ian Cobain reasons that 'as long as public administration in Britain remains such a private affair, hidden carefully from view, we may misunderstand such fundamental matters as our reasons for going to war, our relationship with foreign states and peoples, *and the way that justice has been pursued at home and abroad* [emphasis added]'.[29]

The key point in all of this is that material contained in files retained by the British government, and especially the Ministry of Defence, are crucial to any attempts to uncover the truth of the conflict in Ireland.

Here is a selection of National Archive files which we know to exist on the UDR, some of which are closed until the late 2060s, and as late as 2075:

- DEFE 70/11 UDR: Vetting Feb–Nov 70
- WO 305/4818 1st (Co. Antrim) Battalion, UDR Apl 70–Dec 82
- WO305/4819 3rd (Co. Down) Battalion, UDR Apl 70–Dec. 82
- WO 305/4820 4th (Co. Fermanagh) Battalion, UDR Apl 70–Mar 80
- WO 305/4821 5th (Co. Londonderry) Battalion, UDR Apl 70–Dec 83
- WO 305/4822 8th (Co. Tyrone) Battalion, Dec 71–Dec 83
- WO 305/4823 9th (Co. Antrim) Battalion, UDR Dec 71–Dec 83
- WO 305/4417 10th (City of Belfast) Battalion, UDR Jan 72–Dec 74
- WO 305/5193 10th (City of Belfast) Battalion, UDR Jan 75–Sept 79
- WO 305/4824 11th (Craigavon) Battalion, UDR Jan 81–Mar 84
- WO 305/5433 39th Field Regiment, Royal Artillery/4th Battalion UDR Jan–March 1981
- WO 305/6951 4th/6th (Co. Fermanagh and Co. Tyrone) Battalion, April 1991–Mar 92

Some of those who were bereaved in the conflict want those culpable for the deaths of their loved ones and still alive, or those who bear corporate responsibility for those deaths, to be held accountable through the courts. Others just want an honest acknowledgement by the British state, by republicans, and by loyalists, of their role in the conflict – and acceptance of the hurt that was caused.

Without access to either legal remedies or the repository of secret documents retained by the British government, any attempts towards truth recovery in the context of the conflict are indeed difficult but by no means impossible. Families and campaigners have no intention of giving up.

ENDNOTES

Preface

1   Ken Wharton, *A Long Long War: Voices from the British Army in Northern Ireland 1969–1998* (Solihull: Helion & Company, 2008), pp. 187–9.

Introduction – 'Narrowing the Permissible Lies'

1   'Former Blaenau Gwent Soldier Publishes Book on Experience during Northern Ireland Troubles', *South Wales Argus*, 20 August 2015.
2   Margaret Urwin, *A State in Denial: British Collaboration with Loyalist Paramilitaries* (Cork: Mercier, 2016), p. 286.
3   Aaron Edwards 'Misapplying lessons learned? Analysing the utility of British counterinsurgency strategy in Northern Ireland, 1971–76', *Small Wars & Insurgencies*, 21:2 (2010), p. 304.
4   PRONI, CAB/9/G/89/3, Formation of the Ulster Defence Regiment, November 1969.
5   David McKittrick, Seamus Kelters, Brian Feeney and Chris Thornton, *Lost Lives* (Edinburgh: Mainstream Publishing Company Ltd, 2001), p. 609.
6   Speech by The Queen to the Royal Irish Regiment, Northern Ireland, 2006.
7   'Public statement by the Police Ombudsman pursuant to Section 62 of the Police (Northern Ireland) Act 1988 relating to: Investigation into police handling of certain loyalist paramilitary murders and attempted murders in the north west of Northern Ireland during the period 1989 to 1993', 14 January 2022.
8   Ibid.
9   Chris Ryder, *The Ulster Defence Regiment: An Instrument of Peace* (New edition; London: Mandarin, 1992), p. xvi.
10 John Potter, *A Testimony to Courage: The Regimental History of the Ulster Defence Regiment 1969–1992: The History of the Ulster Defence Regiment 1969–1992* (London: Pen & Sword Books Ltd, 2001).
11 Michael Ignatieff, 'Articles of faith', *Index on Censorship* 25, 5 (1996), p. 113. Thanks to Pádraig Ó Muirigh who first introduced this phrase to me.

Chapter One – 'A Dangerous Species of Ally'

1 Birte Heidemann 'From Postcolonial to Post-Agreement: Theorising Northern Ireland's Negative Liminality' in *Post-Agreement Northern Irish Literature. New Directions in Irish and Irish American Literature* (Palgrave Macmillan, Cham., 2016), p. 17.

2 David Killingray, 'The Idea of a British Imperial African Army', *The Journal of African History* 20, no. 3, 1979, p. 422.

3 Heather J. Sharkey, 'African Colonial States', in John Parker and Richard Reid (eds), *The Oxford Handbook of Modern African History* (Oxford: Oxford University Press, 2013), p. 158.

4 Ibid.

5 Graham Ellison and Jim Smyth, *The Crowned Harp: Policing Northern Ireland* (London: Pluto Press, 2000), p. 10.

6 The Orange Order is a Protestant-only secret society, 'committed to the protection of the principles of the Protestant Reformation and the Glorious Revolution of 1688', which is extremely influential within hard-line political unionism. Their often-intransigent insistence on their right to conduct triumphalist parades across the north has frequently led to powder keg situations in the volatile politics of the area.

7 Allan F. Blackstock, '"A Dangerous Species of Ally": Orangeism and the Irish Yeomanry', *Irish Historical Studies* 30, no. 119, May 1997, p. 405.

8 Ibid., p. 403.

9 Ellison and Smyth, *The Crowned Harp*, p. 10.

10 Blackstock, '"A Dangerous Species of Ally"', p. 405.

11 Ibid.

12 A militia founded in 1912 to oppose, violently if necessary, any moves towards Irish 'Home Rule'. In April 1914 the UVF armed themselves with thousands of guns smuggled into the north of Ireland. Many subsequently served in the British army on the Western Front of the First World War.

13 Ryder, *The Ulster Defence Regiment*, p. 6.

14 Ibid., p. 8.

15 Ibid., p. 9.

16 A 1936 report of the Commission of the National Council of Civil Liberties commented, 'In practice membership of the "B" Specials is confined to members professing the Protestant faith who are also members of the Orange Order – that is, supporters of the Unionist Party.' See Ellison and Smyth, *The Crowned Harp*, p. 11.

17 Ryder, *The Ulster Defence Regiment*, pp. 9–10.

18 Tim Wilson, '"The Most Terrible Assassination That Has Yet Stained the Name of Belfast": The McMahon Murders in Context', *Irish Historical Studies* 37, no. 145, 2010, p. 84.

19 Éamon Phoenix, 'New Light Shed on Stormont's "X" Files', *History Ireland*, no. 4 (Winter 1996).

20   Anne Cadwallader, *Lethal Allies: British Collusion in Ireland* (Mercier: Cork, 2013).

21   Robert Lynch, *The Northern IRA and the Early Years of Partition* (Dublin: Irish Academic Press, 2006), p. 122.

22   Patrick J. Gannon, 'In the Catacombs of Belfast', *Studies: An Irish Quarterly Review* 11, no. 42, June 1922, p. 285.

23   Ibid., p. 291.

24   Kate Holmquist, 'Forgotten Refugees in Their Own Country', *The Irish Times*, 4 May 2005; 'Seeking Refuge 1971', RTÉ broadcast, 13 August 1971.

25   Baron Scarman, 'Violence and Civil Disturbances in Northern Ireland in 1969: Report of Tribunal of Inquiry (Vol. 566)', HM Stationery Office (1972).

26   Ellison and Smyth, *The Crowned Harp*, p. 64.

27   Ibid., p. 59.

28   Bowes Egan and Vincent McCormack, *Burntollet* (London: LRS Publishers, 1969), p. 56.

29   Ryder, *The Ulster Defence Regiment*, p. 24.

30   Egan and McCormack, *Burntollet*, p. 60.

31   Ronald Weitzer, 'Policing a Divided Society: Obstacles to Normalization in Northern Ireland', *Social Problems* 33, no. 1, 1985, p. 43.

32   PRONI, CAB/4/1461, Conclusions of a Meeting of the Cabinet, 15 August 1969.

33   Ibid.

34   NAUK, CJ/3/71 Public Order Royal Ulster Constabulary and Ulster Special Constabulary Correspondence and Papers, 'Belfast', memo dated 18 August 1969.

35   William Beattie Smith, *The British State and the Northern Ireland Crisis, 1969–73: From Violence to Power-sharing* (Washington, D.C.: United States Institute of Peace Press, 2011), p. 70.

36   NAUK, CJ/3/71 Public Order Royal Ulster Constabulary and Ulster Special Constabulary Correspondence And Papers, Home Office memo dated 18 August 1969, 'Confidential, Northern Ireland, "B Specials": Transactions of 15th and 16th August'.

37   NAUK, CJ/3/71 Public Order Royal Ulster Constabulary and Ulster Special Constabulary Correspondence And Papers, Confidential note by I.M. Burns, Assistant Private Secretary to the Home Secretary, 18 August 1969.

38   Beattie Smith, *The British State and the Northern Ireland Crisis, 1969–73*, p. 70.

39   Ibid.

40   James Callaghan, *A House Divided: The Dilemma of Northern Ireland* (London: HarperCollins, 1973), p. 67.

41   NAUK, CJ/3/57, Minutes of the Hunt Committee: List of Witnesses/ Agenda.

42 Ibid.
43 Ibid.
44 Ibid.
45 Ibid.
46 Ibid.
47 Ibid.
48 NAUK, DEFE 70/7 Ulster Defence Regiment – Reorganisation of B Specials (Sept–Nov 69), 'Future of the "B" Specials', 26 September 1969.
49 Potter, *A Testimony to Courage*, p. 14.
50 BBC News 'On This Day' online, '10 October 1969: Ulster's B Specials to Be Disbanded'.
51 Potter, *A Testimony to Courage,* p. 14.
52 NAI, 2001/43/1392, Letter from Mr Kevin Rush, Minister Plenipotentiary, Embassy of Ireland to Great Britain, to Mr Denis Holmes, Counsellor, Department of External Affairs, Regarding a Forthcoming Meeting with Two Labour MPs, Kevin McNamara and John Ryan, 26 November 1969.

Chapter Two – Formation of the New Force

1 Statement by Minister of State for Defence Administration Roy Hattersley in the House of Commons, 12 November 1969.
2 Ryder, *The Ulster Defence Regiment*, p. 37.
3 Potter, *A Testimony to Courage*, p. 44.
4 Ibid.
5 NAUK, WO305-4819 Commander's Diary 3 Batt UDR 1970–1982, entry for March 1971.
6 Potter, *A Testimony to Courage*, p. 45.
7 NAUK, DEFE 70/7 Ulster Defence Regiment – Reorganisation of B Specials (Sept–Nov 69), Army Board Secretariat confidential note, 'The formation of the new Northern Ireland local defence force', 24 October 1969.
8 Statement by Lord Hunt in the House of Lords, 8 December 1969.
9 NAUK, DEFE 70/7 Ulster Defence Regiment – Reorganisation of B Specials (Sept–Nov 69), 'Army Board – The 82nd Meeting – The Formation of the New Northern Ireland Local Defence Force', 24 October 1969.
10 NAUK, DEFE 70/8 UDR Advisory Council (Nov 69–Feb 70), 'Personal – In Confidence', from A.G. Sterling, Head of AG Secretariat, to D.R. Morris, Civilian Adviser to GOC, 13 February 1970.
11 NAUK, DEFE 70/7 Ulster Defence Regiment – Reorganisation of B Specials (Sept–Nov 69, 'Army Board – The 82nd Meeting – The Formation of the New Northern Ireland Local Defence Force', 24 October 1969.
12 Ryder, *The Ulster Defence Regiment*, p. 37.
13 Ibid.
14 Callaghan, *A House Divided*, pp. 109–10.

15   Statement by Minister of State for Defence Administration Roy Hattersley in the House of Commons, 12 November 1969.

16   Statement by Minister of State for Defence Administration Roy Hattersley in the House of Commons, 11 December 1969.

17   PRONI, CAB/4/1485 Conclusions of a Meeting of the Cabinet Held at Stormont Castle on Tuesday, October 14th, 1969 at 10:30 am.

18   PRONI, CAB/9/G/89/1 UDR Formation. Press release, 15 October 1969.

19   Statement by Bernadette Devlin MP in the House of Commons, 19 November 1969.

20   Potter, *A Testimony to Courage*, p. 21.

21   NAUK, DEFE 70/8 UDR Advisory Council (Nov 69–Feb 70), memo from Head of AG Secretariat, 'Ulster Defence Regiment – Debate', 18 November 1969.

22   Ibid.

23   Ibid.

24   John Manley, 'Anti-Catholic Basil Brooke Speech Was "Public Expression of Unionism's Private View"', *The Irish News*, 3 September 2018.

25   NAUK, DEFE 70/8 UDR Advisory Council (Nov 69–Feb 70), Letter from D.R.E. Hopkins, Home Office, to A.G. Sterling, Head of AG Secretariat (MoD), 'Ulster Defence Regiment Advisory Committee on Recruitment', 24 November 1969.

26   NAUK, DEFE 70/8 UDR Advisory Council (Nov 69–Feb 70), memo from AUS (GS), 'Ulster Defence Regiment – Advisory Committee', 1 December 1969.

27   *The Belfast Gazette*, No. 2968, 11 January 1974, p. 13.

28   Harry Bradbeer (dir.), *Enola Holmes* (Netflix, Legendary Entertainment, PCMA Productions, 2020).

29   NAUK, DEFE 70/8 UDR Advisory Council (Nov 69–Feb 70), memo from PS/Min (A) to APS/Secretary of State, 'Ulster Defence Regiment Advisory Council', 21 November 1969.

30   NAUK, DEFE 70/8 UDR Advisory Council (Nov 69–Feb 70), memo from AUS (GS), 'Ulster Defence Regiment – Advisory Committee', 1 December 1969.

31   Henry Patterson, 'The British State and the Rise of the IRA, 1969–71: The View from the Conway Hotel', *Irish Political Studies* 23, no. 4, 1 December 2008, p. 497.

32   Ibid.

33   NAUK, DEFE 70/8 UDR Advisory Council (Nov 69–Feb 70), Letter from J.F. Mayne, APS / Secretary of State, to PS / Minister (A), 'Ulster Defence Regiment Advisory Council', 4 December 1969.

34   NAUK, DEFE 70/8 UDR Advisory Council (Nov 69–Feb 70), Letter from F.G. Guckian to Denis Healey MP, Ministry of Defence, 8 December 1969.

35 NAUK, DEFE 70/8 UDR Advisory Council (Nov 69–Feb 70), Letter from J.F. Mayne, APS / Secretary of State, to MA / CGS, 'Northern Ireland', 10 December 1969.

36 NAUK, DEFE 70/8 UDR Advisory Council (Nov 69–Feb 70), Letter from MA [Military Assistant] to the CGS to APS / Secretary of State, 'Mr. Guckian', 11 December 1969.

37 NAUK, DEFE 70/8 UDR Advisory Council (Nov 69–Feb 70), Letter from PS/Min (A) to Head of AG Secretariat, 'Ulster Defence Regiment Advisory Council', 23 December 1969.

38 NAUK, DEFE 70/8 UDR Advisory Council (Nov 69–Feb 70), memo from Head of AG Secretariat, 'Ulster Defence Regiment – Debate', 18 November 1969.

39 Ibid.

40 NAUK, memo by F.G. Guckian, 'Thoughts on the proposed rapid build-up of the UDR', 10 September 1971 (copy on file with PFC).

41 Ibid.

42 NAUK, Ministry of Defence Telex to Home Office Summarising Meeting between the Two Prime Ministers, 7 September 1971 (copy on file with PFC).

43 NAUK, memo by F.G. Guckian, 'Thoughts on the proposed rapid build-up of the UDR', 10 September 1971 (copy on file with PFC).

44 Ibid.

45 PRONI, CAB/9/G/89/1, 'Draft White Paper on the Proposed Defence Force', n.d.

46 Gearóid Ó Faoleán, 'The Ulster Defence Regiment and the Question of Catholic Recruitment, 1970–1972', *Terrorism and Political Violence* 27, no. 5, 20 October 2015, pp. 843–4.

47 Michael Farrell, *Arming the Protestants: The Formation of the Ulster Special Constabulary and the Royal Ulster Constabulary, 1920–7* (London: Pluto Press, 1983), p. 290.

48 Callaghan, *A House Divided*, p. 132.

49 Sean MacStiofain, *Revolutionary in Ireland* (G. Cremonesi, 1975), pp. 207–8.

50 Ó Faoleán, 'The Ulster Defence Regiment and the Question of Catholic Recruitment, 1970–1972', p. 844.

51 Ibid.

52 Potter, *A Testimony to Courage,* p. 56.

53 Ryder, *The Ulster Defence Regiment*, p. 47.

54 NAI, 2001/43/1392, Note by B. Ó Móráin, 'Third Secretary, Department of External Affairs, Regarding Enrolment in the Ulster Defence Regiment, 3 November 1970.'

55 NAUK, Minutes of 34th Meeting of the UDR Advisory Council, 12 August 1972 (copy on file with PFC).

56 Ryder, *The Ulster Defence Regiment*, p. 46.

57 Potter, *A Testimony to Courage*, p. 60.

58 Ibid.

59 Ó Faoleán, 'The Ulster Defence Regiment and the Question of Catholic Recruitment, 1970–1972', p. 847.

60 McKittrick et al., *Lost Lives*, p. 1494.

61 Potter, *A Testimony to Courage*, p. 60.

62 Ibid. p. 57.

63 Ibid.

64 Ó Faoleán, 'The Ulster Defence Regiment and the Question of Catholic Recruitment, 1970–1972', p. 845.

65 NAUK, CJ 4/5524 Future Organisation of the UDR (1984–85).

66 Potter, *A Testimony to Courage*, pp. 62–3.

67 Ó Faoleán, 'The Ulster Defence Regiment and the Question of Catholic Recruitment, 1970–1972', p. 846.

68 NAUK, Minutes of 34th Meeting of the UDR Advisory Council, 12 August 1972 (copy on file with PFC).

Chapter Three – Citizens of Good Character?

1 PRONI, CAB/9/G/89/3 'Formation of the Ulster Defence Regiment (November 1969), p. 4.

2 Statement by Emanuel Shinwell MP in the House of Commons, 19 November 1969.

3 Potter, *A Testimony to Courage*, p. 26.

4 Statement by Kevin McNamara MP in the House of Commons, 19 November 1969.

5 NAUK, DEFE 24/835, 'Subversion in the UDR', from Director of Security (Army) to BGS(Int); DMO; Head of DS7; Head of DS10 and MA/DCDS I, 20 August 1973.

6 NAUK, DEFE 24/875, memo from David Simmons, US of S (Army) to Lt Col. Bowser, '2 UDR – Members Alleged Criminal Records', 15 May 1974.

7 NAUK, DEFE 24/875, memo from A.W. Stephens, Head of DS10 to Head of DS7, 'Vetting of UDR Applicants', 15 July 1974.

8 The British government has a long-standing, and internationally-binding, legal obligation, agreed between the British and Irish governments following a review by Canadian Judge Peter Cory, to conduct a public inquiry into the murder of Pat Finucane. In place of this, in 2011 the British appointed Desmond de Silva to conduct a review of the case, an evasion of responsibility which the Finucane family described as 'insulting and a farce'. De Silva published his review in 2012 and his conclusions led then Prime Minister David Cameron to apologise for 'frankly shocking levels of collusion'. De Silva shone a light on the role played by the British

state in a very dirty war but ultimately it fell far short of the full-scale independent public inquiry to which the government committed and to which the family is entitled. For a comprehensive analysis of the de Silva review see 'Shining a light on deadly informers: The de Silva report on the murder of Pat Finucane' by Paddy Hillyard and Margaret Urwin, Statewatch, 2 August 2013.

9   Desmond de Silva QC, *The Report of the Patrick Finucane Review*, para. 11.61.

10   Potter, *A Testimony to Courage*, p. 26.

11   Beattie Smith, *The British State and the Northern Ireland Crisis, 1969–73*, p. 257.

12   NAUK, Minutes of the 32nd Meeting of the Advisory Council Held on Monday, 12 June 1972 at 4.00 pm (copy on file with PFC).

13   NAUK, memo from D.L. Ormerod, Commander UDR, 'UDR involvement in UDA', 24 July 1972 (copy on file with PFC).

14   Ibid.

15   'UDRms', *Fortnight*, no. 47 (Fortnight Publications Ltd), 5 October 1972, p. 4.

16   Joe Baker / Glenravel Local History Project, *The Troubles – A Chronology of the Northern Ireland Conflict*, Issue 18, November/December 1972, p. 11.

17   Steve Bruce, *The Red Hand: Protestant Paramilitaries in Northern Ireland* (Oxford: Oxford Paperbacks, 1992), p. 271.

18   Ibid.

19   Ibid., p. 272.

20   Ibid.

21   NAUK, Letter from Lt Col. J.L. Pownall OBE, Ag Secretariat MoD to J.F. Howe, Civil Advisor to the GOC at HQNI Subject Re UDR-UDA Membership, 17 July 1972 (copy on file with PFC).

22   Ibid.

23   Ibid.

24   NAUK, Letter from J.F. Howe, Civil Advisor to the GOC at HQNI to Lt Col. J.L. Pownall OBE, Ag Secretariat MoD Subject Re UDR – Membership of UDA, 31 July 1972 (copy on file with PFC).

25   According to *Lost Lives* (McKittrick et al., 1999), between 1 July 1972 and 31 August 1972 loyalists were responsible for twenty-nine deaths: nineteen in July and ten in August.

26   NAUK, Letter and Accompanying Report from J.B. Bourne to PS (Private Secretary)/Secretary of State, Reference 'Sectarian Assassinations', 23 May 1975 (copy on file with PFC).

27   NAUK, Development of the Ulster Defence Regiment, Confidential Letter from Headquarters Northern Ireland to Ministry of Defence, 12 June 1972 (copy on file with PFC).

28   NAUK, Letter from J.F. Howe, Civil Advisor to the GOC at HQNI, to

Lt Col. J.L. Pownall OBE, Ag Secretariat MoD, 'UDR – Membership of UDA', 31 July 1972 (copy on file with PFC).

29 NAUK, PREM 15/1016, Confidential letter from R.A. Custis, MoD, 29 November 1972 (copy on file with PFC).

30 NAUK, Letter from J.F. Howe, Civil Advisor to the GOC, to PS/ US of S (Army), 'UDR Duties', 2 June 1972 (copy on file with PFC).

31 NAUK, Letter from K.C. MacDonald, Head of Defence Secretariat 7 (MoD) to J.F. Howe, Civil Advisor to the GOC, 'UDR Duties', 21 June 1972 (copy on file with PFC).

32 'Northern Ireland: The Women and the Gunmen', *Time Magazine*, 17 April 1972.

33 NAUK, CJ 4/838, 'Security Forces and UDA', 23 November 1972.

34 NAUK, FCO 87/354, Note of a Meeting at the Northern Ireland Office, Wednesday, 13 November 1974 (copy on file with PFC).

35 NAUK, A Guide to Paramilitary and Associated Organisations, 2 September 1976 (copy on file with PFC).

36 NAUK, CJ 4/266, Draft Paper by General Officer Commanding Northern Ireland [GOC NI], 'Military Operations in the Event of a Renewed IRA Campaign of Violence', 9 July 1972.

37 Ibid.

38 Ibid.

39 Beattie Smith, *The British State and the Northern Ireland Crisis, 1969–73*, p. 258.

40 NAUK, FCO 87/3237 Security in NI (1990), 'Informal Security Discussion – Security Strategic Issues', 18 May 1990s.

41 NAUK, FCO 87/3237 Security in NI (1990), Letter from Peter Brooke (SoS, NI) to Tom King (SoS, Defence) 'Security Force Operations in Northern Ireland', 6 July 1990.

42 Ian S. Wood, *Crimes of Loyalty: A History of the UDA* (Edinburgh: Edinburgh University Press, 2006), p. 108.

43 NAUK, WO305-4746 – File discovered in UK National Archives by Papertrail.pro and shared with the author.

44 NAUK, WO305-4217 Commander's Diary of 3 Infantry Brigade (1 Sept – 30 1973), 'Police Division G – Secret Annex', p. 7, n.d.

45 Ryder, *The Ulster Defence Regiment*, p. 97.

46 Mary Holland, 'Skeletons in the Closet of the UDR', *New Statesman*, April 1980 (copy on file with PFC).

47 Potter, *A Testimony to Courage*, p. 78.

48 Statement by Parliamentary Under-Secretary at the Ministry of Defence Robert Brown MP in the House of Commons, 1 July 1976.

49 Statement by Secretary of State for Northern Ireland Peter Brooke MP in the House of Commons, 17 May 1990.

50 The Historical Enquiries Team was a unit of the Police Service of Northern Ireland (PSNI) established to review all conflict-related deaths.

It was criticised for a lack of independence – it was answerable to the chief constable of the PSNI – and for a partial approach to cases of security force killings. A 2013 review by Her Majesty's Inspectorate of Constabulary (HMIC) found the HET's approach to state involvement cases to be inconsistent with the UK's obligations under Article 2 ECHR. Nevertheless, many bereaved families did engage with the HET, as flawed a process as that was. The HET compiled reports, based mainly on RUC files, that were then given to each family. They sometimes included key information from intelligence sources that helped the PFC/JFF triangulate with other information, discovered independently, to allow us to identify perpetrators.

51 Historical Enquiries Team Review Summary Report concerning the murder of Louis Leonard (copy on file with PFC).
52 Historical Enquiries Team Review Summary Report concerning the murder of John Toland (copy on file with PFC).
53 Historical Enquiries Team Review Summary Report concerning the murders of Brian, John Martin and Anthony Reavey (copy on file with PFC).
54 de Silva, *The Report of the Patrick Finucane Review*, para. 49.
55 Ibid., pp. 253–4.
56 Beattie Smith, *The British State and the Northern Ireland Crisis, 1969–73*, p. 257.
57 Colin Smith, 'Ulster Defence Regiment – Some "Dad's Army" Men Stepping out of Line', *The Observer*, 12 November 1972.

Chapter Four – 'Arming One Section of the Community'

1 NAUK, Minutes of the 32nd Meeting of the Advisory Council Held on Monday, 12 June 1972 at 4.00 pm (copy on file with PFC).
2 NAUK, DEFE 24/822 Ulster Defence Regiment (UDR) – Arms and Armouries – Theft and Loss of Weapons 1972-1975, Loose Minute, 'Northern Ireland Loss of UDR Weapons', from Colonel H.S.L. Dalzell-Payne to PS/US of S (Army), 31 July 1972.
3 NAUK, DEFE 24/822 Ulster Defence Regiment (UDR) – Arms and Armouries – Theft and Loss of Weapons 1972–1975, Loose Minute, 'Northern Ireland Loss of UDR Weapons', from Colonel H.S.L. Dalzell-Payne, to PS/US of S (Army), 19 July 1972 (p. 14/347).
4 NAUK, DEFE 24/822 Ulster Defence Regiment (UDR) – Arms and Armouries – Theft and Loss of Weapons, 1972–1975, Loose Minute from H.S.L. Dalzell-Payne to PS/US of S (Army), 19 July 1972.
5 NAUK, DEFE 24/822 Ulster Defence Regiment (UDR) – Arms and Armouries – Theft and Loss of Weapons 1972–1975, Confidential Background note for reply to PQ 2703A, n.d.
6 NAUK, DEFE 24/822 Ulster Defence Regiment (UDR) – Arms and

Armouries – Theft and Loss of Weapons, 1972–1975, Northern Ireland Losses of UDR Weapons, Loose Minute from F.M.K. Tuck to PS/US of S (Army), 9 August 1972.

7   NAUK, Minutes of 34th Meeting of the UDR Advisory Council, 12 August 1972 (copy on file with PFC).

8   Ibid.

9   'UDRms', *Fortnight*, no. 47 (Fortnight Publications Ltd), 5 October 1972, p. 4.

10 NAUK, DEFE 24/822 Ulster Defence Regiment (UDR) – Arms and Armouries – Theft and Loss of Weapons 1972–1975, memo from APS / US of S (Army), 10 October 1972.

11 NAUK, DEFE 24/822 Ulster Defence Regiment (UDR) – Arms and Armouries – Theft and Loss of Weapons 1972–1975, Reply to APS / US of S (Army) from Col. Dalzell-Payne, 11 October 1972.

12 NAUK, DEFE 24/822 Ulster Defence Regiment (UDR) – Arms and Armouries – Theft and Loss of Weapons 1972–1975, Letter from Nick Evans, Civilian Adviser to the GOC, to Brian McKay, DS7 (MoD), ref: UDR General, 15 March 1973.

13 NAUK, DEFE 24/835 Subversion in the UDR, August 1973.

14 Historical Enquiries Team Review Summary Report concerning the murder of Henry Cunningham (copy on file with PFC).

15 NAUK, DEFE 24/822 Ulster Defence Regiment (UDR) – Arms and Armouries – Theft and Loss of Weapons 1972–1975, memo by Col. H.S.L. Dalzell-Payne, 'Northern Ireland – Raid on TAVR Centre Lurgan', 23 October 1972.

16 NAUK, DEFE 24/822 Ulster Defence Regiment (UDR) – Arms and Armouries – Theft and Loss of Weapons 1972–1975, Letter from Nick Evans, Civilian Adviser to the GOC, to Brian McKay, DS7 (MoD), ref: UDR General, 8 March 1973.

17 NAUK, DEFE 24/822 Ulster Defence Regiment (UDR) – Arms and Armouries – Theft and Loss of Weapons 1972–1975, Memo by Col. C.R. Huxtable, 'Theft of Weapons from UDR Armoury on 23 October 1973', 24 October 1973.

18 Ibid.

19 Ibid.

20 NAUK, DEFE 24/822 Ulster Defence Regiment (UDR) – Arms and Armouries – Theft and Loss of Weapons 1972–1975, Table of weapons losses (copy on file with PFC).

21 Ibid.

22 Ibid.

23 Draft note for PM from SoS re UDR Arms Out Request, 15 June 1972 (copy on file with PFC).

24 NAUK, DEFE 24/822 Ulster Defence Regiment (UDR) – Arms and Armouries – Theft and Loss of Weapons 1972–1975, Note from F.S.

MacDonald, DS7, to PS/US of S (Army), 'UDR Arms', 13 March 1973.

25   Ibid.

26   Ibid.

27   NAUK, DEFE 24/822 Ulster Defence Regiment (UDR) – Arms and Armouries – Theft and Loss of Weapons 1972–1975, Memo from A.P. Cumming-Bruce at DS7, 19 February 1973.

28   NAUK, DEFE 24/822 Ulster Defence Regiment (UDR) – Arms and Armouries – Theft and Loss of Weapons 1972–1975, Draft reply to PQ 3141A, 'Notes for Supplementaries', n.d.

29   NAUK, DEFE 24/822 Ulster Defence Regiment (UDR) – Arms and Armouries – Theft and Loss of Weapons 1972-1975, Letter to NIO from J.F. Howe, Civil Adviser to GOC, 25 September 1972.

30   Ibid.

31   NAUK, DEFE 24/822 Ulster Defence Regiment (UDR) – Arms and Armouries – Theft and Loss of Weapons 1972-1975, Letter to Bernadette Devlin MP, from David Howell (NIO), 20 October 1972.

32   NAUK, DEFE 24/822 Ulster Defence Regiment (UDR) – Arms and Armouries – Theft and Loss of Weapons 1972-1975, Letter from David Simmons, DS10, to J.F. Howe, Civil Advisor to the GOC, 9 January 1973.

33   NAUK, DEFE 24/822 Ulster Defence Regiment (UDR) – Arms and Armouries – Theft and Loss of Weapons 1972-1975, Memo from APS / US of S (Army) to Head of DS10, 28 February 1973.

34   See Cadwallader, *Lethal Allies*.

35   HET report into the death of Denis Mullen (copy on file with the PFC).

36   Cadwallader, *Lethal Allies,* pp. 122.

37   Historical Enquiries Team Review Summary Report concerning the murders of Peter and Jane McKearney (copy on file with the PFC).

38   Ibid.

39   Ibid.

40   Ibid.

41   Ibid.

42   Historical Enquiries Team Review Summary Report concerning the murder of Trevor Brecknell (copy on file with the PFC).

43   Name known to the PFC but cannot be used for legal reasons.

44   Ibid.

45   The breech of every gun leaves its own distinct pattern. Doctoring the breechblock may have been an attempt to obscure ballistic evidence.

46   Historical Enquiries Team Review Summary Report concerning the murders of Brian, John Martin and Anthony Reavey.

47   Ibid.

48   Historical Enquiries Team Review Summary Report concerning the murder of Frederick McLoughlin (copy on file with PFC).

49   Historical Enquiries Team Review Summary Report concerning the murder of Patsy McNeice (copy on file with PFC).

50 Joseph Lutton, recorded in the Historical Enquiries Team Review Summary Report concerning the murder of Frederick McLoughlin.
51 At the time of writing, Beattie had also been found guilty of intimidating the family of one of his victims.
52 'Operation Denton', as it is known, under Boutcher, was set up after four years of legal arguments, culminating in the Appeal Court ordering an analysis of all the 'Glenanne Gang' killings, to be compliant with Article 2 of the European Convention of Human Rights.
53 Historical Enquiries Team Review Summary Report concerning the attack on the Rock Bar (copy on file with PFC).
54 NAI: 2017/10/47 TAOIS – Complaints against RUC (Jan–Apl 1987), Note by David O'Donoghue, 'Loyalist and republican paramilitaries', 10 April 1987.
55 de Silva, 'The Report of the Patrick Finucane Review', para.57

Chapter Five – Subversion in the UDR

1 Urwin, *A State in Denial*, p. 50.
2 NAUK, CJ4/266 Draft Paper by General Officer Commanding Northern Ireland [GOC NI], 'Military Operations in the Event of a Renewed IRA Campaign of Violence', 9 July 1972.
3 The JIC may be familiar to readers who recall its role in compiling the dossier on weapons of mass destruction in Iraq, which was used to justify the war prosecuted by the UK and US against Iraq in 2003.
4 Steven McCaffery, 'UDR the top source of arms "for Protestant extremists"', *The Irish News*, 2 May 2006.
5 NAUK, DEFE 24/835 Subversion in the UDR, August 1973.
6 Ibid.
7 NAUK, DEFE 70/246 Ulster Defence Regiment Advisory Council-Minutes of Meetings 1971–1973, Minutes of the 37th Meeting of the UDR Advisory Council held on Tuesday 28th November 1972 at 4.00pm, p. 5.
8 NAUK, DEFE 70/246 Ulster Defence Regiment Advisory Council-Minutes of Meetings 1971–1973, Minutes of the 38th Meeting of the UDR Advisory Council held on Thursday, 11th January 1973 at 4.00pm, p. 4.
9 NAUK, DEFE 70/246 Ulster Defence Regiment Advisory Council-Minutes of Meetings 1971–1973, Minutes of the 42nd Meeting of the UDR Advisory Council held on Friday, 6th July 1973 at 4.00pm, p. 4.
10 DEFE 70/246 Ulster Defence Regiment Advisory Council-Minutes of Meetings 1971–1973, Minutes of the 40th Meeting of the UDR Advisory Council held on Friday 13th April 1973 at 4.00pm, p. 4.
11 NAUK, DEFE 70/246 Ulster Defence Regiment Advisory Council-Minutes of Meetings 1971–1973, Minutes of the 42nd Meeting of the

UDR Advisory Council held on Friday, 6th July 1973 at 4.00pm, p. 4.

12 Steven McCaffery, 'Former Politician Talks About His Life in the UDA, UDR and the RUC', *The Irish News*, 15 May 2006.

13 According to 'Annex E' of *Subversion in the UDR*, the weapon was also used in a kidnapping, while the 'seven' attempted murders referred to involve drive-by shootings at groups of Catholic youths.

14 NAUK, DEFE 24/835 Subversion in the UDR.

15 'UDI' here stands for a 'Unilateral Declaration of Independence'.

16 The phrase 'perhaps under a Labour government' has been crossed out by a pen-stroke. It is unclear who was responsible, though evidently this was thought too starkly partisan for what is intended to be a dispassionate report.

17 NAUK, DEFE 24/835 Subversion in the UDR.

18 NAUK, DEFE 24/877, Untitled loose memo (copy on file with PFC).

19 NAUK, DEFE 24/877 Op Chantry Reinforcements – Reception and Initial Deployment, 30 November 1973.

20 The IRA had also put in place a contingency plan to take over parts of Belfast in the event of a major escalation of hostilities, which author Martin Dillon also confusingly called 'a doomsday plan' (see Martin Dillon, *The Dirty War*, p. 72). After the army had discovered these IRA plans in a raid on a house in Belfast, it seems the British government made plans to use them in their defence at the European Court of Human Rights (see CJ 4/608 – European Commission on Human Rights – Use of IRA Plot Material), in which the Republic of Ireland had argued the UK had breached the European Convention on Human Rights and Fundamental Freedoms.

21 NAUK, DEFE 13/835, Minute from Head of DS10 (D.E. Johnston) to Assistant Private Secretary to the Secretary of State, 6 October 1975.

Chapter Six – A Question of Loyalty

1 NAUK, Letter from K.C. MacDonald, 'Head of Defence Secretariat 7 (MoD) to J.F. Howe, Civil Advisor to the GOC, UDR Duties', 21 June 1972 (copy on file with PFC).

2 Tim Pat Coogan, *The Troubles: Ireland's Ordeal 1966–1996 and the Search for Peace* (Boulder, Co.: Denver Museum, 1996), p. 154.

3 'Funeral of John Black', *News Letter*, 30 June 1972.

4 Tom Buckley, 'Double Troubles of Northern Ireland – A Visit with the Protestant Militants', *New York Times*, 10 December 1972.

5 NAUK, WO305-4250 P1 – HQ 39th Infantry Brigade (May 1972), Confidential memo, 'INTSUM No. 74 Covering Period 24–30 May 1972', 31 May 1972, p. 6.

6 Urwin, *A State in Denial*, pp. 46–7.

7 Coogan, *The Troubles*, p. 155.

8   McKittrick et al., *Lost Lives*, p. 238.
9   Ken Wharton, *The Bloodiest Year 1972: British Soldiers in Northern Ireland, in Their Own Words* (The History Press, 2011), p. 196.
10 Ibid.
11 Wood, *Crimes of Loyalty*, p. 107.
12 Untitled article, *Fortnight*, No. 49 (2 November 1972).
13 Christopher Sweeney, 'Ulstermen Establish Subversive Group', *The Times*, 15 March 1974.
14 Urwin, *A State in Denial*, p. 112.
15 Merlyn Rees, 'Mistakes Were Made in Security Policy', *Belfast Telegraph*, 11 August 1994.
16 NAUK, CJ 4/1300, Brief for meeting with Messrs Logue, Duffy, O'Donoghue about the UDR, 4.00pm, Monday, 24 June (copy on file with PFC).
17 Ibid.
18 Ibid.
19 Don Anderson, *Fourteen May Days: The Inside Story of the Loyalist Strike of 1974* (Dublin: Gill & Macmillan, 1994), p. 135.
20 Urwin, *A State in Denial*, p. 119.
21 NAUK, FCO 87/342, Note of a Meeting between the Secretary of State and Representatives of the UWC Strike Co-Ordinating Committee Held at Stormont Castle on Wednesday 7 August 1974 (copy on file with PFC). For a useful explanation of the various loyalist factions, the reader might consult Margaret Urwin's *A State In Denial*, or 'A Glossary of Terms Related to the Conflict' hosted by the CAIN Archive. The CAIN Archive is a collection of information and source material on 'the Troubles' and politics in Northern Ireland from 1968 to the present. CAIN is located in Ulster University.
22 NAUK, FCO 87/342, Note of a Meeting between the Secretary of State and Representatives of the UWC Strike Co-Ordinating Committee Held at Stormont Castle on Wednesday, 7 August 1974 (copy on file with PFC).
23 Ibid.
24 NAUK, DEFE 24/1197, Confidential Draft to PS/US of S (Army), Full-Time Element in the Ulster Defence Regiment, 31 October 1974 (copy on file with PFC).
25 NAUK, CJ 4/1300, Restricted Draft Minute From Mr Barker to Mr Chesterton Re: The Ulster Defence Regiment, January 1976 (copy on file with PFC).
26 'UVF Say "Our Boys are in the UDR"', *Sunday News*, 31 August 1975.
27 NAUK, PREM 16/520, Memo 'Mrs. Thatcher's Call on the Prime Minister on 10 September', 11 September 1975.
28 NAI, 2008/79/3059, Northern Ireland – Assessment of Minority's Position in a Breakdown Situation.
29 Ibid.

30 Cadwallader, *Lethal Allies*, p. 117.
31 NAUK, CJ 4/799, Contingency Planning in the Event of an Emergency, Memo from Mr Leach to Mr Abbott, 'The UDR and the Catholic Community', 9 September 1975.
32 Urwin, *A State in Denial*, p. 155.
33 Ibid., p. 164.
34 'A Conversation with Sam Thompson', *Shared Ireland Podcast*, 23 October 2019.

Chapter Seven – The Roadblock Killings

1 John Brewer, Rick Wilford, Adrian Guelke, Ian Hume, and Edward Moxon-Browne, *The Police, Public Order and the State: Policing in Great Britain, Northern Ireland, the Irish Republic, the USA, Israel, South Africa and China* (2nd ed.; London: Palgrave Macmillan UK, 1996), p. 66.
2 Mary Minihan, 'State Papers: INLA Described by Catholic Priests as "Bunch of Lunatics"', *The Irish Times*, 31 December 2015.
3 Urwin, M., *Fermanagh: From Plantation to Peace Process* (Dublin: Wordwell Books, 2021), pp. 169–71; 'Kelly Family Challenges PSNI Investigation'.
4 Pat Fahy, 'Kelly Murder Remains a Dark Stain on Policing and Justice Systems', *Irish News*, 14 November 2018.
5 A registered charity, working closely with human rights and victims' groups that represent families affected by the conflict, helping families access official information from archives.
6 Pat Fahy, 'Kelly Murder Remains a Dark Stain on Policing and Justice Systems', *Irish News*, 14 November 2018.
7 NAUK, FCO 87/3237 Security in NI (1990), note from P.N. Bell, Security Policy and Operations Division (NIO), 'The Minister's Visit to Strabane and Castlederg – 10 April 1990', 11 April 1990.
8 NAI, 2016/52/9 Meeting Between the Taoiseach and the Church of Ireland, 17 January 1986, p. 4.
9 NAUK, CJ 4/1666 Ulster Defence Regiment – Ministerial and Official Visits, Future Role 1976–77, Confidential memo from J.H.G. Leahy to Mr. Stephens, 'Increase in UDR Conrates', 20 December 1976.
10 Ibid.
11 NAUK, CJ 4/6325 Security UDR (1985–86), Letter from A.W. Stephens to Mr Innes, 'UDR and Mr. Mallon', 2 January 1986.
12 NAUK, CJ 4/5522 UDR (1984–85), 'Meeting to discuss the UDR held on 13 February 1985', p. 4.
13 NAUK, loose memo – British Govt Legal Advice on UDA Roadblocks (copy on file with PFC).
14 Urwin, *A State in Denial*, p. 251.

15 NAUK, loose memo – British Govt Legal Advice on UDA Roadblocks (copy on file with PFC).

16 NAUK, DEFE 24/822 Ulster Defence Regiment (UDR) – Arms and Armouries – Theft and Loss of Weapons 1972–1975, NI 13/20/E01(S) 'Miss Bernadette Devlin MP – Questions on the Ulster Defence Regiment'.

17 Urwin, *A State in Denial*, p. 155.

18 Cadwallader, *Lethal Allies,* p. 100.

19 Historical Enquiries Team Review Summary Report concerning the murder of F.J. O'Toole (copy on file with PFC).

20 Ibid.

21 Cadwallader, *Lethal Allies*, p. 101.

22 Ibid., p. 102.

23 NAUK, WO305-4684 – 3rd Infantry Brigade HQ (Aug. 1975), Secret Annex 'Extremist Protestant Activity, 4 August 1975.

24 Cadwallader, *Lethal Allies*, p. 102.

25 Ibid., p. 103.

26 NAUK, CJ 4/1047, Letter to Harding (FCO) from Janes (NIO) on a meeting with Irish Ambassador, 13 August 1975.

27 Ibid.

28 NAUK, FCO 87/423, Memo to Harding (FCO) from Janes (NIO) on a meeting with Irish Ambassador, 12 September 1975.

29 Historical Enquiries Team Review Summary Report concerning the murder of F.J. O'Toole.

30 Ibid.

31 Ibid.

32 Ibid.

33 Cadwallader, *Lethal Allies*, p. 60.

34 Ibid.

35 Historical Enquiries Team Review Summary Report concerning the murder of F.J. O'Toole.

36 Cadwallader, *Lethal Allies*, pp. 36–8.

37 Ibid., p. 158.

38 Martin Doyle, 'A ghost estate and an empty grave: "I don't think Northern Ireland was worth one life"', *The Irish Times*, 1 January 2022.

39 Gerry Moriarty, 'Loyalism's most prolific sectarian killer may have enjoyed indefensible relationship with RUC officers', *The Irish Times*, 25 October 2013.

40 McKittrick et al., *Lost Lives*, p. 398.

41 Justice Henry Barron, *Interim Report on the Report of the Independent Commission of Inquiry into the Dublin and Monaghan Bombings* (Joint Oireachtas Committee on Justice, Equality, Defence and Women's Rights, Dublin, 2003).

42 Historical Enquiries Team Review Summary Report concerning the murder of F.J. O'Toole.

43 Ibid.
44 Ibid.
45 Ibid.
46 Ibid.
47 Freya McClements, 'I was glad to see that it did come out that it was collusion', *The Irish Times*, 20 December 2021.
48 Cadwallader, *Lethal Allies*, p. 112.
49 NAUK, WO305-4684 – 3rd Infantry Brigade HQ (Aug. 1975), Log Sheet, 25 August 1975.
50 Cadwallader, *Lethal Allies*, p. 112.
51 Ibid.
52 Ibid., p. 114.
53 Ibid., p. 115.
54 Ibid., pp. 116–17.
55 Ibid., p. 117.
56 NAUK, PREM 16/520, Secretary of State to Prime Minister, 28 August 1975.

Chapter Eight – Life and Death in the UDR

1   Statement by Under-Secretary of State for Defence Ian Gilmour in the House of Commons, 11 March 1971.
2   Ryder, *The Ulster Defence Regiment*, p. 49.
3   NAUK, 'Development of the Ulster Defence Regiment', Confidential Letter from Headquarters Northern Ireland to Ministry of Defence, 12 June 1972 (copy on file with PFC)'.
4   NAUK, 'UDR Duties', Memo from John Howe, Civil Advisor to GOC Northern Ireland, to the Undersecretary of State (US of S) (Army) and to the UDR Steering Committee, 2 June 1972 (copy on file with PFC).
5   Ryder, *The Ulster Defence Regiment*, p. 49.
6   NAUK, DEFE 13/835, Secret Annex A 'The Ulster Defence Regiment', from AUS (GS) to PS/US of S (ARMY), 19 March 1974 (copy on file with PFC).
7   NAUK, DEFE 13/835, Minute from Vice-Chief of the General Staff to Undersecretary of State (Army), 17 April 1974.
8   Ryder, *The Ulster Defence Regiment*, p. 86.
9   James Dingley, *Combating Terrorism in Northern Ireland* (Abingdon: Routledge, 2009), p. 63.
10 Ó Faoleán, 'The Ulster Defence Regiment and the Question of Catholic Recruitment, 1970–1972', p. 848.
11 NAUK, DEFE 13/835, Minute from Vice-Chief of the General Staff to Undersecretary of State (Army), 17 April 1974.
12 Ibid.
13 NAUK, DEFE 13/835, 'The UDR and Intelligence', Letter from the

Secretary of State for Northern Ireland to the Secretary of State for Defence, 2 October 1974.

14 Peter R. Neumann, 'The Myth of Ulsterization in British Security Policy in Northern Ireland', *Studies in Conflict & Terrorism* 26, no. 5, 1 September 2003, p. 365.

15 Peter Taylor, *Stalker: The Search for the Truth* (London and Boston: Faber & Faber, 1987), p. 30.

16 NAI, 2017/10/47 TAOIS – Complaints against RUC (Jan–April 1987).

17 'Justice in Jeopardy?' Up Close, Ulster Television, 2021 (www.itv.com/utvprogrammes/articles/up-close-justice-in-jeopardy).

18 Faligot, in Neumann, 'The Myth of Ulsterization in British Security Policy in Northern Ireland', p. 366.

19 Ibid.

20 Ellison and Smyth, *The Crowned Harp*, p. 82.

21 McGarry & O'Leary, in Neumann, 'The Myth of Ulsterization in British Security Policy in Northern Ireland', p. 366.

22 Michael Dewar, *The British Army in Northern Ireland* (2nd revised edition; London: Weidenfeld Military, 1996), p. 140.

23 Neumann, 'The Myth of Ulsterization in British Security Policy in Northern Ireland', p. 369.

24 NAUK, DEFE 11/917, 'Situation in Northern Ireland', Confidential annex to Chiefs of Staff Committee meeting, 14 September 1976.

25 Author of *Britain's Long War: British Strategy in the Northern Ireland Conflict, 1969–98* (London: Palgrave Macmillan, 2003), now Professor of Security Studies at King's College London.

26 Neumann, 'The Myth of Ulsterization in British Security Policy in Northern Ireland', p. 369.

27 NAUK, CJ 4/4800 P1, Future Organisation of UDR (1980–83), Letter from Richard Jackson, Civil Adviser to GOC to Frances Elliott, 'NIO – UDR Appraisal', 28 Oct. 1980.

28 Hugo Arnold, 'Crime, Ulsterisation and the Future of the UDR', *Fortnight*, 7 October 1985, p. 4.

29 Ellison and Smyth, *The Crowned Harp*, p. 82.

30 Ryder, *The Ulster Defence Regiment*, pp. 85–6.

31 Ibid., p. 86.

32 NAUK, WO305-4819 Commander's Diary 3 Batt UDR 1970–1982, entry for 18 February 1976.

33 Ibid.

34 Ibid.

35 NAUK, CJ 4/5524 Future Organisation of the UDR (1984–85), Minute by Nicholas Scott for Secretary of State (L&B), 18 January 1985.

36 Ibid.

37 NAUK, CJ 4/5524 Future Organisation of the UDR (1984–85), 'The 1984 Security Review – The Future of the UDR', p. 5.

38 Ryder, *The Ulster Defence Regiment*, pp. 87–8.

39 Urwin, *Fermanagh*, pp. 136–46.

40 Edward Burke, *An Army of Tribes: British Army Cohesion, Deviancy and Murder in Northern Ireland* (Liverpool: Liverpool University Press, 2018), p. 236.

41 Ibid., p. 275.

42 Peter Robinson, *Hands Off The UDR* (Belfast: Democratic Unionist Party, 1990), p. 3.

43 Wharton, *A Long Long War*, pp. 442–3.

44 Joseph S. Robinson, '"We Have Long Memories in This Area": Ulster Defence Regiment Place-Memory along the Irish Border', *Memory Studies*, 27 May 2020, p. 206.

45 Statement by Mervyn Storey MLA in the Northern Ireland Assembly, 24 May 2010, 'Fortieth Anniversary of Disbanding of B-Specials and Formation of UDR'.

46 'Roll of Honour' on the website of the Ulster Defence Regiment Association.

47 Conflict Trauma Resource Centre, 'Legacy of War, Experiences of Members of the Ulster Defence Regiment', report for Veteran Services Northern Ireland, p. 6 (copy on file with PFC).

48 Wharton, *A Long Long War*, pp. 442–3.

49 BBC Northern Ireland, *Legacy: A Collection of Personal Testimonies from People Affected by the Troubles in Northern Ireland* (Belfast: Elucidate Consultancy, 2007), p. 46.

50 Urwin, *Fermanagh*, p. 123–4.

51 Ibid., p. 124.

52 Ibid.

53 Statement by Under-Secretary of State for Defence for the Army, Peter Blaker, to House of Commons, 6 July 1973.

54 Ibid.

55 Ryder, *The Ulster Defence Regiment*, p. 64.

56 Potter, *A Testimony to Courage*, p. 115.

57 Ryder, *The Ulster Defence Regiment*, p. 66.

58 Potter, *A Testimony to Courage*, p. 116.

59 Ibid., p. 117.

60 Ibid., p. 119.

61 Ibid., p. 120.

62 Ryder, *The Ulster Defence Regiment*, p. 75.

63 Wharton, *A Long Long War*, p. 195.

64 Ibid., pp. 298–9.

65 Ryder, *The Ulster Defence Regiment*, p. 63.

66 NAUK, Development of the Ulster Defence Regiment, Confidential Letter from Headquarters Northern Ireland to Ministry of Defence, 12 June 1972 (copy on file with PFC)'.

67   Urwin, *Fermanagh*, p. 202.

68   Ibid.

69   Veteran Services Northern Ireland, 'UDR' (copy on file with PFC).

70   Meath Peace Group Talks: No. 60 – 'The Legacy of War – Experiences of UDR Families', 10 April 2006.

71   Ibid.

72   Ibid.

73   Rebecca Black, 'Trauma of IRA Murder Continues to Haunt Generations of a Family 40 Years Later', *Belfast Telegraph*, 17 January 2021.

74   Ryder, *The Ulster Defence Regiment*, p. 181.

75   Tweet on 14 January 2021 by SEFF – South East Fermanagh Foundation – (@SEFFLisnaskea), 'SEFF Remembers Samuel Millar'. https://twitter.com/SEFFLisnaskea/status/1349865318479503362?s=20

Chapter Nine – Criminality in the UDR

1   Miller, *Rethinking Northern Ireland*, p. 108.

2   'UDRms', *Fortnight*, no. 47 (Fortnight Publications Ltd), 5 October 1972, p. 4.

3   'UDR: Too Many Bad Apples', *Hibernia*, 3 December 1976.

4   Ryder, *The Ulster Defence Regiment*, pp. 181–2.

5   NAUK, DEFE 70/599 Ulster Defence Regiment: Criminal and Security Investigations of 10 UDR, 'Involvement of Members with Paramilitary Organisations'.

6   NAUK, DEFE 70/599, Note by Capt. J.W. Jubb for HQNI, 'Crime/Security 10 UDR', 11 November 1978.

7   Ibid.

8   Ibid.

9   Ibid.

10   NAUK, DEFE 70/599, Note by Capt. J.W. Jubb, for HQNI, 'Security Investigations 10 UDR', 24 February 1978.

11   NAUK, DEFE 70/599, Minutes of a meeting held at HQNI on 24 February 1978 to discuss a defensive press brief on current investigations at 10 UDR, 25 February 1978.

12   Ibid.

13   Ibid.

14   NAUK, DEFE 70/599, Note by Lt Col. J.R.E. Laird, for GOC, to Col. G.G. Strong, Directorate of Security (Army), 'Investigations at 10 UDR Belfast', 27 February 1978.

15   Ibid.

16   Martin Dillon, *The Shankill Butchers: A Case Study of Mass Murder* (new edition; Cornerstone Digital, 2009).

17   BBC Northern Ireland online, 'Shankill Butchers held Belfast in grip of terror', 28 March 2011.

18   NAUK, DEFE 70/599, Memo from Capt. Guthrie to HQNI, 'Crime/ Security – 10 UDR', 7 March 1978.
19   NAUK, CJ 4/1300, Confidential memo from P.T.E. England, Deputy Under-Secretary of State, to Major General D.T. Young, Commander Land Forces (HQNI), 'DUS/11/0572', 5 November 1975.
20   Ibid.
21   NAUK, DEFE 70/599, 'Malpractice within 10 UDR' (signatory unclear), 2 March 1978.
22   NAUK, DEFE 70/599, note from J. Dromgoole, AUS (GS), to APS / S of S, 'UDR Irregularities', 2 March 1978.
23   NAUK, DEFE 70/599, AUS (GS) minute No. 95/78, 2 March 1978.
24   NAUK, DEFE 70/599, loose note (copy on file with PFC).
25   NAUK, DEFE 70/599, 'UDR Irregularities' 11 May 1978.
26   NAUK, DEFE 70/599, note by Capt. Guthrie, for GOC, to Directorate of Security (Army), 'UDR personnel connected with paramilitary organisations – 10 UDR', 14 November 1978.
27   Ibid.
28   NAUK, DEFE 13/835, Minute from Head of DS10 (D.E. Johnston) to Assistant Private Secretary to the Secretary of State, 6 October 1975.
29   NAUK, CJ 4/2530, Confidential note from Buxton to Stephens, 'The Province Reserve UDR Force (PRUDR)', 2 February 1978.
30   Ryder, *The Ulster Defence Regiment*, p. 181.
31   Ibid.
32   Dillon, *The Shankill Butchers*, p. 258.
33   Ryder, *The Ulster Defence Regiment*, p. 183.
34   NAUK, CJ 4/4546 Incidents Involving the UDR (1975–1983), Handwritten note to Walsh (NIO), 22 February 1979.
35   NAUK, CJ 4/4546 Incidents Involving the UDR (1975–1983), Note to Walsh from S.M. Pope, Division 1 (B), 22 February 1979.
36   'UDR's Rotten Apples', *The Phoenix*, 30 March 1984.
37   Ibid.
38   NAUK, 'Criminal Charges Against a Member of the UDR', note from D.B. Omand, DS10, to APS / Secretary of State, PS / US of S (Army), and others, 4 June 1975 (copy on file with PFC).
39   NAUK, CJ 4/7560 Prosecution of Members of the Security Forces in NI (1983–88) (1), note from G.W. Davies, Law and Order Division, 17 June 1987.
40   NAUK, CJ 4/7560 Prosecution of Members of the Security Forces in NI (1983–88) (1), 'Note for the Record' by S.G. Brearley, 11 May 1988.
41   Urwin, *A State in Denial*, p. 195.
42   PRONI, CRCT/3/2/3/506 R v McClelland, McConnell & McConnell, Bill No. 496/81 (copy on file with PFC).
43   Connla Young, 'UDA Killer of Catholic Man in 1980 Was Former Prison Officer', *The Irish News*, 23 August 2016.

44 Anne Cadwallader's *Lethal Allies* is the definitive work on this gang of killers and is a highly recommended read.

45 NAUK, WO305-4218 Commander's Diary, 3rd Infantry Brigade (October 1973), Brigade Log Sheet for 24 October 1973.

46 NAUK, WO305-4212 Commander's Diary, 3rd Infantry Brigade (April 1973), NIREP One 17 April 1973.

47 NAUK, WO305-4212 Commander's Diary, 3rd Infantry Brigade (April 1973), Annex A to HQ 3 INF BDE, 24 April 1973.

48 For an in-depth look at this gang's activities, see Urwin's *Fermanagh*.

49 CJ4/1069, Memo from T.C. Barker to Under-secretary of State for Northern Ireland, 18 May 1976.

50 'Bomb Charge Man in UDR, Court Told', *The Irish Times*, 21 October 1976.

51 NAUK, CJ 4/1304, Memo to PUS from T.C. Barker, 'George Samuel Farrell', 25 May 1976'.

52 NAUK, CJ 4/6791 Involvement of UDR in Serious Crime (1979–87), Minute from Buxton to Stephens, 19 March 1979.

53 NAUK, CJ 4/6791 Involvement of UDR in Serious Crime (1979–87), Letter to Prime Minister by Paschal J. O'Hare, 6 December 1983.

54 NAUK, CJ 4/6791 Involvement of UDR in Serious Crime (1979–87), Letter from P. Coulson, Law and Order Division, to Buxton, on offences committed by UDR members, 4 February 1985.

55 It should be remembered that Mallon drew attention to UDR involvement in the murder of Farmer and McCartney at an early stage.

56 NAUK, CJ 4/5522 UDR (1984–85), Letter from Sadie Johnston, Law & Order Division, to Mr Blackwell, 'Controversial Cases Involving the UDR', 24 January 1985.

57 NAUK, CJ 4/6791 Involvement of UDR in Serious Crime (1979–87), handwritten note on copy of letter from S.G. Brearley to PS / Secretary of State (B&L), 'Mr. Peter Utley', copy dated 21 March 1985.

58 NAUK, CJ 4/6791 Involvement of UDR in Serious Crime (1979–87), Letter from P. Coulson, Law and Order Division, to Buxton, on offences committed by UDR members, 4 February 1985.

59 NAUK, 'CJ 4/5524 Future Organisation of the UDR (1984–85), Letter from Merifield to Coulson, 'Meeting on UDR', 30 January 1985.

60 NAUK, CJ 4/6791 Involvement of UDR in Serious Crime (1979–87), Letter from S.G. Brearley, SIL Division, to Mr Bickham, 'Conviction of Members of the UDR', 5 February 1985.

61 NAUK, CJ 4/6791 Involvement of UDR in Serious Crime (1979–87), Note for the Record by S.G. Brearley, 'Conviction of Members of the Security Forces', 7 March 1985.

62 NAI, 2015/51/1355 'Ulster Defence Regiment', 30 January 1985; NAUK, CJ 4/7560 Prosecution of Members of the Security Forces in NI (1983–88) (1), note from (Miss) S. Johnston, Law & Order Division, to Mr

Dalzell, 'Arrest of Part-Time Member of 2 UDR', 30 June 1987.

63 Monica McWilliams, 'Violence against Women and Political Conflict: The Northern Ireland Experience', *Critical Criminology* 8, no. 1, 1 March 1997, pp. 81–2.

64 NAUK, CJ 4/4546 Incidents Involving the UDR (1975–1983), note from P.W.J. Buxton, to PS / Secretary of State (B), 'Personal Protection Weapons for UDR Members', 21 May 1981.

65 McWilliams, 'Violence against Women and Political Conflict', p. 84.

66 Ibid.

67 NAUK, WO305-4213 3rd Infantry Brigade (May 1973), COMCEN 3 INF BDE, 18 May 1973.

68 Ryan Miller, 'Domestic violence in NI is epidemic', *SCOPE NI*, 13 October 2020.

69 Susan McKay, 'The guns are gone, but misogyny still stalks Northern Ireland', *The Guardian*, 1 December 2021.

70 Private Jimmy Graham was killed while driving a school bus in Derrylin, County Fermanagh, in 1985. As discussed in Chapter Eight, he was the third of three brothers, all part-time UDR members, killed by the IRA.

71 NAUK, CJ 4/5524 Future Organisation of the UDR (1984–85), Letter from MoD to DA Hill, UDR Criminal Offences, 29 March 1985.

72 NAUK, CJ 4/5807 Anglo-Irish Talks UDR & Security Forces (1985), Letter from Alan Goodison, British Embassy, Dublin, to A.D.S. Goodall, Deputy Under-Secretary of State (FCO), 'Involvement of UDR Members in Criminal Activities, Controversial Shootings and Harassment, 1970–1985', 2 August 1985.

73 Ibid.

74 NAUK, CJ 4/5808 Anglo-Irish Talks UDR & Security Forces (1985), Confidential memo from P.W.J. Buxton to Mr. Stephens, 'Involvement of UDR Members in Criminal and Other Activities', 16 August 1985.

75 Ryder, *The Ulster Defence Regiment*, pp. 183–4.

Chapter Ten – 'An Aspiration Unlikely to be Fulfilled'

1 NAUK, PREM 19/80, hand-written note by Prime Minister. 'PM's Notes on NIO', 13 July 1979.

2 NAUK, CJ 4/4545 UDR Admin and Staffing, Letter from P. Coulson (L&O Div) to Mr Brooker, 'UDR Training on the Isle of Man', 16 February 1983.

3 NAUK, CJ 4/5157 – UDR (1982–84), restricted memo from G.D. Fergusson to Mr Hill, 'Visit by UDR Band to USA', 30 January 1984.

4 NAUK, CJ 4/5524 Future Organisation of the UDR (1984–85), Draft discussion paper by P.W.J. Buxton, 'Ulster Defence Regiment', 14 November 1984, p. 3.

5   Éamon Phoenix, 'British Concerned over UDR Credibility', *The Irish Times*, 2 January 2017.

6   NAUK, CJ 4/5157 UDR (1982–84), note by Allan Perceval, CIO at HQNI, 'Sunday Times Possible Article about the Disbandment of the UDR', 15 October 1984.

7   NAUK, CJ 4/5524 Future Organisation of the UDR (1984–85), Confidential memo from Paul Coulson, Law and Order Division to Mr Buxton, 'UDR', 15 November 1984.

8   NAUK, CJ 4/2530, Memo from P.W.J. Buxton, 'Compromise of a UDR Operational Order', 22 May 1978.

9   NAUK, CJ 4/5157 Ulster Defence Regiment: General File, Letter from D.J. Coffey (MoD) to Cabinet Office, 'Proposed Amendment to the House of Commons Disqualification Act', 16 May 1984.

10 NAUK, FCO 87/2353 The Ulster Defence Regiment (UDR), Letter from A.D.S. Goodall (FCO) to A.N. Nicholls (MoD), 'Defence White Paper: The Ulster Defence Regiment', 6 February 1986.

11 NAUK, FCO 87/3237 Security in NI (1990), Confidential note from P.N. Bell, Security Policy and Operations Division, 'Visit to 4 UDR Enniskillen', 14 December 1989.

12 NAUK, CJ 4/3063 Studies into the Future Role of the UDR (1979–80), 'Civil Affairs Report – Prepared for 10th (City of Belfast) Battalion, Ulster Defence Regiment, by Major P.H.S. Newel and Major A.F. Roberts',

13 This was the threatened 'United Unionist Action Council' strike in May 1977, for which all eleven battalions of UDR were placed on one of the longest callouts experienced by the UDR.

14 NAUK, CJ 4/5524 Future Organisation of the UDR (1984–85), 'Note of a meeting held on 12 March to discuss the UDR', 15 March 1985.

15 NAUK, CJ 4/5524 Future Organisation of the UDR, 'Meeting to discuss the UDR held on 13 February 1985', note by J.A. Daniell, Private Secretary, 15 February 1985.

16 NAUK, CJ 4/5807 Anglo-Irish Talks UDR & Security Forces (1985), Secret memo, 'Associated Measures: The UDR', enclosed with letter from N.H. Nicholls (MoD) to Christopher Mallaby, 4 July 1985.

17 NAUK, DEFE 24/3005 UDR – General (1976), 'Memo from W.D. Reeves (Head of DS14) to various', 12 May 1976.

18 Michael Savage, 'Fifty Years on, What Is the Legacy of Enoch Powell's "Rivers of Blood" Speech?', *The Observer*, 15 April 2018.

19 NAUK, WO305-4819 Commander's Diary 3 Batt UDR 1970-1982, entry for 22 September 1977.

20 Ibid., entry for 20 July 1982.

21 Ibid., entry for 10 September 1982.

22 NAUK, CJ 4/6326 UDR General (1985–86), Letter from Tom King, Secretary of State for Northern Ireland, to George Younger, Secretary of State for Defence, 24 April 1986.

23 NAUK, CJ 4/6326 UDR General (1985–86), Letter from Tom King, Secretary of State for Northern Ireland, to George Younger, Secretary of State for Defence, 24 April 1986.

24 Dubbed by sympathisers 'The UDR Four', the men were found guilty on 1 July 1986. In 1991 three of the men were released on appeal after interview notes were found to have been altered by the RUC. However, the conviction of one, Neil Latimer, stood and he spent fourteen years in prison before being released under the Good Friday Agreement.

25 NAUK, CJ 4/5157 UDR (1982–84). Confidential note from Paul Coulson to Mr Brown, 'Loss of Sensitive Documents by an Officer in 10 UDR', 22 October 1982.

26 NAUK, CJ 4/5157 UDR (1982–84). Restricted note by A.R. Brown, Law and Order Division, 11 January 1983, p. 3.

27 NAUK, CJ 4/5522 UDR (1984–85), note by T.C. McKane, civil adviser to the GOC, 'UDR Study Period: 16-17 November 1985', 20 November 1985.

28 Ibid.

29 NAUK, FCO 87/2142 UDR (1985), Briefing note sent by D.A. Hill (NIO) to British Embassy, Dublin, 'UDR: Notes for use by Ministers in answer to questions', 1 May 1985, p. 3.

30 Ibid.

31 Ibid.

32 Mary Holland, 'Skeletons in the Closet of the UDR', *New Statesman*, April 1980.

33 Sinn Féin, *The Ulster Defence Regiment: The Loyalist Militia* (Dublin: Sinn Féin, 1990), p. 18.

34 'Iran's Long Game', BBC Radio Four, 21 April 2020. Producer: Zak Brophy.

35 Rolston, '"An Effective Mask for Terror": Democracy, Death Squads and Northern Ireland', *Crime, Law and Social Change*, vol. 44, iss. 2, p. 198.

36 Ibid., p. 185.

37 Ibid., p. 186.

38 Ibid., p. 191.

39 Huw Bennett, '"Smoke Without Fire"? Allegations Against the British Army in Northern Ireland, 1972–5', *Twentieth Century British History* 24, no. 2, 1 June 2013, p. 516.

40 Seán Murray (dir.), *Unquiet Graves* (Relapse Pictures, 2015).

41 PRONI, CAB/9/G/89/3, Formation of the Ulster Defence Regiment, November 1969.

42 Edward Burke, 'Counter-Insurgency against "Kith and Kin"? The British Army in Northern Ireland, 1970–76', *The Journal of Imperial and Commonwealth History* 43, no. 4, 8 August 2015, p. 660.

43 Ibid., p. 662.

44 John Newsinger, 'Hearts and minds: The myth and reality of British

counter-insurgency', *International Socialism*, Issue 148, 5 October 2015.

45   Ed Davey, 'Metropolitan Police "Stockpiling" Plastic Bullets', *BBC News*, 3 May 2012.

46   NAUK, DEFE 70/2208 Western Europe NI UDR and RUC (Oct 1988–Nov 1989), Confidential note from M.L. Scicluna, Head of GS Sec, to PS / Secretary of State, 'Ulster Defence Regiment – Baton Round Guns', 14 November 1988.

47   Ibid.

48   NAUK, DEFE 70/2208 Western Europe NI UDR and RUC (Oct 1988–Nov 1989), Reply from Foreign Secretary Geoffrey Howe, to Secretary of State for Defence, 'FCS/88/239 Ulster Defence Regiment: Baton Round Guns', 29 December 1988.

49   NAUK, DEFE 70/2208 Western Europe NI UDR and RUC (Oct 1988–Nov 1989), Letter from J.S. Wall, Private Secretary to the Foreign Secretary, to S.J. Leach (NIO), 'UDR Baton Round Guns', 3 March 1989.

50   NAUK, DEFE 70/2208 Western Europe NI UDR and RUC (Oct 1988–Nov 1989), Letter from Lieutenant General Sir John Waters, GOC, HQNI, to Secretary of State for Northern Ireland, Peter Brooke, 24 September 1989.

51   NAUK, DEFE 70/2208 Western Europe NI UDR and RUC (Oct 1988–Nov 1989), Letter from Lieutenant General Sir John Waters, GOC, HQNI, to Secretary of State for Northern Ireland, Peter Brooke, 24 September 1989.

52   Cate McCurry, 'Taoiseach Urged British to Defer Move to Equip UDR with Plastic Bullets in 1989', *Belfast Telegraph*, 29 December 2019.

53   NAI, 2020/26/35 Anglo-Irish Section Weekly Brief week ending 22/06/90, Note from Declan O'Donovan, 'Briefing by British Army', 20 June 1990.

54   Ibid.

55   NAUK, DEFE 24/3001 UDR – appraisal (1981), Confidential memo from J.T. Cliffe, Head of DS15 (L), to PS / Secretary of State, 14 May 1981.

56   NAUK, CJ 4/4545 UDR Admin and Staffing, Brief by Colin Davenport, Head of Law & Order Division (NIO) to PS / Secretary of State (L&B), 'UDR "Call-Out"', 11 December 1981.

Chapter Eleven – The Demise of the UDR

1   NAUK, DEFE 24/3001 UDR – Appraisal (1981), Secret memo from CGS to US of S (Army) 'UDR Appraisal', 13 February 1981.

2   Ibid, p. 1.

3   NAUK, CJ 4/4800 P1 – Future Organisation of UDR (1980–83), Secret memo from I.M. Burns, Division 1 (NIO), to PS/PUS (B), 'IMB/80/12/16 Policy Appraisal of the Ulster Defence Regiment', 9 December 1980.

4   NAUK, CJ 4/4800 P2 – Future Organisation of UDR (1980–83)', from

I.M. Burns to Mr Blelloch, 'IMB/81/2/65 UDR Appraisal', 6 February 1981.

5   NAUK, CJ 4/4800 P1 – Future Organisation of UDR (1980–83)', 'A Policy Appraisal of the Ulster Defence Regiment: Note by NIO', pp. 13–14.

6   NAUK, CJ 4/4800 P1 – Future Organisation of UDR (1980–83), Secret memo from I.M. Burns, Division 1 (NIO), to PS/PUS (B), 'IMB/80/12/16 Policy Appraisal of the Ulster Defence Regiment', 9 December 1980.

7   Ibid.

8   Ibid.

9   NAUK, CJ 4/4800 P1 – Future Organisation of UDR (1980–83), Note from Brigadier B.W. Davies, HQNI, to I.M. Burns, Division 1 (NIO), 11 December 1980.

10 NAUK, CJ 4/4800 P1 – Future Organisation of UDR (1980–83), Confidential memo from I.M. Burns, Division 1 (NIO), to PS/PUS (B), 'IMB/80/12/16 Policy Appraisal of the Ulster Defence Regiment', 15 December 1980.

11 NAUK, CJ 4/4800 P1 – Future Organisation of UDR (1980–83), Confidential memo from R.L. Smith, PS/PUS (B), to Mr Burns, 'Policy Appraisal of the Ulster Defence Regiment', 22 December 1980.

12 NAUK, CJ 4/4800 P1 – Future Organisation of UDR (1980–83), Secret memo from I.M. Burns, 'IMB/81/1/10 – Note for the Record – Policy Appraisal of the Ulster Defence Regiment', 8 January 1981.

13 NAUK, CJ 4/4800 P1 – Future Organisation of UDR (1980–83), 'UDR Appraisal', p. 3 (partial copy only on file with PFC).

14 Ibid, pp. 9–10.

15 Ibid., p. 11.

16 Ciara Quinn, 'Paul (17) Suffered 50 Wounds in UDR Shooting', *Andersonstown News*, 26 January 2015.

17 NAI, 2015/51/1355 'Ulster Defence Regiment', 30 January 1985, p. 1.

18 Ibid., p. 2.

19 Ibid., pp. 2–3.

20 Shane Hickey, 'Margaret Thatcher Doubted Irish Resolve to Combat Terrorism', *The Irish* Times, 24 July 2018.

21 John Bew, 'Anglo-Irish Agreement a Triumph of Persistence and Backdoor Diplomacy', *The Irish Times*, 30 December 2014.

22 NAUK, FCO 87/1966 Anglo-Irish Agreement Reaction in ROI (1985). Confidential telegram from Goodison, British embassy, Dublin, to FCO, 'GRS 180 – DFA Representations about the UDR', December 1985 (n.d.).

23 Éamon Phoenix, 'British Concerned over UDR Credibility', *The Irish Times*, 2 January 2017.

24 NAUK, CJ 4/5807 Anglo-Irish talks UDR & security forces (1985), Secret & Personal note from A.D.S. Goodall, FCO, to N.H. Nicholls, MoD, 'Anglo-Irish Relations: UDR', 2 August 1985.

25 NAUK, CJ 4/5807 Anglo-Irish talks UDR & security forces (1985), note to J.A. Daniell, MoD, from A.D.S. Goodall, FCO, 'UDR Associated Measures', 16 July 1985.

26 David Goodall, 'Margaret Thatcher's Moods, Garret FitzGerald's Outburst – a Diplomat Looks Back', *The Irish Times*, 25 July 2021.

27 NAUK, CJ 4/5807 Anglo-Irish talks UDR & security forces (1985), note by D. Brennan, NIO, 'UDR Associated Measures', 16 July 1985.

28 NAUK, FCO 87/2142 UDR (1985), Briefing note sent by D.A. Hill (NIO) to British Embassy, Dublin, 'UDR: Notes for use by Ministers in answer to questions', 1 May 1985, p. 2.

29 NAUK, DEFE 70/2208 Western Europe NI UDR and RUC (Oct 1988–Nov 1989), 'UK Eyes A Secret – Loose Minute – UDR Policy and Security', Confidential Annex K, 22 September 1989.

30 de Silva, *The Report of the Patrick Finucane Review*, para. 11.30.

31 Ibid., para. 11.52.

32 Ibid., para. 11.59.

33 Stevens Enquiry: Overview and Recommendations, 17 April 2003 (https://cain.ulster.ac.uk/issues/collusion/stevens3/stevens3summary.htm).

34 Ibid.

35 In August 1987, a UDR colour sergeant stole weapons from Palace Barracks, which he sold to Ken Barrett. Barrett, a UDA member, pleaded guilty in 2004 to Pat Finucane's murder. The weapons stolen included a 9 mm Browning pistol that was subsequently used in that murder. The colour sergeant was himself convicted in 1988 for his role in the theft (de Silva Review, para. 57).

36 Stevens Enquiry: Overview and Recommendations, 17 April 2003 (https://cain.ulster.ac.uk/issues/collusion/stevens3/stevens3summary.htm).

37 Ibid.

38 NAUK, DEFE 70/2208 Western Europe NI UDR and RUC (Oct 1988–Nov 1989), 'Press Release: Statement by Mr. Stevens', 8 October 1989.

39 NAUK, DEFE 70/2208 Western Europe NI UDR and RUC (Oct 1988–Nov 1989), 'PQ 6908: Briefing for PM's Questions on 17 October – UDR Leaks: Guardian Article of 16 October', 16 October 1989.

40 NAUK, DEFE 70/2208 Western Europe NI UDR and RUC (Oct 1988–Nov 1989), Letter to General Sir John Chapple, Chief of the General Staff, from Lt Gen. Sir David Young, Colonel Commandant Ulster Defence Regiment, 16 October 1989.

41 NAUK, DEFE 70/2208 Western Europe NI UDR and RUC (Oct 1988–Nov 1989), Letter to Secretary of State for Northern Ireland from Colonel Faulkner, Colonel Commandant Ulster Defence Regiment, 16 November 1989.

42 NAUK, DEFE 70/2208 Western Europe NI UDR and RUC (Oct 1988–Nov 1989), Loose Minute by W.P. Cassell, Head of GS Sec, 'Panorama Programme on the UDR', 20 October 1989.

43 NAUK, DEFE 70/2208 Western Europe NI UDR and RUC (Oct 1988–Nov 1989), Letter to Secretary of State for Defence from Secretary of State for Northern Ireland, 20 October 1989.

44 NAUK, DEFE 70/2208 Western Europe NI UDR and RUC (Oct 1988–Nov 1989), 'Secret UK Eyes A Draft – Operational Policy for the UDR in the 1990s.'

45 Ibid., p. 15.

46 Ryder, *The Ulster Defence Regiment*, pp. 240–1.

47 Fearghal McGarry, *The Rising: Ireland: Easter 1916* (2nd ed.; Oxford: OUP, 2017), p. 184.

Chapter 12 – Sinning Quietly

1   James Loughlin, 'Northern Ireland and British Fascism in the Inter-War Years', *Irish Historical Studies* 29, no. 116, 1995, p. 544.

2   James Loughlin (Liverpool: Liverpool University Press, 2019), pp. 7–8.

3   The B Specials' shadow extends over community relations to the present day. In 2016 it emerged that around £350,000 had been paid to the Ulster Special Constabulary Association over the previous ten years (Connla Young, *Irish News*, 2 May 2016). In November 2019 at a meeting of Mid & East Antrim Council, DUP alderman John Carson said, 'It's just a terrible thing we haven't the B Specials around today' (local news report, on file with PFC). In 2021, a Council-funded 're-enactment' of a B Specials' VCP, while largely ignored locally, drew criticism for being 'inappropriate' (Brian Hutton, *The Irish Times*, 16 October 2021).

4   Seán Murray (dir.), *Unquiet Graves* (Relapse Pictures, 2015).

5   Ellison and Smyth, *The Crowned Harp*, pp. 66–7.

6   Ibid., p. 162.

7   Statewatch, 'NI: Reforming the UDR?', 1 September 1991 (www.statewatch.org/statewatch-database/ni-reforming-the-udr/).

8   Wood, 'Crimes of Loyalty – A History of the UDA', p. 108.

9   Anne Mandeville, 'Organizational format and state violence: the case of the Ulster Defense Regiment in Northern Ireland', *Cultures & Conflicts*, Volume 9–10, Issue 1–2, January 1993, p. 14.

10 NAUK, DEFE 24/835 Subversion in the UDR, August 1973.

11 NAUK, DEFE 24/875 UDR: Recruitment, intelligence, Secret draft introduction brief for US of S (Army), 'The Ulster Defence Regiment', by A.P. Cumming-Bruce, DS7, 12 March 1974.

12 Dan Sabbagh, Rowena Mason and Jessica Elgot, 'Britain fears US forces may pull out of Kabul airport within days', *The Guardian*, 18 August 2021.

13 NAUK, FCO 87/2353, Memo to A.D.E. Goodall from G.E. Clarke, 2 January 1986.

14 Farrell, *Arming the Protestants*, pp. 290–1.

15   Ian Cobain, *The History Thieves: Secrets, Lies and the Shaping of a Modern Nation* (London: Portobello Books Ltd, 2017), p. 147.

16   National Archives, 'Takedown and Reclosure Policy'.

17   Cobain, *The History Thieves*, p. xii.

18   Ibid.

19   Ibid., pp. 110–11.

20   Ian Cobain, *Cruel Britannia: A Secret History of Torture* (London: Portobello Books Ltd, 2013), p. 87.

21   Cobain, *The History Thieves*, p. xv.

22   'Spotlight on the Troubles: A Secret History, Series 1, Episode 7', BBC One, 22 October 2019.

23   Ian Cobain, 'Ministry of Defence holds 66,000 files in breach of 30-year rule', *The Guardian*, 6 October 2013.

24   Anne Cadwallader, 'DECLASSIFIED UK OP-ED: Impunity for Killings in Service of the State: The UK Government's Latest Scheme', *Daily Maverick*, 26 July 2021.

25   At a public event on 22 November 2021, discussing the UK government's legacy proposals organised by the School of Law at Queen's University Belfast, the CAJ, and the Bingham Centre for the Rule of Law.

26   'United & Disgusted Relatives', *Tyrone Courier*, 3 November 2021, pp. 1, 30–31.

27   Statement by CAJ (Committee on the Administration of Justice) 'New report finds proposed UK government amnesty cannot deliver truth for victims of The Troubles', 7 September 2021.

28   Cobain, *The History Thieves*, pp. xv–xvi.

29   Ibid., p. xiii.

REFERENCES

Academic Papers

Bennett, Huw, '"Smoke Without Fire"? Allegations Against the British Army in Northern Ireland, 1972–5', *Twentieth Century British History* 24, no. 2, 1 June 2013, p. 516.

Burke, Edward, 'Counter-Insurgency against "Kith and Kin"? The British Army in Northern Ireland, 1970–76', *The Journal of Imperial and Commonwealth History* 43, no. 4, 8 August 2015, p. 660.

Davey, Ed, 'Metropolitan Police "Stockpiling" Plastic Bullets', *BBC News*, 3 May 2012.

Edwards, Aaron, 'Misapplying lessons learned? Analysing the utility of British counterinsurgency strategy in Northern Ireland, 1971–76', *Small Wars & Insurgencies*, 21:2 (2010), p. 304.

Gannon, Patrick J., 'In the Catacombs of Belfast', *Studies: An Irish Quarterly Review* 11, no. 42, June 1922, p. 285.

Ignatieff, Michael, 'Articles of Faith', *Index on Censorship* 25, 5 (1996), p. 113.

Killingray, David, 'The Idea of a British Imperial African Army', *The Journal of African History* 20, no. 3, 1979, p. 422.

Loughlin, James, 'Northern Ireland and British Fascism in the Inter-War Years', *Irish Historical Studies* 29, no. 116, 1995, p. 544.

Mandeville, Anne, 'Organizational format and state violence: the case of the Ulster Defense Regiment in Northern Ireland', *Cultures & Conflicts*, vols 9–10, Issue 1–2, January 1993, p. 14.

McWilliams, Monica, 'Violence against Women and Political Conflict: The Northern Ireland Experience', *Critical Criminology* 8, no. 1, 1 March 1997, pp. 81–2.

Neumann, Peter R., 'The Myth of Ulsterization in British Security Policy in Northern Ireland', *Studies in Conflict & Terrorism* 26, no. 5, 1 September 2003, p. 365.

Ó Faoleán, Gearóid, 'The Ulster Defence Regiment and the Question of Catholic Recruitment, 1970–1972', *Terrorism and Political Violence* 27, no. 5, 20 October 2015, pp. 843–4.

Patterson, Henry, 'The British State and the Rise of the IRA, 1969–71: The View from the Conway Hotel', *Irish Political Studies* 23, no. 4, 1 December 2008, p. 497.

Phoenix, Éamon, 'New Light Shed on Stormonts "X" Files', *History Ireland*, iss. 4, vol. 4 (Winter 1996).

Robinson, Joseph S., '"We Have Long Memories in This Area": Ulster Defence Regiment Place-Memory along the Irish Border', *Memory Studies*, 27 May 2020, p. 206.

Rolston, Bill, '"An Effective Mask for Terror": Democracy, Death Squads and Northern Ireland', *Crime, Law and Social Change*, vol. 44, iss. 2, p. 198.

Weitzer, Robert, 'Policing a Divided Society: Obstacles to Normalization in Northern Ireland', *Social Problems* 33, no. 1, 1985, p. 43.

Wilson, Tim, '"The Most Terrible Assassination That Has Yet Stained the Name of Belfast": The McMahon Murders in Context', *Irish Historical Studies* 37, no. 145, 2010, p. 84.

Books & Pamphlets

Adorno, Theodor W. and Pickford, Henry, *Critical Models: Interventions and Catchwords* (annotated edition; New York: Columbia University Press, 2005), p. 89.

Anderson, Don, *Fourteen May Days: The Inside Story of the Loyalist Strike of 1974* (Dublin: Gill & Macmillan, 1994), p. 135.

BBC Northern Ireland, *Legacy: A Collection of Personal Testimonies from People Affected by the Troubles in Northern Ireland* (Belfast: Elucidate Consultancy, 2007), p. 46.

Brewer, John; Wilford, Rick; Guelke, Adrian; Hume, Ian and Moxon-Browne, Edward, *The Police, Public Order and the State: Policing in Great Britain, Northern Ireland, the Irish Republic, the USA, Israel, South Africa and China* (2nd ed.; London: Palgrave Macmillan UK, 1996), p. 66.

Bruce, Steve, *The Red Hand: Protestant Paramilitaries in Northern Ireland* (Oxford: Oxford Paperbacks, 1992).

Burke, Edward, *An Army of Tribes: British Army Cohesion, Deviancy and Murder in Northern Ireland* (Liverpool: Liverpool University Press, 2018), p. 236.

Cadwallader, Anne, *Lethal Allies: British Collusion in Ireland* (Mercier: Cork, 2013).

Callaghan, James, *A House Divided: The Dilemma of Northern Ireland* (London: HarperCollins, 1973), p. 67.

Cobain, Ian, *Cruel Britannia: A Secret History of Torture* (London: Portobello Books Ltd, 2013), p. 87.

Cobain, Ian, *The History Thieves: Secrets, Lies and the Shaping of a Modern Nation* (London: Portobello Books Ltd, 2017), p. xii.

Coogan, Tim Pat, *The Troubles: Ireland's Ordeal 1966–1996 and the Search for Peace* (Boulder, Co.: Denver Museum, 1996), p. 154.

Dewar, Michael, *The British Army in Northern Ireland* (2nd revised edition; London: Weidenfeld Military, 1996), p. 140.

Dillon, Martin, *The Dirty War* (London: Arrow Books Ltd, 1990).

Dillon, Martin, *The Shankill Butchers: A Case Study of Mass Murder* (new edition; Cornerstone Digital, 2009).

Dingley, James, *Combating Terrorism in Northern Ireland* (Abingdon: Routledge, 2009), p. 63.

Egan, Bowes and McCormack, Vincent, *Burntollet* (London: LRS Publishers, 1969), p. 56.

Ellison, Graham and Smyth, Jim, *The Crowned Harp: Policing Northern Ireland* (London: Pluto Press, 2000), p. 10.

Farrell, Michael, *Arming the Protestants: The Formation of the Ulster Special Constabulary and the Royal Ulster Constabulary, 1920–7* (London: Pluto Press, 1983), p. 290.

Heidemann, Birte, 'From Postcolonial to Post-Agreement: Theorising Northern Ireland's Negative Liminality', in idem, *Post-Agreement Northern Irish Literature. New Directions in Irish and Irish American Literature* (Cham: Springer International Publishing, Palgrave Macmillan, 2016), p. 17.

Loughlin, James, *Fascism and Constitutional Conflict: The British Extreme Right and Ulster in the Twentieth Century* (Liverpool: Liverpool University Press, 2019), pp. 7–8.

Lynch, Robert, *The Northern IRA and the Early Years of Partition* (Dublin: Irish Academic Press, 2006), p. 122.

MacStiofain, Sean, *Revolutionary in Ireland* (London: G. Cremonesi, 1975), pp. 207–8.

McGarry, Fearghal, *The Rising: Ireland: Easter 1916* (2nd ed.; Oxford: OUP, 2017), p. 184.

McKittrick, David; Kelters, Seamus; Feeney, Brian and Thornton, Chris, *Lost Lives* (Edinburgh: Mainstream Publishing Company Ltd, 2001).

Miller, David, *Rethinking Northern Ireland: Culture, Ideology and Colonialism* (London: Routledge, 1998).

Potter, John, *A Testimony to Courage: The Regimental History of the Ulster Defence Regiment 1969–1992: The History of the Ulster Defence Regiment 1969–1992* (London: Pen & Sword Books Ltd, 2001).

Robinson, Peter, *Hands Off the UDR* (Belfast: Democratic Unionist Party, 1990), p. 3.

Ryder, Chris, *The Ulster Defence Regiment: An Instrument of Peace* (New edition; London: Mandarin, 1992), p. xvi.

Sharkey, Heather J., 'African Colonial States', in John Parker and Richard Reid (eds), *The Oxford Handbook of Modern African History* (Oxford: Oxford University Press, 2013), p. 158.

Sinn Féin, *The Ulster Defence Regiment: The Loyalist Militia* (Dublin: Sinn Féin, 1990), p. 18.

Smith, William Beattie, *The British State and the Northern Ireland Crisis, 1969–73: From Violence to Power-sharing* (Washington, D.C: United States Institute of Peace Press, 2011), p. 70.

Taylor, Peter, *Stalker: The Search for the Truth* (London and Boston: Faber & Faber, 1987), p. 30.

Urwin, Margaret, *A State in Denial: British Collaboration with Loyalist Paramilitaries* (Cork: Mercier, 2016), p. 286.

Urwin, Margaret, *Fermanagh: From Plantation to Peace Process* (Dublin: Wordwell Books, 2021).

Wharton, Ken, *A Long Long War: Voices from the British Army in Northern Ireland 1969–1998* (Solihull: Helion & Company, 2008), pp. 187–9.

Wharton, Ken, *The Bloodiest Year 1972: British Soldiers in Northern Ireland, in Their Own Words* (Stroud: The History Press, 2011).

Wood, Ian S., *Crimes of Loyalty: A History of the UDA* (Edinburgh: Edinburgh University Press, 2006), p. 108.

Magazine & News Articles

Arnold, Hugo, Crime, 'Ulsterisation and the Future of the UDR', *Fortnight*, 7 October 1985.

Baker, Joe / Glenravel Local History Project, 'The Troubles', *A Chronology of the Northern Ireland Conflict*, Issue 18, November/December 1972.

The Belfast Gazette, No. 2968, 11 January 1974.

Bew, John, 'Anglo-Irish Agreement a Triumph of Persistence and Backdoor Diplomacy', *The Irish Times*, 30 December 2014.

Black, Rebecca, 'Trauma of IRA Murder Continues to Haunt Generations of a Family 40 Years Later', *Belfast Telegraph*, 17 January 2021.

'Bomb Charge Man in UDR, Court Told', *The Irish Times*, 21 October 1976.

Buckley, Tom, 'Double Troubles of Northern Ireland – A Visit with the Protestant Militants', *New York Times*, 10 December 1972.

Cadwallader, Anne, 'DECLASSIFIED UK OP-ED: Impunity for Killings in Service of the State: The UK Governments Latest Scheme', *Daily Maverick*, 26 July 2021.

Cobain, Ian, 'Ministry of Defence holds 66,000 files in breach of 30-year rule', *The Guardian*, 6 October 2013.

Davey, Ed, 'Metropolitan Police "Stockpiling" Plastic Bullets', *BBC News*, 3 May 2012.

'"Doomsday" plan for North revealed in archives', *The Irish Times*, 1 January 2005.

Fahy, Pat, 'Kelly Murder Remains a Dark Stain on Policing and Justice Systems', *Irish News*, 14 November 2018.

'Former Blaenau Gwent Soldier Publishes Book on Experience during Northern Ireland Troubles', *South Wales Argus*, 20 August 2015.

'Funeral of John Black', *News Letter*, 30 June 1972.

'Germany disbands Stasi records agency but saves files', *DW (Deutsche Welle)*, 17 June 2021.

Goodall, David, 'Margaret Thatcher's Moods, Garret FitzGerald's Outburst – a Diplomat Looks Back', *The Irish Times*, 25 July 2021.

Hickey, Shane, 'Margaret Thatcher Doubted Irish Resolve to Combat Terrorism', *The Irish Times*, 24 July 2018.

Holland, Mary, 'Skeletons in the Closet of the UDR', *New Statesman*, April 1980 (copy on file with PFC).

Lewis, Brandon, 'Do Our Critics Have a Better Way to Tackle the Legacy of the Troubles?', *The Telegraph*, 17 July 2021.

Manley, John, 'Anti-Catholic Basil Brooke Speech Was "Public Expression of Unionisms Private View"', *The Irish News*, 3 September 2018.

McCaffery, Steven, 'Former Politician Talks About His Life in the UDA, UDR and the RUC', *The Irish News*, 15 May 2006.

McCaffery, Steven, 'UDR the top source of arms "for Protestant extremists"', *The Irish News*, 2 May 2006.

McCurry, Cate, 'Taoiseach Urged British to Defer Move to Equip UDR with Plastic Bullets in 1989', *Belfast Telegraph*, 29 December 2019.

McKay, Susan, 'The guns are gone, but misogyny still stalks Northern Ireland', *The Guardian*, 1 December 2021.

Miller, Ryan, 'Domestic violence in NI is epidemic', *SCOPE NI*, 13 October 2020.

Minihan, Mary, 'State Papers: INLA Described by Catholic Priests as "Bunch of Lunatics"', *The Irish Times*, 31 December 2015.

Moriarty, Gerry, 'Loyalism's most prolific sectarian killer may have enjoyed indefensible relationship with RUC officers', *The Irish Times*, 25 October 2013.

Newsinger, John, 'Hearts and minds: The myth and reality of British counter-insurgency', *International Socialism*, Issue 148, 5 October 2015.

'Northern Ireland: The Women and the Gunmen', *Time Magazine*, 17 April 1972.

Phoenix, Éamon, 'British Concerned over UDR Credibility', *The Irish Times*, 2 January 2017.

Quinn, Ciara, 'Paul (17) Suffered 50 Wounds in UDR Shooting', *Andersonstown News*, 26 January 2015.

Rees, Merlyn, 'Mistakes Were Made in Security Policy', *Belfast Telegraph*, 11 August 1994.

Sabbagh, Dan; Mason, Rowena and Elgot, Jessica, 'Britain fears US forces may pull out of Kabul airport within days', *The Guardian*, 18 August 2021.

Savage, Michael, 'Fifty Years on, What Is the Legacy of Enoch Powell's "Rivers of Blood" Speech?', *The Observer*, 15 April 2018.

Smith, Colin, 'Ulster Defence Regiment – Some "Dads Army" Men Stepping out of Line', *The Observer*, 12 November 1972.

Sweeney, Christopher, 'Ulstermen Establish Subversive Group', *The Times*, 15 March 1974.

'UDR: Too Many Bad Apples', *Hibernia*, 3 December 1976.

'UDRms', *Fortnight*, no. 47 (Fortnight Publications Ltd), 5 October 1972.

'UDR's Rotten Apples', *The Phoenix*, 30 March 1984.

'United & Disgusted Relatives', *Tyrone Courier*, 3 November 2021.

Untitled article, *Fortnight*, No. 49 (2 November 1972).

'UVF Say "Our Boys are in the UDR"', *Sunday News*, 31 August 1975.

Young, Connla, 'UDA Killer of Catholic Man in 1980 Was Former Prison Officer', *The Irish News*, 23 August 2016.

Other Media

'10 October 1969: Ulsters B Specials to Be Disbanded', *On This Day,* BBC News online.

'A Conversation with Sam Thompson', *Shared Ireland* Podcast, 23 October 2019.

Enola Holmes, dir. Harry Bradbeer (Netflix, Legendary Entertainment, PCMA Productions, 2020).

Holmquist, Kate, 'Forgotten Refugees in Their Own Country', *The Irish Times*, 4 May 2005; *Seeking Refuge 1971*, RTÉ broadcast, 13 August 1971.

Iran's Long Game, BBC Radio Four, 21 April 2020. Producer: Zak Brophy.

Justice in Jeopardy? Up Close, Ulster Television, 2021.

Roll of Honour, www.royal-irish.com/sites/default/files/attachments/udr_roll_of_honour.pdf.

'SEFF Remembers Samuel Millar', Tweet on 14 January 2021 by South East Fermanagh Foundation (@SEFFLisnaskea)

'Shankill Butchers held Belfast in grip of terror', BBC Northern Ireland online, 28 March 2011.

Spotlight on the Troubles: A Secret History, Series 1, Episode 7, BBC One, 22 October 2019.

Statewatch, NI: Reforming the UDR?, 1 September 1991.

Unquiet Graves, dir. Seán Murray (Relapse Pictures, 2015).

Reports

Baron Scarman, 'Violence and Civil Disturbances in Northern Ireland in 1969: Report of Tribunal of Inquiry (Vol. 566)', HM Stationery Office (1972).

Conflict Trauma Resource Centre, 'Legacy of War, Experiences of Members of the Ulster Defence Regiment', report for Veteran Services Northern Ireland, p. 6 (copy on file with PFC).

Desmond de Silva QC, 'The Report of the Patrick Finucane Review', para. 11.61.

Historical Enquiries Team Review, 'Summary Report concerning the attack on the Rock Bar'.

Historical Enquiries Team Review, 'Summary Report concerning the murders of Brian, John Martin, and Anthony Reavey'.

Historical Enquiries Team Review, 'Summary Report concerning the murder of Denis Mullen'.

Historical Enquiries Team Review, 'Summary Report concerning the murder of F.J. O'Toole'.

Historical Enquiries Team Review, 'Summary Report concerning the murder of Frederick McLoughlin' (copy on file with the PFC).

Historical Enquiries Team Review, 'Summary Report concerning the murder of Henry Cunningham'.

Historical Enquiries Team Review, 'Summary Report concerning the murder of John Toland'.

Historical Enquiries Team Review, 'Summary Report concerning the murder of Louis Leonard'.

Historical Enquiries Team Review, 'Summary Report concerning the murder of Patsy McNeice' (copy on file with PFC).

Historical Enquiries Team Review, 'Summary Report concerning the murders of Peter and Jane McKearney' (copy on file with the PFC).

Historical Enquiries Team Review, 'Summary Report concerning the murder of Trevor Brecknell (copy on file with the PFC).

Justice Henry Barron, 'Interim Report on the Report of the Independent Commission of Inquiry into the Dublin and Monaghan Bombings' (Joint Oireachtas Committee on Justice, Equality, Defence and Womens Rights, Dublin, 2003).

'Meath Peace Group Talks: No. 60 – The Legacy of War – Experiences of UDR Families, 10 April 2006' (copy on file at PFC).

'Stevens Enquiry: Overview and Recommendations', 17 April 2003 (https://cain.ulster.ac.uk/issues/collusion/stevens3/stevens3summary.htm).

Veteran Services Northern Ireland, 'UDR' (copy on file with PFC).

Statements, Speeches

Northern Ireland Office, 'Addressing the legacy of Northern Ireland's past', Command Paper, 14 July 2021.

Statement by Bernadette Devlin MP in the House of Commons, 19 November 1969.

Statement by CAJ (Committee on the Administration of Justice), 'New report finds proposed UK government amnesty cannot deliver truth for victims of The Troubles', 7 September 2021.

Statement by Emanuel Shinwell MP in the House of Commons, 19 November 1969.

Statement by July 2021, Brandon Lewis, Secretary of State for Northern Ireland, to House of Commons, 14 July 2021.

Statement by Kevin McNamara MP in the House of Commons, 19 November 1969.

Statement by Lord Hunt in the House of Lords, 8 December 1969.

Statement by Mervyn Storey MLA in the Northern Ireland Assembly, 24 May 2010. Fortieth Anniversary of Disbanding of B-Specials and Formation of UDR.

Statement by Minister of State for Defence Administration Roy Hattersley in the House of Commons, 11 December 1969.

Statement by Minister of State for Defence Administration Roy Hattersley in the House of Commons, 12 November 1969.

Statement by Parliamentary Under-Secretary at the Ministry of Defence Robert Brown MP in the House of Commons, 1 July 1976.

Statement by Secretary of State for Northern Ireland Peter Brooke MP in the House of Commons, 17 May 1990.

Statement by Under-Secretary of State for Defence for the Army, Peter Blaker, to House of Commons, 6 July 1973.

Statement by Under-Secretary of State for Defence Ian Gilmour in the House of Commons, 11 March 1971.

Speech by The Queen to the Royal Irish Regiment, Northern Ireland, 2006.

Declassified Files

Draft note for PM from SoS re UDR Arms Out Request, 15 June 1972 (copy on file with PFC).

NAI, 2001/43/1392, Letter from Mr Kevin Rush, Minister Plenipotentiary, Embassy of Ireland to Great Britain, to Mr Denis Holmes, Counsellor, Department of External Affairs, Regarding a Forthcoming Meeting with Two Labour MPs, Kevin McNamara and John Ryan, 26 November 1969.

NAI, 2001/43/1392, Note by B. Ó Móráin, Third Secretary, Department of External Affairs, Regarding Enrolment in the Ulster Defence Regiment, 3 November 1970.

NAI, 2008/79/3059, Northern Ireland – Assessment of Minority's Position in a Breakdown Situation.

NAI, 2015/51/1355 Ulster Defence Regiment, 30 January 1985.

NAI, 2015/51/1355 Ulster Defence Regiment, 30 January 1985; NAUK, CJ 4/7560 Prosecution of Members of the Security Forces in NI (1983–88) (1), note from (Miss) S. Johnston, Law & Order Division, to Mr Dalzell, Arrest of Part-Time Member of 2 UDR, 30 June 1987.

NAI, 2016/52/9 Meeting Between the Taoiseach and the Church of Ireland, 17 January 1986, p. 4.

NAI, 2017/10/47 TAOIS – Complaints against RUC (Jan–Apl 1987), Note by David O'Donoghue, Loyalist and republican paramilitaries, 10 April 1987.

NAI, 2017/10/47 TAOIS – Complaints against RUC (Jan–Apl 1987).

NAI, 2020/26/35 Anglo-Irish Section Weekly Brief week ending 22/06/90, Note from Declan O'Donovan, Briefing by British Army, 20 June 1990.

NAUK, A Guide to Paramilitary and Associated Organisations, 2 September 1976 (copy on file with PFC).

NAUK, CJ 3/57 Minutes of the Hunt Committee: List of Witnesses/Agenda.

NAUK, CJ 3/71 Public Order Royal Ulster Constabulary and Ulster Special Constabulary Correspondence and Papers, Belfast, Memo dated 18 August 1969.

NAUK, CJ 3/71 Public Order Royal Ulster Constabulary and Ulster Special Constabulary Correspondence and Papers, Confidential note by I.M. Burns, Assistant Private Secretary to the Home Secretary, 18 August 1969.

NAUK, CJ 3/71 Public Order Royal Ulster Constabulary and Ulster Special Constabulary Correspondence and Papers, Home Office memo dated 18 August 1969, Confidential, Northern Ireland, 'B Specials': Transactions of 15th and 16th August.

NAUK, CJ 4/608 European Commission on Human Rights – Use of IRA Plot Material (May–June 1974).

NAUK, CJ 4/1047, Letter to Harding (FCO) from Janes (NIO) on a meeting with Irish Ambassador, 13 August 1975.

NAUK, CJ 4/1069, Memo from T.C. Barker to Under-Secretary of State for Northern Ireland, 18 May 1976.

NAUK, CJ 4/1300, Brief for meeting with Messrs Logue, Duffy, O'Donoghue about the UDR, 4.00 pm Monday 24 June (copy on file with PFC).

NAUK, CJ 4/1300, Confidential memo from P.T.E. England, Deputy Under-Secretary of State, to Major General D.T. Young, Commander Land Forces (HQNI), DUS/11/0572, 5 November 1975.

NAUK, CJ 4/1300, Restricted Draft Minute from Mr Barker to Mr Chesterton Re: The Ulster Defence Regiment, January 1976 (copy on file with PFC).

NAUK, CJ 4/1304, Memo to PUS from T.C. Barker, George Samuel Farrell, 25 May 1976.

NAUK, CJ 4/1666 Ulster Defence Regiment – Ministerial and Official Visits, Future Role 1976-77, Confidential memo from J.H.G. Leahy to Mr Stephens, Increase in UDR Conrates, 20 December 1976.

NAUK, CJ 4/2530, Confidential note from Buxton to Stephens, The Province Reserve UDR Force (PRUDR), 2 February 1978.

NAUK, CJ 4/2530, Memo from P.W.J. Buxton, Compromise of a UDR Operational Order, 22 May 1978.

NAUK, CJ 4/266 Draft Paper by General Officer Commanding Northern Ireland [GOC NI], Military Operations in the Event of a Renewed IRA Campaign of Violence, 9 July 1972.

NAUK, CJ 4/266, Draft Paper by General Officer Commanding Northern Ireland [GOC NI], Military Operations in the Event of a Renewed IRA Campaign of Violence, 9 July 1972.

NAUK, CJ 4/3063 Studies into the Future Role of the UDR (1979–80), Civil Affairs Report – Prepared for 10th (City of Belfast) Battalion, Ulster Defence Regiment, by Major P.H.S. Newel and Major A.F. Roberts.

NAUK, CJ 4/4545 UDR Admin and Staffing, Brief by Colin Davenport, Head of Law & Order Division (NIO) to PS / Secretary of State (L&B), UDR 'Call-Out', 11 December 1981.

NAUK, CJ 4/4545 UDR Admin and Staffing, Letter from P. Coulson (L&O Div) to Mr Brooker, UDR Training on the Isle of Man, 16 February 1983.

NAUK, CJ 4/4546 Incidents Involving the UDR (1975–1983), handwritten note to Walsh (NIO), 22 February 1979.

NAUK, CJ 4/4546 Incidents Involving the UDR (1975–1983), Note from P.W.J. Buxton to PS / Secretary of State (B), Personal Protection Weapons for UDR Members, 21 May 1981.

NAUK, CJ 4/4546 Incidents Involving the UDR (1975–1983), Note to Walsh from S.M. Pope, Division 1 (B), 22 February 1979.

NAUK, CJ 4/4800 P1 – Future Organisation of UDR (1980–83), A Policy Appraisal of the Ulster Defence Regiment: Note by NIO, pp. 13–14.

NAUK, CJ 4/4800 P1 – Future Organisation of UDR (1980–83), Confidential memo from I.M. Burns, Division 1 (NIO), to PS/PUS (B), IMB/80/12/16 Policy Appraisal of the Ulster Defence Regiment, 15 December 1980.

NAUK, CJ 4/4800 P1 – Future Organisation of UDR (1980–83), Confidential memo from R.L. Smith, PS/PUS (B), to Mr Burns, Policy Appraisal of the Ulster Defence Regiment, 22 December 1980.

NAUK, CJ 4/4800 P1 – Future Organisation of UDR (1980–83), Note from Brigadier B.W. Davies, HQNI, to I.M. Burns, Division 1 (NIO), 11 December 1980.

NAUK, CJ 4/4800 P1 – Future Organisation of UDR (1980–83), Secret memo from I.M. Burns, Division 1 (NIO), to PS/PUS (B), IMB/80/12/16 Policy Appraisal of the Ulster Defence Regiment, 9 December 1980.

NAUK, CJ 4/4800 P1 – Future Organisation of UDR (1980–83), Secret memo from I.M. Burns, IMB/81/1/10 – Note for the Record – Policy Appraisal of the Ulster Defence Regiment, 8 January 1981.

NAUK, CJ 4/4800 P1 – Future Organisation of UDR (1980–83), UDR Appraisal (partial copy only on file with PFC).

NAUK, CJ 4/4800 P1, Future Organisation of UDR (1980–83), Letter from Richard

Jackson, Civil Adviser to GOC to Frances Elliott, NIO – UDR Appraisal, 28 Oct 1980.

NAUK, CJ 4/4800 P2 – Future Organisation of UDR (1980-83), from I.M. Burns to Mr Blelloch, IMB/81/2/65 UDR Appraisal, 6 February 1981.

NAUK, CJ 4/5157 UDR (1982–84), Confidential note from Paul Coulson to Mr Brown, Loss of Sensitive Documents by an Officer in 10 UDR, 22 October 1982.

NAUK, CJ 4/5157 UDR (1982–84), Note by Allan Perceval, CIO at HQNI, Sunday Times Possible Article about the Disbandment of the UDR, 15 October 1984.

NAUK, CJ 4/5157 UDR (1982–84), Restricted memo from G.D. Fergusson to Mr Hill, Visit by UDR Band to USA, 30 January 1984.

NAUK, CJ 4/5157 UDR (1982–84), Restricted note by A.R. Brown, Law and Order Division, 11 January 1983.

NAUK, CJ 4/5157 Ulster Defence Regiment: General File, Letter from D.J. Coffey (MoD) to Cabinet Office, Proposed Amendment to the House of Commons Disqualification Act, 16 May 1984.

NAUK, CJ 4/5522 UDR (1984–85), Letter from Sadie Johnston, Law & Order Division, to Mr Blackwell, Controversial Cases Involving the UDR, 24 January 1985.

NAUK, CJ 4/5522 UDR (1984–85), Meeting to discuss the UDR held on 13 February 1985.

NAUK, CJ 4/5522 UDR (1984–85), Note by T.C. McKane, civil adviser to the GOC, UDR Study Period: 16–17 November 1985, 20 November 1985.

NAUK, CJ 4/5524 Future Organisation of the UDR (1984–85), Confidential memo from Paul Coulson, Law and Order Division to Mr Buxton, UDR, 15 November 1984.

NAUK, CJ 4/5524 Future Organisation of the UDR (1984–85), Draft discussion paper by P.W.J. Buxton, Ulster Defence Regiment, 14 November 1984.

NAUK, CJ 4/5524 Future Organisation of the UDR (1984–85), Letter from Merifield to Coulson, Meeting on UDR, 30 January 1985.

NAUK, CJ 4/5524 Future Organisation of the UDR (1984–85), Letter from MoD to D.A. Hill, UDR Criminal Offences, 29 March 1985.

NAUK, CJ 4/5524 Future Organisation of the UDR (1984–85), Meeting to discuss the UDR held on 13 February 1985, Note by J.A. Daniell, Private Secretary, 15 February 1985.

NAUK, CJ 4/5524 Future Organisation of the UDR (1984–85), Minute by Nicholas Scott for Secretary of State (L&B), 18 January 1985.

NAUK, CJ 4/5524 Future Organisation of the UDR (1984–85), Note of a meeting held on 12 March to discuss the UDR, 15 March 1985.

NAUK, CJ 4/5524 Future Organisation of the UDR (1984–85), The 1984 Security Review – The Future of the UDR, p. 5.

NAUK, CJ 4/5524 Future Organisation of the UDR (1984–85).

NAUK, CJ 4/5807 Anglo-Irish Talks UDR & Security Forces (1985), Letter from Alan Goodison, British Embassy, Dublin, to A.D.S. Goodall, Deputy Under-Secretary of State (FCO), Involvement of UDR Members in Criminal Activities,

Controversial Shootings and Harassment, 1970–1985, 2 August 1985.

NAUK, CJ 4/5807 Anglo-Irish talks UDR & Security Forces (1985), Note by D. Brennan, NIO, UDR Associated Measures, 16 July 1985.

NAUK, CJ 4/5807 Anglo-Irish talks UDR & Security Forces (1985), Note to J.A. Daniell, MoD, from A.D.S. Goodall, FCO, UDR Associated Measures, 16 July 1985.

NAUK, CJ 4/5807 Anglo-Irish talks UDR & Security Forces (1985), Secret & Personal note from A.D.S. Goodall, FCO, to N.H. Nicholls, MoD, Anglo-Irish Relations: UDR, 2 August 1985.

NAUK, CJ 4/5807 Anglo-Irish Talks UDR & Security Forces (1985), Secret memo, Associated Measures: The UDR, enclosed with letter from N.H. Nicholls (MoD) to Christopher Mallaby, 4 July 1985.

NAUK, CJ 4/5808 Anglo-Irish Talks UDR & Security Forces (1985). Confidential memo from P.W.J. Buxton to Mr Stephens, Involvement of UDR Members in Criminal and Other Activities, 16 August 1985.

NAUK, CJ 4/6325 Security UDR (1985-86), Letter from A.W. Stephens to Mr Innes, UDR and Mr Mallon, 2 January 1986.

NAUK, CJ 4/6326 UDR General (1985–86), Letter from Tom King, Secretary of State for Northern Ireland, to George Younger, Secretary of State for Defence, 24 April 1986.

NAUK, CJ 4/6791 Involvement of UDR in Serious Crime (1979–87), Handwritten note on copy of letter from S.G. Brearley to PS / Secretary of State (B&L), Mr Peter Utley, copy dated 21 March 1985.

NAUK, CJ 4/6791 Involvement of UDR in Serious Crime (1979–87), Letter from P. Coulson, Law and Order Division, to Buxton, on offences committed by UDR members, 4 February 1985.

NAUK, CJ 4/6791 Involvement of UDR in Serious Crime (1979–87), Letter from S.G. Brearley, SIL Division, to Mr Bickham, Conviction of Members of the UDR, 5 February 1985.

NAUK, CJ 4/6791 Involvement of UDR in Serious Crime (1979–87), Letter to Prime Minister by Paschal J. O'Hare, 6 December 1983.

NAUK, CJ 4/6791 Involvement of UDR in Serious Crime (1979–87), Minute from Buxton to Stephens, 19 March 1979.

NAUK, CJ 4/6791 Involvement of UDR in Serious Crime (1979–87), Note for the Record by S.G. Brearley, Conviction of Members of the Security Forces, 7 March 1985.

NAUK, CJ 4/7560 Prosecution of Members of the Security Forces in NI (1983–88) (1), Note for the Record by S.G. Brearley, 11 May 1988.

NAUK, CJ 4/7560 Prosecution of Members of the Security Forces in NI (1983–88) (1), Note from G.W. Davies, Law and Order Division, 17 June 1987.

NAUK, CJ 4/7560 Prosecution of Members of the Security Forces in NI (1983–88) (1), Note from (Miss) S. Johnston, Law & Order Division, to Mr Dalzell, Arrest of Part-Time Member of 2 UDR, 30 June 1987.

NAUK, CJ 4/799 Contingency Planning in the Event of an Emergency, Memo from Mr Leach to Mr Abbott, The UDR and the Catholic Community, 9 September 1975.

NAUK, CJ 4/838 Security Forces and UDA, 23 November 1972.

NAUK, 'Criminal Charges Against a Member of the UDR', Note from D.B. Omand, DS10, to APS / Secretary of State, PS / US of S (Army), and others, 4 June 1975 (copy on file with PFC).

NAUK, DEFE 11/917, Situation in Northern Ireland, Confidential annex to Chiefs of Staff Committee meeting, 14 September 1976.

NAUK, DEFE 13/835, Letter from the Secretary of State for Northern Ireland to the Secretary of State for Defence, The UDR and Intelligence, 2 October 1974.

NAUK, DEFE 13/835, Minute from Head of DS10 (D.E. Johnston) to Assistant Private Secretary to the Secretary of State, 6 October 1975.

NAUK, DEFE 13/835, Minute from Vice-Chief of the General Staff to Undersecretary of State (Army), 17 April 1974.

NAUK, DEFE 13/835, Secret Annex A The Ulster Defence Regiment, from AUS (GS) to PS/US of S (ARMY), 19 March 1974 (copy on file with PFC).

NAUK, DEFE 24/877 Op Chantry Reinforcements – Reception and Initial Deployment, 30 November 1973.

NAUK, DEFE 24/3001 UDR – Appraisal (1981), Confidential memo from J.T. Cliffe, Head of DS15 (L), to PS / Secretary of State, 14 May 1981.

NAUK, DEFE 24/3001 UDR – Appraisal (1981), Secret memo from CGS to US of S (Army), UDR Appraisal, 13 February 1981.

NAUK, DEFE 24/3005 UDR – General (1976), Memo from W.D. Reeves (Head of DS14) to various, 12 May 1976.

NAUK, DEFE 24/822 Ulster Defence Regiment (UDR) – Arms and Armouries – Theft and Loss of Weapons 1972–1975, Confidential Background note for reply to PQ 2703A, n.d.

NAUK, DEFE 24/822 Ulster Defence Regiment (UDR) – Arms and Armouries – Theft and Loss of Weapons 1972–1975, Draft reply to PQ 3141A, Notes for Supplementaries, n.d.

NAUK, DEFE 24/822 Ulster Defence Regiment (UDR) – Arms and Armouries – Theft and Loss of Weapons 1972–1975, Letter from Nick Evans, Civilian Adviser to the GOC, to Brian McKay, DS7 (MoD), ref: UDR General, 15 March 1973.

NAUK, DEFE 24/822 Ulster Defence Regiment (UDR) – Arms and Armouries – Theft and Loss of Weapons 1972–1975, Letter from Nick Evans, Civilian Adviser to the GOC, to Brian McKay, DS7 (MoD), ref: UDR General, 8 March 1973.

NAUK, DEFE 24/822 Ulster Defence Regiment (UDR) – Arms and Armouries – Theft and Loss of Weapons 1972–1975, Letter to Bernadette Devlin MP, from David Howell (NIO), 20 October 1972.

NAUK, DEFE 24/822 Ulster Defence Regiment (UDR) – Arms and Armouries – Theft and Loss of Weapons 1972–1975, Letter to NIO from J.F. Howe, Civil Adviser to GOC, 25 September 1972.

NAUK, DEFE 24/822 Ulster Defence Regiment (UDR) – Arms and Armouries – Theft and Loss of Weapons 1972–1975, Loose Minute, 'Northern Ireland Loss of UDR Weapons', from Colonel H.S.L. Dalzell-Payne to PS/US of S (Army), 19 July 1972.

NAUK, DEFE 24/822 Ulster Defence Regiment (UDR) – Arms and Armouries – Theft and Loss of Weapons 1972–1975, Loose Minute, Northern Ireland Loss of UDR Weapons, from Colonel H.S.L. Dalzell-Payne to PS/US of S (Army), 31 July 1972.

NAUK, DEFE 24/822 Ulster Defence Regiment (UDR) – Arms and Armouries – Theft and Loss of Weapons, 1972–1975, Northern Ireland Losses of UDR Weapons, Loose Minute from F.M.K. Tuck to PS/US of S (Army), 9 August 1972.

NAUK, DEFE 24/822 Ulster Defence Regiment (UDR) – Arms and Armouries – Theft and Loss of Weapons 1972–1975, Memo from A.P. Cumming-Bruce at DS7, 19 February 1973.

NAUK, DEFE 24/822 Ulster Defence Regiment (UDR) – Arms and Armouries – Theft and Loss of Weapons 1972–1975, Memo from APS / US of S (Army), 10 October 1972.

NAUK, DEFE 24/822 Ulster Defence Regiment (UDR) – Arms and Armouries – Theft and Loss of Weapons 1972–1975, NI 13/20/E01(S) Miss Bernadette Devlin MP – Questions on the Ulster Defence Regiment.

NAUK, DEFE 24/822 Ulster Defence Regiment (UDR) – Arms and Armouries – Theft and Loss of Weapons 1972–1975, Note from F.S. MacDonald, DS7, to PS/US of S (Army), UDR Arms, 13 March 1973.

NAUK, DEFE 24/822 Ulster Defence Regiment (UDR) – Arms and Armouries – Theft and Loss of Weapons 1972–1975, Reply to APS / US of S (Army) from Col. Dalzell-Payne, 11 October 1972.

NAUK, DEFE 24/822 Ulster Defence Regiment (UDR) – Arms and Armouries – Theft and Loss of Weapons 1972–1975, Table of weapons losses (copy on file with PFC).

NAUK, DEFE 24/822 Ulster Defence Regiment (UDR) – Arms and Armouries – Theft and Loss of Weapons, 1972–1975, Loose minute from H.S.L. Dalzell-Payne to PS/US of S (Army), 19 July 1972.

NAUK, DEFE 24/822 Ulster Defence Regiment (UDR) – Arms and Armouries – Theft and Loss of Weapons 1972–1975, Loose minute to PS. US of S Northern Ireland, Losses of UDR Weapons – Comparison of Losses of Weapons Between Battalions of UDR and Incidents of Suspected Collusion, 1 August 1972.

NAUK, DEFE 24/822 Ulster Defence Regiment (UDR) – Arms and Armouries – Theft and Loss of Weapons 1972–1975, Letter from David Simmons, DS10, to J.F. Howe, Civil Advisor to the GOC, 9 January 1973.

NAUK, DEFE 24/822 Ulster Defence Regiment (UDR) – Arms and Armouries – Theft and Loss of Weapons 1972–1975, Memo by Col. C.R. Huxtable, Theft of Weapons from UDR Armoury on 23 October 1973, 24 October 1973.

NAUK, DEFE 24/822 Ulster Defence Regiment (UDR) – Arms and Armouries – Theft and Loss of Weapons 1972–1975, Memo by Col. H.S.L. Dalzell-Payne, Northern Ireland – Raid on TAVR Centre Lurgan, 23 October 1972.

NAUK, DEFE 24/822 Ulster Defence Regiment (UDR) – Arms and Armouries – Theft and Loss of Weapons 1972–1975, Memo from APS / US of S (Army) to Head of DS10, 28 February 1973.

NAUK, DEFE 24/835 Subversion in the UDR.

NAUK, DEFE 24/835, Subversion in the UDR, from Director of Security (Army) to BGS(Int); DMO; Head of DS7; Head of DS10 and MA/DCDS I, 20 August 1973.

NAUK, DEFE 24/875, Memo from A.W. Stephens, Head of DS10 to Head of DS7, Vetting of UDR Applicants, 15 July 1974.

NAUK, DEFE 24/875, Memo from David Simmons, US of S (Army) to Lt. Col. Bowser, 2 UDR – Members Alleged Criminal Records, 15 May 1974.

NAUK, DEFE 24/875, Secret draft introduction brief for US of S (Army), The Ulster Defence Regiment, by A.P. Cumming-Bruce, DS7, 12 March 1974.

NAUK, DEFE 24/877, Untitled loose memo (copy on file with PFC).

NAUK, DEFE 70/2208 Western Europe NI UDR and RUC (Oct 1988–Nov 1989), Confidential note from M.L. Scicluna, Head of GS Sec, to PS / Secretary of State, Ulster Defence Regiment – Baton Round Guns, 14 November 1988.

NAUK, DEFE 70/2208 Western Europe NI UDR and RUC (Oct 1988–Nov 1989), Letter from J.S. Wall, Private Secretary to the Foreign Secretary, to S.J. Leach (NIO), UDR Baton Round Guns, 3 March 1989.

NAUK, DEFE 70/2208 Western Europe NI UDR and RUC (Oct 1988–Nov 1989), Letter to General Sir John Chapple, Chief of the General Staff, from Lt Gen. Sir David Young, Colonel Commandant Ulster Defence Regiment, 16 October 1989.

NAUK, DEFE 70/2208 Western Europe NI UDR and RUC (Oct 1988–Nov 1989), Letter to Secretary of State for Defence from Secretary of State for Northern Ireland, 20 October 1989.

NAUK, DEFE 70/2208 Western Europe NI UDR and RUC (Oct 1988–Nov 1989), Letter to Secretary of State for Northern Ireland from Colonel Faulkner, Colonel Commandant Ulster Defence Regiment, 16 November 1989.

NAUK, DEFE 70/2208 Western Europe NI UDR and RUC (Oct 1988–Nov 1989), Loose minute by W.P. Cassell, Head of GS Sec, Panorama Programme on the UDR, 20 October 1989.

NAUK, DEFE 70/2208 Western Europe NI UDR and RUC (Oct 1988–Nov 1989), PQ 6908: Briefing for PMs Questions on 17 October – UDR Leaks: Guardian Article of 16 October, 16 October 1989.

NAUK, DEFE 70/2208 Western Europe NI UDR and RUC (Oct 1988–Nov 1989), Press Release: Statement by Mr Stevens, 8 October 1989.

NAUK, DEFE 70/2208 Western Europe NI UDR and RUC (Oct 1988–Nov 1989), Secret UK Eyes A Draft – Operational Policy for the UDR in the 1990s.

NAUK, DEFE 70/2208 Western Europe NI UDR and RUC (Oct 1988–Nov 1989), UK Eyes A Secret – Loose Minute – UDR Policy and Security, Confidential Annex K, 22 September 1989.

NAUK, DEFE 70/246 Ulster Defence Regiment Advisory Council – Minutes of Meetings 1971–1973, Minutes of the 37th Meeting of the UDR Advisory Council held on Tuesday 28th November 1972 at 4.00 pm, p. 5.

NAUK, DEFE 70/246 Ulster Defence Regiment Advisory Council – Minutes of Meetings 1971–1973, Minutes of the 38th Meeting of the UDR Advisory Council held on Thursday, 11th January 1973 at 4.00 pm, p. 4.

NAUK, DEFE 70/246 Ulster Defence Regiment Advisory Council – Minutes of

Meetings 1971–1973, Minutes of the 40th Meeting of the UDR Advisory Council held on Friday 13th April 1973 at 4.00 pm, p. 4.

NAUK, DEFE 70/246 Ulster Defence Regiment Advisory Council – Minutes of Meetings 1971–1973, Minutes of the 42nd Meeting of the UDR Advisory Council held on Friday, 6th July 1973 at 4.00 pm, p. 4.

NAUK, DEFE 70/599 Ulster Defence Regiment: Criminal and Security Investigations of 10 UDR, Involvement of Members with Paramilitary Organisations.

NAUK, DEFE 70/599, AUS (GS) minute No. 95/78, 2 March 1978.

NAUK, DEFE 70/599, Loose note (copy on file with PFC).

NAUK, DEFE 70/599, Malpractice within 10 UDR (signatory unclear), 2 March 1978.

NAUK, DEFE 70/599, Memo from Capt. Guthrie to HQNI, Crime/Security – 10 UDR, 7 March 1978.

NAUK, DEFE 70/599, Minutes of a meeting held at HQNI on 24 February 1978 to discuss a defensive press brief on current investigations at 10 UDR, 25 February 1978.

NAUK, DEFE 70/599, Note by Capt. Guthrie, for GOC, to Directorate of Security (Army), UDR personnel connected with paramilitary organisations – 10 UDR, 14 November 1978.

NAUK, DEFE 70/599, Note by Capt. J.W. Jubb for HQNI, Crime/Security 10 UDR 11 November 1978.

NAUK, DEFE 70/599, Note by Capt. J.W. Jubb, for HQNI, Security Investigations 10 UDR, 24 February 1978.

NAUK, DEFE 70/599, Note by Lt Col. J.R.E. Laird, for GOC, to Col. G.G. Strong, Directorate of Security (Army), Investigations at 10 UDR Belfast, 27 February 1978.

NAUK, DEFE 70/599, Note from J. Dromgoole, AUS (GS), to APS / S of S, UDR Irregularities, 2 March 1978.

NAUK, DEFE 70/599, UDR Irregularities, 11 May 1978.

NAUK, DEFE 70/7 Ulster Defence Regiment – Reorganisation of B Specials (Sept–Nov 69), Army Board – The 82nd Meeting – The Formation of the New Northern Ireland Local Defence Force, 24 October 1969.

NAUK, DEFE 70/7 Ulster Defence Regiment – Reorganisation of B Specials (Sept–Nov 69), Army Board – The 82nd Meeting – The Formation of the New Northern Ireland Local Defence Force, 24 October 1969.

NAUK, DEFE 70/7 Ulster Defence Regiment – Reorganisation of B Specials (Sept–Nov 69), Army Board Secretariat confidential note, The formation of the new Northern Ireland local defence force, 24 October 1969.

NAUK, DEFE 70/7 Ulster Defence Regiment – Reorganisation of B Specials (Sept–Nov 69), Future of the 'B' Specials, 26 September 1969.

NAUK, DEFE 70/8 UDR Advisory Council (Nov 69–Feb 70), Letter from D.R.E. Hopkins, Home Office, to A.G. Sterling, Head of AG Secretariat (MoD), Ulster Defence Regiment Advisory Committee on Recruitment, 24 November 1969.

NAUK, DEFE 70/8 UDR Advisory Council (Nov 69–Feb 70), Letter from F.G. Guckian to Denis Healey MP, Ministry of Defence, 8 December 1969.

NAUK, DEFE 70/8 UDR Advisory Council (Nov 69–Feb 70), Letter from J.F. Mayne, APS / Secretary of State, to MA / CGS, Northern Ireland, 10 December 1969.

NAUK, DEFE 70/8 UDR Advisory Council (Nov 69–Feb 70), Letter from J.F. Mayne, APS / Secretary of State, to PS / Minister (A), Ulster Defence Regiment Advisory Council, 4 December 1969.

NAUK, DEFE 70/8 UDR Advisory Council (Nov 69–Feb 70), Letter from MA [Military Assistant] to the CGS to APS / Secretary of State, Mr Guckian, 11 December 1969.

NAUK, DEFE 70/8 UDR Advisory Council (Nov 69–Feb 70), Letter from PS/Min (A) to Head of AG Secretariat, Ulster Defence Regiment Advisory Council, 23 December 1969.

NAUK, DEFE 70/8 UDR Advisory Council (Nov 69–Feb 70), Memo from AUS (GS), Ulster Defence Regiment – Advisory Committee, 1 December 1969.

NAUK, DEFE 70/8 UDR Advisory Council (Nov 69–Feb 70), Memo from Head of AG Secretariat, Ulster Defence Regiment – Debate, 18 November 1969.

NAUK, DEFE 70/8 UDR Advisory Council (Nov 69–Feb 70), Memo from PS/Min (A) to APS/Secretary of State, Ulster Defence Regiment Advisory Council, 21 November 1969.

NAUK, DEFE 70/8 UDR Advisory Council (Nov 69–Feb 70), Personal – In Confidence, from A.G. Sterling, Head of AG Secretariat, to D.R. Morris, Civilian Adviser to GOC, 13 February 1970.

NAUK, DEFE 70/2208 Western Europe NI UDR and RUC (Oct 1988–Nov 1989), Letter from Lieutenant General Sir John Waters, GOC, HQNI, to Secretary of State for Northern Ireland, Peter Brooke, 24 September 1989.

NAUK, DEFE 70/2208 Western Europe NI UDR and RUC (Oct 1988–Nov 1989), Letter from Lieutenant General Sir John Waters, GOC, HQNI, to Secretary of State for Northern Ireland, Peter Brooke, 24 September 1989.

NAUK, DEFE 70/2208 Western Europe NI UDR and RUC (Oct 1988–Nov 1989), Reply from Foreign Secretary Geoffrey Howe, to Secretary of State for Defence, FCS/88/239 Ulster Defence Regiment: Baton Round Guns, 29 December 1988.

NAUK, Development of the Ulster Defence Regiment, Confidential Letter from Headquarters Northern Ireland to Ministry of Defence, 12 June 1972 (copy on file with PFC).

NAUK, FCO 87/1966 Anglo-Irish Agreement Reaction in ROI (1985), Confidential telegram from Goodison, British embassy, Dublin, to FCO, GRS 180 – DFA Representations about the UDR, December 1985 (n.d.).

NAUK, FCO 87/2142 UDR (1985), Briefing note sent by D.A. Hill (NIO) to British Embassy, Dublin, UDR: Notes for use by Ministers in answer to questions, 1 May 1985.

NAUK, FCO 87/2142 UDR (1985), Cover letter sent by D.A. Hill (NIO) to British Embassy, Dublin, UDR: Notes for use by Ministers in answer to questions, 1 May 1985.

NAUK, FCO 87/2353, Memo to A.D.E. Goodall from G.E. Clarke, 2 January 1986.

NAUK, FCO 87/2353 The Ulster Defence Regiment (UDR), Letter from A.D.S.

Goodall (FCO) to A.N. Nicholls (MoD), Defence White Paper: The Ulster Defence Regiment, 6 February 1986.

NAUK, FCO 87/3237 Security in NI (1990), Confidential note from P.N. Bell, Security Policy and Operations Division, Visit to 4 UDR Enniskillen, 14 December 1989.

NAUK, FCO 87/3237 Security in NI (1990), Informal Security Discussion – Security Strategic Issues, 18 May 1990s.

NAUK, FCO 87/3237 Security in NI (1990), Letter from Peter Brooke (SoS, NI) to Tom King (SoS, Defence) Security Force Operations in Northern Ireland, 6 July 1990.

NAUK, FCO 87/3237 Security in NI (1990), Note from P.N. Bell, Security Policy and Operations Division (NIO), The Ministers Visit to Strabane and Castlederg – 10 April 1990, 11 April 1990.

NAUK, FCO 87/342, Note of a Meeting between the Secretary of State and Representatives of the UWC Strike Co-Ordinating Committee Held at Stormont Castle on Wednesday, 7 August 1974 (copy on file with PFC).

NAUK, FCO 87/354, Note of a Meeting at the Northern Ireland Office, Wednesday, 13 November 1974 (copy on file with PFC).

NAUK, FCO 87/423, From J.D.W. Janes in the NIO to G.W. Harding in the FCO, 29 December 1975.

NAUK, FCO 87/423, Memo to Harding (FCO) from Janes (NIO) on a meeting with Irish Ambassador, 12 September 1975.

NAUK, Letter and Accompanying Report from J.B. Bourne to PS / Secretary of State, Reference 'Sectarian Assassinations', 23 May 1975 (copy on file with PFC).

NAUK, Letter from J.F. Howe, Civil Advisor to the GOC, to PS / US of S (Army), UDR Duties, 2 June 1972 (copy on file with PFC).

NAUK, Letter from J.F. Howe, Civil Advisor to the GOC at HQNI, to Lt Col. J.L. Pownall OBE, Ag Secretariat MoD, UDR – Membership of UDA, 31 July 1972 (copy on file with PFC).

NAUK, Letter from K.C. MacDonald, Head of Defence Secretariat 7 (MoD) to J.F. Howe, Civil Advisor to the GOC, UDR Duties, 21 June 1972 (copy on file with PFC).

NAUK, Letter from Lt Col. J.L. Pownall OBE, Ag Secretariat MoD to J.F. Howe, Civil Advisor to the GOC at HQNI Subject Re UDR-UDA Membership, 17 July 1972 (copy on file with PFC).

NAUK, Loose memo – British Govt Legal Advice on UDA Roadblocks (copy on file with PFC).

NAUK, Memo by F.G. Guckian, Thoughts on the proposed rapid build-up of the UDR, 10 September 1971 (copy on file with PFC).

NAUK, Memo from D.L. Ormerod, Commander UDR, UDR involvement in UDA, 24 July 1972 (copy on file with PFC)

NAUK, Ministry of Defence Telex to Home Office Summarising Meeting between the Two Prime Ministers, 7 September 1971 (copy on file with PFC).

NAUK, Minutes of 34th Meeting of the UDR Advisory Council, 12 August 1972 (copy on file with PFC).

NAUK, Minutes of the 32nd Meeting of the Advisory Council Held on Monday, 12 June 1972 at 4.00 pm (copy on file with PFC).

NAUK, Oral Reply to Parliamentary Question PQ 3141A, 30 November 1972 (copy on file with PFC).

NAUK. PREM 15/1016, Confidential letter from R.A. Custis, MoD, 29 November 1972 (copy on file with PFC).

NAUK, PREM 16/520, Memo Mrs Thatcher's Call on the Prime Minister on 10 September, 11 September 1975.

NAUK, PREM 16/520, Secretary of State to Prime Minister, 28 August 1975.

NAUK, PREM 19/80, Handwritten note by Prime Minister, PMs Notes on NIO, 13 July 1979.

NAUK, UDR Duties, Memo from John Howe, Civil Advisor to GOC Northern Ireland, to the Undersecretary of State (US of S) (Army) and to the UDR Steering Committee, 2 June 1972 (copy on file with PFC).

NAUK, WO305-4212 Commander's Diary, 3rd Infantry Brigade (April 1973), Annex A to HQ 3 INF BDE, 24 April 1973.

NAUK, WO305-4212 Commander's Diary, 3rd Infantry Brigade (April 1973), NIREP One 17 April 1973.

NAUK, WO305-4213 – 3rd Infantry Brigade (May 1973), COMCEN 3 INF BDE, 18 May 1973.

NAUK, WO305-4217 Commander's Diary of 3 Infantry Brigade (1 Sept – 30 1973), Police Division G – Secret Annex, n.d.

NAUK, WO305-4218 Commander's Diary, 3rd Infantry Brigade (October 1973), Brigade Log Sheet for 24 October 1973.

NAUK, WO305-4746.

NAUK, WO305-4250 P1 – HQ 39th Infantry Brigade (May 1972), Confidential memo, INTSUM No. 74 Covering Period 24–30 May 1972, 31 May 1972.

NAUK, WO305-4819 Commander's Diary 3 Batt UDR 1970–1982, Entry for 10 September 1982.

NAUK, WO305-4819 Commander's Diary 3 Batt UDR 1970–1982, Entry for 18 February 1976.

NAUK, WO305-4819 Commander's Diary 3 Batt UDR 1970–1982, Entry for 20 July 1982.

NAUK, WO305-4819 Commander's Diary 3 Batt UDR 1970–1982, Entry for 22 September 1977.

NAUK, WO305-4819 Commander's Diary 3 Batt UDR 1970–1982, Entry for March 1971.

PRONI, CAB/4/1461, Conclusions of a Meeting of the Cabinet, 15 August 1969.

PRONI, CAB/4/1485, Conclusions of a Meeting of the Cabinet Held at Stormont Castle on Tuesday, 14 October 1969 at 10:30 a.m.

PRONI, CAB/9/G/89/1, Draft White Paper on the Proposed Defence Force, n.d.

PRONI, CAB/9/G/89/1, UDR Formation, Press release, 15 October 1969.

PRONI, CAB/9/G/89/3, Formation of the Ulster Defence Regiment (November 1969).

PRONI, CRCT/3/2/3/506 R v McClelland, McConnell & McConnell, Bill No. 496/81.

INDEX